The Student's Guide to

EUROPEAN
INTEGRATION

T0355629

The Student's Guide to

EUROPEAN INTEGRATION

FOR STUDENTS, BY STUDENTS

Edited by
Jorge Juan Fernández García
Jess Clayton
Christopher Hobley

polity

The right of Jorge Juan Fernández García, Jess E. Clayton and Christopher Hobley to be identified as authors of the editorial material has been asserted in accordance with the UK Copyright, Designs and Patents Act 1988.

First published in 2004 by Polity Press in association with Blackwell Publishing Ltd.

Editorial office:
Polity Press
65 Bridge Street
Cambridge CB2 1UR, UK

Marketing and production:
Blackwell Publishing Ltd
108 Cowley Road
Oxford OX4 1JF, UK

Distributed in the USA by
Blackwell Publishing Inc.
350 Main Street
Malden, MA 02148, USA

A catalogue record for this book is available from the British Library.

Library of Congress Cataloging-in-Publication Data

The Student's Guide to European Integration : for students, by students / edited by Jorge Juan Fernández García, Jess E. Clayton, Christopher Hobley.
        p. cm.
ISBN 0-7456-2980-6 (hard. : alk. paper) — ISBN 0-7456-2981-4 (pbk. : alk. paper)
1. European Union. I. Fernández García, Jorge Juan. II. Clayton, Jess E. III. Hobley, Christopher.

JN30 .S8 2003
341.242′2–dc21
2003004581

Typeset in 10.5 on 12.5 pt Times New Roman
by Kolam Information Services Pvt. Ltd, Pondicherry, India
Printed and bound in Great Britain by TJ International, Padstow, Cornwall

For further information on Polity, visit our website: www.polity.co.uk

Contents

Part VII Conclusion   **291**

Acknowledgements

This book would not have been possible without the contributions of all the authors, and the editors would therefore like to thank each individual who contributed to this volume. This book is a direct result of their hard work, understanding and enthusiasm for European integration. We would also like to extend our gratitude to Daniel Engel, Paul Sturgess, Amar Reganti and Esra Bulut for their initial contributions to the project. Moreover, we would like to extend special thanks to Elias Corossis for his excellent contribution explaining the European models of capitalism.

The London School of Economics has provided the authors with an inspiring learning experience and much academic support outside the classroom. We would like to acknowledge the academic support of Dr Andreas Staab and Dr Alain Guyomarch, who encouraged this project during its initial phases, as well as the assistance of many other professors at the LSE during the later stages of the project. In particular, Dr Andrés Rodriguez Pose, Dr Robert Hancké, Dr Damian Chalmers, Dr Simona Talani and Dr Richard Bronk deserve special recognition for their generosity in reading and critiquing our finalized chapters.

Academic kudos and thanks must also be extended to our enthusiastic team of Ph.D. students, who meticulously read our chapters and provided valuable feedback: Mar Rubio on policy issues, Dr Joan Costa on economics, Cristina Secades on legal issues, and especially Diego Muro for his hard work on so many chapters. The academic calibre and readability of our volume is a direct result of their assistance.

Recognition must also be given to those who, through their practical and professional experiences, used their expertise to help us. In particular, we acknowledge the assistance of Dr Alexander Stubb for his feedback on Flexible Integration; Hugh Pullen for his comments on Environmental Policy; Mia Forbes-Pirie for her critique of Competition Policy and legal analysis of our law section; Miriam Alt for her research on the Single Market; Dharmender Singh for his assistance with European

Parliament issues; Albert Massot and Alex Ruiz for their help with the CAP; and Roser Serra and Dr Francesc Morata for their assistance on Regional Policy. In addition, we would like to thank Nancy Worthmann Clayton and Mary Fletcher-Gomez for their editorial assistance on all the chapters and Bjørn Høyland for his invaluable assistance in updating and extending our bibliographies.

Particular recognition must be given to Jean Whittaker and Wendy Pattison at the LSE European Institute, for helping us keep track of materials, receive faxes, and track down professors; Sylvia Cornforth of the LSE Academic Publications Office, whose hard work helped us to find the right publisher; as well as Louise Knight, Rachel Kerr and the people at Polity for their constant assistance and prompt answers to our queries.

Most importantly, we would also like to thank our families, whose invaluable support during this project helped us to overcome obstacles and reach our final goal. Their understanding and encouragement has been critical to the success of this project.

A special thank you goes to Jorge Juan Fernández García for his endless optimism and tireless commitment to the project.

Any weaknesses and errors that remain are the responsibility of the editors.

Abbreviations

.

ACP	African/Caribbean/Pacific countries	CIS	Commonwealth of Independent States (former USSR)
AER	Assembly of European Regions	CJTF	Combined Joint Task Forces
AG	Advocate-General	CM	Common Market
AWGI	Ad Hoc Working Group on Immigration	CMO	Common Market Organization
Benelux	Belgium, Netherlands and Luxembourg	COMECON	Council for Mutual Economic Assistance
BWS	Bretton Woods System	COPA	Confederation of Professional Agricultural Organizations
CAP	Common Agricultural Policy		
CC	closer co-operation	CoR	Committee of the Regions
CCP	Common Commercial Policy	COREPER	Committee of Permanent Representatives
CEECs	Central and Eastern European countries	CSF	Community Support Framework
CEN	European Standards Committee	CU	customs union
CENELEC	European Electrotechnical Standardization Committee	DG	Directorate-General
		EAGGF	European Agricultural Guidance and Guarantee Fund
CET	Common External Tariff	EAP	Environmental Action Programme
CFI	Court of First Instance		
CFSP	Common Foreign and Security Policy	EBRD	European Bank for Reconstruction and Development
CI	Community Initiative		

EC	European Community	EPU	European Political Union
ECB	European Central Bank	ER	exchange rate
ECHO	EC Humanitarian Office	ERDF	European Regional
ECHR	European Court of Human		Development Fund
	Rights	ERM	exchange rate mechanism
ECHR	European Convention on	ERP	European Recovery
	Human Rights		Programme (Marshall Plan)
ECJ	European Court of Justice	ERT	European Round Table of
ECOFIN	Council of Economic and		Industrialists
	Finance Ministers	ESC	Economic and Social
ECSC	European Coal and Steel		Committee
	Community	ESCB	European System of Central
ECU	European Currency Unit		Banks
EDC	European Defence	ESDI	European Security and
	Community		Defence Identity
EDF	European Development	ESDP	European Security and
	Fund		Defence Policy
EEA	European Economic	ESF	European Social Fund
	Area	ETIS	European Telecom
EEA	European Environmental		Standards Institute
	Agency	ETUC	European Trade Union
EEB	European Environmental		Confederation
	Bureau	EU	European Union
EEC	European Economic	EUMC	EU Military Committee
	Community	EUMS	EU Military Staff
EFTA	European Free Trade	EURATOM	European Atomic Energy
	Association		Community
EIB	European Investment Bank	EUROPOL	European Police Office
EIS	European Information	FDI	Foreign Direct Investment
	Service	FIFG	Financial Instrument for
EMCF	European Monetary Co-		Fisheries Guidance
	operation Fund	FTA	free trade area
EMI	European Monetary	G7	Group of 7 (Western
	Institute		industrialized economic
EMS	European Monetary System		powers)
EMU	Economic and Monetary	G8	Group of 7 plus Russia
	Union	GAC	General Affairs Council
EN	European Norms	GATT	General Agreement on
EP	European Parliament		Tariffs and Trade
EPC	European Political	GDP	gross domestic product
	Community	GNP	gross national product
EPP	European People's Party	GSP	Growth and Stability
EPU	European Payments Union		Pact

GSP	Generalized System of Preferences	PES	Party of European Socialists
HOSG	Heads of State and/or Government	PHARE	Poland and Hungary: Action for the Reconstruction of the Economy (*Pologne et Hongrie: assistance pour la restructuration économique*)
IBRD	International Bank for Reconstruction and Development (World Bank)		
IGC	Intergovernmental Conference	PPP	purchasing power parity
IMPs	Integrated Mediterranean Programmes	PSC	Political and Security Committee
ISD	Investment Services Directive	QMV	Qualified Majority Voting
		QR	quantitative restrictions
ISPA	Instrument for Structural Policy for Pre-Accession	R&D	Research and Development
		RRF	rapid reaction force
JHA	Justice and Home Affairs	SAP	Social Action Programme
M&A	mergers and acquisitions	SAPARD	Special Accession Programme for Agriculture and Rural Development
MEP	Member of the European Parliament		
MLG	multi-level governance	SEA	Single European Act
MNC	multi-national company	SIM	Single Internal Market
NAFTA	North American Free Trade Area	SIS	Schengen Information System
NATO	North Atlantic Treaty Organization	SME	small and medium-sized enterprise
NGO	non-governmental organization	SMP	Single Market Programme
		TACIS	Technical Assistance to the Commonwealth of Independent States
NTB	non-tariff barrier		
NUTS	nomenclature of territorial units for statistics	TEN	trans-European network
OCA	optimum currency area	TEU	Treaty on European Union (Maastricht Treaty)
OECD	Organization for Economic Co-operation and Development		
		TREN	DG for Transport and Energy Policy
OEEC	Organization for European Economic Co-operation	Trevi Group	Intergovernmental group on international crime (*Terrorisme, Radicalisme, Extrémisme et Violence Internationale*)
OPEC	Organization of Petroleum Exporting Countries		
OSCE	Organization for Security and Co-operation in Europe		
		UN	United Nations

UNICE	Union of Industrial and Employers' Confederation of Europe (*Union des Confédérations de l'Industrie et des Employeurs d'Europe*)	VAT	value-added tax
		VER	voluntary export restriction
		WEU	Western European Union
		WTA	World Trade Agreement
		WTO	World Trade Organization

Supportive website: *http://www.abdn.ac.uk/pir/sources/eurogide.htm* A glossary of EU terms and acronyms.

Basic Statistics on Current EU Member States

Current EU members	Total population (millions), 2001	Area (thousand sq. km)	GDP (billion €), 2001	GDP growth (annual %), 2001	GDP per capita (€), 2001	GDP per capita as % of EU-15 average (PPS)	Inflation, (GDP deflator, annual %), 2001	Unemployment rate (% of total labour force), 2001
Austria	8.1	82.7	211.86	0.7	26,156	112.7	2.3	3.6
Belgium	10.3	32.8	254.28	0.7	24,687	105.8	2.4	6.6
Denmark	5.4	42.4	180.42	1.7	33,411	118.2	2.3	4.3
Finland	5.2	304.6	135.98	1.4	26,150	104.3	2.7	9.1
France	59.5	550.1	1463.72	1.0	24,600	101.5	1.8	8.5
Germany	82.2	349.3	2071.20	0.4	25,197	103.7	2.4	7.7
Greece	10.6	128.9	130.93	3.5	12,352	69.9	3.7	10.5
Ireland	3.8	69.9	114.48	3.3	30,126	119.7	4.0	3.9
Italy	57.8	294.1	1216.69	0.4	21,050	104.2	2.3	9.4
Luxembourg	0.4	2.6	21.51	0.1	53,775	192.0	2.4	2.0
Netherlands	16.0	33.9	429.17	0.2	26,823	111.1	5.1	2.5
Portugal	10.0	91.5	122.71	0.7	11,271	73.4	4.4	4.1
Spain	39.5	499.4	651.64	1.9	16,497	83.0	2.8	10.6
Sweden	8.9	411.6	244.23	1.6	27,442	99.4	2.7	4.9
UK	59.8	241.6	1593.40	1.6	26,645	102.2	1.2	5.0
EU average	**25.2**	**209.0**	**589.48**	**0.9**	**24,546**	**100.0**	**2.8**	**6.2**

Source: Eurostat, http://europa.eu.int/comm/eurostat/public/datashop and related Eurostat sources.

Basic Statistics on Prospective EU Member States

Prospective EU members	Total population (millions), 2001	Area (thousand sq. km)	GDP (billion €), 2001	GDP growth (annual %), 2001	GDP per capita (€), 2001	GDP per capita as % of EU-15 average	Inflation, (GDP deflator, annual %), 2001	Unemployment rate (% of total labour force), 2001
Bulgaria	8.2	110.6	15.2	4.0	1,900	8.0	7.5*	17.5*
Cyprus	0.8	9.2	10.2	4.0	15,100	61.5	1.9∧	3.0∧
Czech Republic	10.3	77.3	6.3	3.3	6,200	25.3	4.7*	8.5*
Estonia	1.4	42.3	61.7	5.0	4,500	18.3	5.8	12.4
Hungary	10.2	92.3	57.8	3.8	5,700	23.2	9.2*	6.5*
Latvia	2.4	62.1	8.5	7.7	3,600	14.7	2.5	7.6*
Lithuania	3.5	64.8	13.4	5.9	3,800	15.5	1.3*	12.5*
Malta	0.4	0.3	4.1	−0.8	10,300	42.0	2.8*	4.5~
Poland	38.6	304.4	196.7	1.1	5,100	20.8	5.3*	16.7*
Romania	22.6	230.3	44.4	5.3	2,000	8.1	34.5*	9.1
Slovakia	5.4	48.1	22.9	3.3	4,200	17.1	7.4*	19.8*
Slovenia	2.0	20.1	21.0	3.0	10,500	42.8	8.4*	11.5*
Turkey	67.4	769.6	164.6	−7.4	4,200	17.1	69.0	10.6
Average of candidates	**13.3**	**140.9**	**48.2**	**2.9**	**5,930**	**24.2**	**12.3**	**10.8**
EU average	**25.2**	**209.0**	**589.48**	**0.9**	**24,546**	**100.0**	**2.8**	**6.2**

∧ Data for Cyprus: inflation for Greek Cypriot area, 1.9% (2001 est.) and Turkish Cypriot area, 53.2% (2000 est.); unemployment for Greek Cypriot area, 3% (2001 est.) and Turkish Cypriot area, 5.6% (1999 est.).

* Data reflect the official estimate for 2001.

~ Data from 2000.

Source: Eurostat, http://europa.eu.int/comm/eurostat/public/datashop and the World Fact Book 2001, http://www.cia.gov/cia/publications/factbook.

Introduction – or How to Use this Book

When we first started studying European integration, we found it surprisingly difficult to understand the various aspects of the subject. Ordinary economic and political science textbooks on European integration did not provide us with the information we needed as intelligent – but uninformed – readers and academic articles on the subject assumed a very high level of prior knowledge. Upon finishing our degrees, we realized that, as former students, we had the knowledge to write a book that addressed the needs of students new to this subject – in other words, to create the book that we had needed at the beginning of our studies.

Because this is an introductory volume, we do not claim to provide all the relevant information on the subject; instead, we have outlined the facts you need to know in order to understand the subject and the issues that are most relevant to the current academic debate. Each chapter acts as an independent introduction to a particular topic. It is written based on the assumption that the reader has limited previous knowledge of the subject. In addition, we have written the chapters in a straightforward manner, with a bibliography at the end of each, rather than complicated footnotes referencing other volumes at the bottom of every page. Furthermore, we have designed each chapter so that the reader can quickly find the information they need, without having to read the book from cover to cover.

All chapters (with the exception of chapters 1 and 23) are divided into identical sections:

- An initial paragraph (or two) set in a tinted box, briefly outlining why the subject is important to the topic of European integration.
- A section entitled *The facts*, highlighting the most important aspects of the subject and including the basic facts and figures that students need to know in order to understand the literature.
- A section entitled *The problems/issues*, discussing the major areas of academic controversy, by addressing political science, economic as well as legal issues.

- A section entitled *Who wins/who loses*, examining the point of view of the main actors (such as national governments or citizens), in order to establish the distributional gains and losses from a particular policy – not only financially but also in terms of power, sovereignty, etc.
- A section entitled *Food for thought*, providing the reader with further avenues of inquiry. As it is difficult to address every aspect of each subject exhaustively, this section introduces ideas that need to be mentioned, but could not be expanded upon in the text.
- A *student-to-student tip*, offering helpful information based on the personal experience of the author on the best approach to the subject.
- A *summary*, identifying key information throughout the chapter and intended as a quick overview of the main issues.
- A *selected bibliography*, providing a list of books and articles that students have found useful, in a prioritized rather than alphabetical order. It also contains articles by most of the academics mentioned in the chapter, and identifies any 'seminal works' on a subject.
- A list of *supportive websites* most relevant to the subject area.

This structure allows readers to target the information they need on each subject, without having to read unnecessary, complicated text. If another chapter in the book offers more information about a subject mentioned, the name of this chapter is noted in italics, in addition to cross-referencing in the index: for example, (see *Regional Policy*).

There are also some aspects unique to this study of European integration that you should know about before you begin.

- The European Union may be referred to as the EEC, the EC, the EU or the Community, depending on the historical context and the preference of the particular author.
- While this volume sometimes refers to individual treaties (such as the Treaties of Rome or the Nice Treaty), the term 'Treaty' may be used generally to refer to the consolidated contents of all the treaties.
- The Treaty on European Union (TEU) was signed in 1992 during the Intergovernmental Conference at Maastricht; therefore, this document is often referred to as the Maastricht Treaty. In this volume, it may be referred to either way.
- Following the TEU, the Treaty is divided into three sections, known as 'Pillars': the first, (Community), Pillar deals with most EU policies; the second Pillar pertains to the CFSP; the third Pillar deals with some aspects of JHA. Decision-making procedures differ significantly within each Pillar.
- The Articles of the Treaty were renumbered in 1997 in the Treaty of Amsterdam; therefore older literature often uses the older numbering system. In order to facilitate the use of all the literature, this volume uses the new numbering, placing the older article designation in parentheses: for example, Article 234 (ex-Article 177).

- The Community currency used before the introduction of the euro (€) in 1999 was called the ECU.
- The various policy departments of the EU Commission (known as Directorates-General, or DGs) were formerly numbered, but are now named using descriptive titles. While this volume uses the names of the DGs, older literature may refer to the numbering system. Please note that when referring to EU policy areas (i.e. Regional Policy), the name of that policy will be capitalized; when referring to the policy areas in general, there will be no capitalization.

Selected bibliography

Academic textbooks

Tsoukalis, L. (1997) *The New European Economy Revisited*, 3rd edn, Oxford: Oxford University Press.
  Tsoukalis presents an outstanding account of the political economy issues surrounding the European integration process, although he focuses more on politics than economics.
Wallace, H. and W. Wallace (eds) (2000) *Policy-Making in the European Union*, 4th edn, Oxford: Oxford University Press.
  The authors provide an excellent supportive resource, compiling essays by several academics on EU integration.
Artis, L. and N. Lee (eds) (1997) *The Economics of the European Union: Policy and Analysis*, Oxford: Oxford University Press.
  This is a useful book for analysing the EU from an economic point of view.
Bainbridge, T. (1999) *The Penguin Companion to the European Union*, 2nd edn, Harmondsworth: Penguin.
  This is an exceptionally clear reference work, which is useful for finding specific bits of information, rather than providing a comprehensive introduction to the subject area.

Newspapers and magazines

The Financial Times: *http://www.ft.com*
  The *FT* offers some free and some subscription-based online access, and its news coverage and analysis are excellent. Although the *FT* is very good at presenting different arguments, it does so from a liberal standpoint. Search the *Specials* if you want more in-depth analysis (e.g. Europe Reinvented), and the *Surveys* for country analysis. Check also *www.ft.com/brussels/*.
The Economist: *http://www.economist.com*
  Every weekly edition contains a section on European issues, ranging from four to ten pages. These pages are worth reviewing either in hard copy or online. The *Economist* special surveys on various topics offer insight into integration issues. Some of the best ones can be accessed free online (http://www. economist.com/surveys/): the *EU* (23 Oct. 1999), *Models of European Capitalism* (12 Feb. 2000), *A Constitution for Europe* (28 Oct. 2000) and *EU Enlargement* (19 May 2001). The quarterly *Economist Intelligence Unit (EIU) Country Reports* provide the information needed to perform country analysis for essays.
The Week in Europe: *http://www.cec.org.uk/press/we/latest.htm*
  This publication provides concise information weekly on the latest developments in the EU. PDF versions of the publication can be downloaded free of charge.
The European Voice: *http://www.european-voice.com*
  This is a weekly newspaper covering EU affairs, published by the Economist Group.

Official publications from the European Union

Fontaine, P., *Europe in 10 points*. European Documentation.
Borchardt, K-D., *The ABC of Community Law*. European Documentation.
Borchardt, K-D., *Europe from A to Z*. European Documentation.

All three can be ordered free from the European Commission's Representation in the UK (www.cec.org.uk)
The European Union: A Guide for Americans, by the Delegation of the EU Commission to the United States (*http://www.eurunion.org/infores/euguide/euguide.htm*)

All of these publications are official sources, and therefore are biased in favour of the EU.

Other written sources

The European Public Affairs Directory, Landmarks sa/nv. This annually updated directory contains the names and contact details of thousands of professionals working in or around the EU. The *EPAD* is usually available at university libraries, and is an essential source for those conducting original research.
The *Monitoring European Integration* reports from the Centre for Economic Policy Research (www.cepr.org) are an annual series of reports on the progress of economic integration in Europe.

Electronic sources

Portals

Portals are websites that give selected and evaluated links to other relevant websites. In many cases, portals can be more efficient than search engines for finding quality information.

http://eiop.or.at/euroint/ EuroInternet provides up-to-date details of where to find information on the Internet related to all issues concerning European integration. It has an amazing pool of resources, and we strongly recommend that you start all searches here.
http://www.euroguide.org Euroguide is developed by Essex County Libraries with input from 146 public library authorities, offering access to sources of very updated EU information on the web.
http://www.eurunion.org This is a very useful website, particularly the section on EU Law and the policy overviews.
http://www.europeanaccess.co.uk/addinfo/eotihome.htm *Europe on the Internet* provides a substantial, comprehensive and structured list of websites with European information. Also available at this site is *The Web Directory: Europe on the Internet*.
http://www.eia.org.uk The page 'Websites for EU Information' on the European Information Association portal provides access to many EU-related sites.
http://www.ex.ac.uk/library/internet/eurostudies.html This is a comprehensive listing of Internet resources, with brief annotations provided by the European Documentation Centre at the University of Exeter.

Official EU server

http://www.europa.eu.int *Europa* is the official EU server, the first place to search for official documents, press releases, etc. Unfortunately, it can be relatively difficult to navigate. In particular, the search engine on the site should be used only for very specific queries. Below are some of the most relevant features of the site:

- *What's New in Europa*, a section of the *Europa* website, which is updated daily – *http://europa.eu.int/geninfo/whatsnew.htm*
- *European Commission official documents*, a list of all official Commission documents, including all White and Green Papers, the *Bulletin of the European Union* (monthly), and the *General Report on the Activities of the Union* (annual) – *http://europa.eu.int/comm/off/index_en.htm*
- *The Economic and Financial Affairs Documentation* is the source of a variety of documents, such as information on European economic trends and the EU economy, replacing its predecessor, the Annual Economic Report. It is also the source for the *Convergence Report* and the *Broad Economic Policy Guidelines*. Reports and studies, economic papers, euro papers and enlargement papers can be found at: *http://europa.eu.int/comm/economy_finance/document/docum_en.htm*
- *EU Commission Press Room* offers a service that sends daily email updates on EU issues directly to personal email accounts – *http://europa.eu.int/comm/press_room/index_en.cfm*
- *SCAD Plus* contains an index and overview of many important EU policies and programmes. It is best used in conjunction with the EP Fact Sheets, listed below – *http://europa.eu.int/scadplus/*

http://www.europarl.eu.int   An excellent but under-used official resource, whose mostly interesting features are:

- *EP Research DG*. It is a well-kept secret that the EP has its own Research DG, which provides extremely useful studies and background documents – *http://www.europarl.eu.int/studies/default_en.htm* and *http://www.europarl.eu.int/workingpapers/default_en.htm*
- *EP Fact Sheets* provides an excellent encyclopaedic *Fact Sheets on the EU*, which cover all aspects of EU policy and include details of legal documents and EP involvement. It is an excellent initial resource when approaching new subject areas – *http://www.europarl.eu.int/factsheets/default_en.htm*
- *The Legislative Observatory of the EP* is a useful site for following current legislative developments; it offers information on what stage of the decision-making process any particular piece of legislation is at. The search engine is difficult to use, so specific queries are best – *http://wwwdb.europarl.eu.int/dors/oeil/en/default.htm*

http://www.cec.org.uk   The website of the EU Commission Representation in the UK, it provides interesting briefings on all policy fields, and is a very good starting point for research on most policies.

http://www.fco.gov.uk/eu/   The UK Foreign Office site provides a section called *Facts, not Myths*, offering information for an informed debate on British membership in the EU. The Foreign Office recognizes that 'much of the information that people read about Europe in the United Kingdom is misleading or inaccurate'.

http://www.parliament.uk   The research done by the UK Parliament is fresh, up-to-date and an expression of the state of the debate in the least pro-European EU country. The site aims at providing politically impartial and factual information, as well as a range of opinions on each subject covered:

- *House of Commons Research Papers Library* is extremely useful, and follows academic as well as newspaper debates – *http://www.parliament.uk/commons/lib/research/rpintro.htm*
- *House of Lords Select Committees' Reports on the European Union* are not plentiful, but offer in-depth studies of certain EU issues. They have been created by the UK House of Lords to aid in decision making – *http://www.publications.parliament.uk/pa/ld/ldeucom.htm*

Statistics

http://europa.eu.int/comm/eurostat/ Euro-Indicators from *Eurostat*, the official EU Statistical Office, furnishes up-to-date economic indicators on all fifteen member states. Unfortunately, specific queries cost €15–30, so we recommend obtaining information from the OECD or the World Bank as well.

http://www.oecd.org/statistics/ This provides a wide range of economic statistics for the thirty member countries of the OECD.

http://www.worldbank.org/data/ The World Bank also provides good statistics on fifty-four indicators for 207 countries.

http://www.abcnews.go.com/reference/countryprofiles/countryprofiles_index.html Country information at this site is extremely useful to support essays with accurate economic data.

http://www.odci.gov/cia/publications/factbook/index.html The *CIA World Fact Book* provides country profiles and a great deal of useful statistical information on all officially recognized countries. However, all financial data are provided in US dollars, which must then be converted into euros for comparison with statistics from other EU sources. See http://www.x-rates.com to convert euros to US dollars on a daily or monthly basis by year from 1990.

http://www.imf.org The International Monetary Fund (IMF) offers very interesting working documents and country information.

Think tanks

http://europa.eu.int/comm/cdp/index_en.htm The Forward Studies Unit (FSU) is a think tank of the EU Commission. White Papers and working documents can be found here.

http://www.theepc.be The European Policy Centre provides invaluable information regarding current issues.

http://www.wrr.nl This is the site for the Netherlands Scientific Council for Government Policy, which has a selection of excellent working documents.

http://www.tepsa.be The Trans-European Policy Studies Association is a Belgian site, with sections called *Documents online* and *Recent Papers* providing working documents and materials.

http://www.enepri.org The European Network of Economic Policy Research Institutes comprises ten leading economic research institutes (the CEPS and the CPB are the best ones), offering interesting working papers.

http://www.britainineurope.org.uk *Britain in Europe* is an interesting site, providing a good pamphlet on exposing all the straight-banana and euro urban myths.

http://www.freebritain.co.uk   This nationalistic anti-Europe site provides a complete list of Euro-sceptic web resources. It is a good source for those interested in critiques of EU integration.

Universities and academic organizations

http://netguide.coleurop.be/   The College of Europe website has links to virtually all aspects of EU affairs. It is the best portal for non-official sources.

http://www.iue.it   This is the home-page of the European University Institute in Florence, which has an interesting collection of studies and analyses: *Publications from the European University Institute, Florence*, provides access to the EUI Working Papers, the Jean Monnet Chair Papers, and the EIB Lecture Series. The Jean Monnet Lectures are particularly useful – *http://www.iue.it/PUB/*.

http://www.eucenters.org   The Network of European Union Centres provides a pool of resources from ten European Union Centres hosted by academic institutions throughout the USA.

http://www.indiana.edu/~west/   This is a vast up-to-date pool of resources from Indiana University.

http://www.columbia.edu/cu/lweb/indiv/lehman/guides/westoid.html   It is extremely useful to find EU web resources from Columbia University.

http://www.lib.berkeley.edu/GSSI/eu.html   This site contains a helpful list of EU Internet resources from the University of California at Berkeley.

http://www.theclasslist.com/ecsa   The European Community Studies Association (ECSA) is the premier EU studies scholarly and professional association world-wide. It publishes the *ECSA Review Fora*, from the US section of ECSA, which are sets of commissioned essays on timely topics in EU affairs and EU studies.

Online journals

http://www.eiop.or.at/erpa/   EIoP is a common access point for the following online working paper series in the field of European integration research. It offers recent academic papers in a variety of subjects and a very user-friendly data base, and includes:

- Online publications on European research, Robert Schuman Centre and Academy of European Law at the European University Institute, Florence.
- MPIfG Discussion Papers and MPIfG Working Papers, Max Planck Institute for the Study of Societies (MPIfG), Cologne.
- Jean Monnet Working Papers, Harvard Law School.
- European Integration online Papers (EIoP) ECSA-Austria.
- Advanced Research on the Europeanization of the Nation-State (ARENA), Oslo.
- Working Papers, Mannheim Centre for European Social Research (MZES).

Other useful links

http://www.useu.be The site of the US Mission to the EU, it provides a great deal of factual information and excellent links to other sites.

http://news.bbc.co.uk/hi/english/static/in_depth/europe/2001/inside_europe/ The BBC provides an excellent compilation of interesting information on the EU.

http://www.eurunion.org/legislat/home.htm An introduction to EU basics, as well as EU law and policy overviews, are available here.

http://eurotext.ulst.ac.uk/ The *Academic Introductions* provides basic information on the different topics from leading academics in their fields.

http://www.euobserver.com The *EU Observer* offers updates on the activities of European institutions.

http://www.eubusiness.com This online European business information service provides very up-to-date news in all policy fields.

http://www.euractiv.com This information source is focused on EU news, policy positions and EU actors.

Political map of Europe, 2002

Part I

BASIC BACKGROUND

I

A History of European Integration

Jess Clayton

The European Union (EU) is a historical project based on the desire to promote peace and stability in Europe through economic integration. However, the development of the EU since the end of World War II has been neither linear nor consistent, and historians have constructed many explanations for this uneven development throughout the EU's fifty-year history. One of the more useful concepts introduced to explain this phenomenon is known as 'deepening versus widening':

- *Deepening* refers to EU integration in terms of policy development and the creation of institutions.
- *Widening* refers to EU integration in terms of increased EU membership through enlargement.

While not the only engine for EU development, deepening and widening can be viewed as a vehicle by which the EU has reached its present state. However, it is important to realize that while deepening sometimes leads to widening (and vice versa), this is not consistently the case. In fact, history has demonstrated that deepening can block widening, and widening can inhibit deepening. Moreover, deepening and widening can result in unexpected developments within the EU. This chapter will provide a brief overview of EU history, by highlighting major events in EU integration, in terms of deepening and widening.

A   The Golden Age and the origins of the European Community (1945–1969)

The reconstruction of Europe after World War II initiated a period of dynamic economic growth in Europe that is often referred to as the 'Golden Age', which lasted from 1950 to 1969. This period witnessed a rapid increase in intra-EC trade, the rise of state-supported industries (known as 'national champions'), and a mixed economy in the EEC member states (see *Economic Theories of Regional Integration*). While the economic boom assisted the initial success of the European Communities, it also hid many of the institutional deficiencies and economic barriers which characterized the EEC.

I   The Schuman Plan and the creation of the European Coal and Steel Community (ECSC)

The physical devastation of Europe after World War II inspired some world leaders to devise a constructive and peaceful way to rebuild the continent. While the US-funded European Recovery Programme (known as the Marshall Plan) provided money for reconstruction, it did not offer a long-term solution to the political antagonism between European nations. The creation of an economic community composed of European nations was only one of several proposals that aimed at rebuilding Europe and ensuring future peace and prosperity. However, the Schuman Plan (created by Jean Monnet, but presented by French Foreign Minister Robert Schuman) had several distinct advantages over the other ideas put forward:

- It focused on joint control over the means of creating war: namely, coal and steel production.
- It created the institutional basis for economic co-operation between France and Germany.
- It acted as a stimulus to the economy, particularly in the manufacturing sectors.
- It provided economic disincentives for conflicts between members of that organization.

In other words, Monnet proposed a way in which Germany could add to the prosperity of Europe while simultaneously preventing German rearmament and subsequent European conflicts.

The Schuman Plan became the basis for the ECSC, which was established in April 1951 through the ratification of the Treaty of Paris by France, Germany, Italy and the Benelux countries (Belgium, the Netherlands and Luxembourg). The founding principle behind this organization – namely, that political ends could be achieved through economic means – is still a guiding principle of the current EU. Moreover, many institutions created for the ECSC (such as the High Authority) provided the framework for such Community institutions as the European Commission and the European Court of Justice (ECJ).

The Schuman Plan and the ECSC provide examples of both deepening and widening. By expanding the customs union created by the Benelux countries in 1944 to include the two large economic powers of France and Germany, the ECSC demonstrated the importance of widening to increase the economic viability of a customs union. Through the political structure developed in the Schuman Plan, Monnet provided a framework for greater economic co-operation between all member states, as well as the possibility for further integration in other areas.

2   The Treaties of Rome and the creation of the European Economic Community (EEC)

The success of the ECSC during the economic boom of reconstruction led to the creation of the European Economic Community (EEC) through the ratification of the Treaties of Rome in March 1957. One of the primary motivations behind the expansion of the ECSC into the EEC came from France. The customs union in coal and steel production had led to greater prosperity in the manufacturing sectors, in which Germany held a dominant position. However, France still had a largely agricultural economy, which did not benefit directly from the elimination of barriers to trade instituted by the ECSC. Therefore, in proposing the expansion of the current organization to include agriculture, France hoped to increase its economic benefits from the project. Therefore, the Treaties of Rome created two new organizations to complement the ECSC: the EEC and EURATOM (the European Atomic Energy Community). In contrast to the restricted scope of the Treaty of Paris, the EEC Treaty envisioned a common market within Europe based on the free movement of goods, services, capital and labour. These goals were to be achieved through the elimination of trade barriers between the member states (see *Economic Theories of Regional Integration*). Importantly, the EEC now included a common policy on agriculture (see *Common Agricultural Policy*).

The creation of the EEC demonstrates a significant deepening of the Community. The initial success in the fields of coal and steel production led to the desire for co-operation in agriculture. This in turn led to the first common policy in the Community: namely, the Common Agricultural Policy (CAP), which still accounts for as much as half of the EU budget. Expanding the scope of the Community to include all aspects of the economy resulted in the need to create a common external tariff (CET) and an EU-level competition policy (see *External Policies* and *Competition Policy*).

At the same time, the rapid deepening of the EEC also instigated a response from non-member states which would temporarily prevent the widening of the EEC. Led by the UK, seven countries that were not members of the EEC joined together to create the European Free Trade Association (EFTA) in January 1960. Unlike the EEC, EFTA allowed members to conduct external trade policies independently, and excluded agricultural goods from its customs union. In addition, EFTA was much more intergovernmental than the EEC. Partly as a result of EFTA, the first enlargement of the EEC (to include three members of EFTA) did not take place until 1973.

3   The Empty Chair crisis and the Luxembourg Compromise

The Treaty of Rome was an ambitious document that called for the expansion of several supranational institutions and the transfer of competences from the national governments to the Community decision-makers. During the early 1960s, the Commission sought to gain the political power necessary to act as the administrative head of the Community. However, the development of this level of supranationalism disturbed many member states – in particular, France, which had traditionally led the development of the Community since its conception by Jean Monnet. Under the leadership of President Charles de Gaulle, France began demanding that the Community remain more intergovernmental (see *Theories of European Integration*). Yet in 1965, intergovernmentalism was being challenged in several areas:

- The European Assembly (the precursor to the European Parliament) wished to develop into a more legitimate legislature, and desired some control over the EU budget.
- The EU Commission was requesting an independent source of revenue from import duties and agricultural levies, so that the EU budget would be less dependent on the member states.
- The EEC was attempting to finalize the co-ordination of national governments in the creation of the CAP, which was favoured by France but generally opposed by Germany.
- The Treaty had established a timetable for the use of qualified majority voting (QMV), to begin in 1966, which would replace unanimity voting in some policy areas (see *Institutional Processes*).

Therefore, when the Commission proposed a package deal instituting the CAP, in co-ordination with EU revenues from tariffs and levies under the control of the European Assembly, de Gaulle refused to compromise. While France was the main proponent of the CAP, de Gaulle was unwilling to cede any more power to the EEC in the form of an independent budget or, more importantly, through the use of QMV. When in July 1965 the other five member states rejected France's counter-proposals on these issues, the French delegation walked out of the Council of Ministers, and boycotted Community activities for seven months. This led to an impasse that was only resolved through the Luxembourg Compromise in January 1966. The compromise allowed for the *de facto* retention of unanimity for the protection of vital national interests, whenever QMV was used.

The Luxembourg Compromise demonstrates how rapid deepening in the Community can lead to situations which result in policies that severely restrict further deepening. While the compromise resulted in EU budgetary 'own resources' (see *The EU Budget*) and the CAP, it did so only by sacrificing the broad implementation of QMV until the 1980s. The maintenance of the national veto resulted in 'lowest-common-denominator' decision making within the EEC, as member states used the threat of veto to resist policy compromises (see *The Single Market*). This is one reason why the development of the Community slowed to a stand-still during the 1970s.

B   The Oil Crises and Stagflation (1970–1979)

The third decade of the European project was characterized by a global economic slowdown and a corresponding slowdown in European integration. The recession resulting from the two oil crises caused member states to turn away from joint projects in order to protect their own struggling economies. Moreover, the Luxembourg Compromise led to lowest-common-denominator decision making, which slowed the process of product harmonization. Despite the dismal economic atmosphere, the 1970s did result in several important developments in the EEC. The collapse of the Bretton Woods monetary system forced the EU to create its own form of monetary co-operation. In addition, the first enlargement served to solidify the importance of the EEC as the primary form of economic co-operation in Europe, at the expense of the further development of EFTA. Both developments would act as springboards for rapid widening and deepening in the 1980s.

I   Global economic crisis

The economic expansion and low levels of unemployment which had assisted the development of the EEC since the end of World War II collapsed in the 1970s. The recession was triggered by the dramatic rise in oil prices resulting from the policies of the OPEC cartel in 1973–4 and 1978–9. Higher oil prices led to higher production costs, especially in Europe, which was particularly dependent on foreign oil as a source of energy. This situation resulted in the simultaneous rise in both unemployment and inflation throughout Europe, a situation known as 'stagflation'. In addition, the collapse of the Bretton Woods monetary system in 1971 undermined the stability of all the European currencies (see *Economic and Monetary Union*).

The recession might have been shorter and milder, however, had not the internal structure of most European economies proved too inflexible to cope effectively with the rapid change in the global economic environment. Two factors in particular caused these structural inflexibilities:

- *Keynesianism*: the monetary policy used throughout Europe in the 1960s, which controls the economy by supporting the domestic demand for goods through government spending and by focusing on reducing unemployment. However, as the system relies on a closed economy, Keynesian monetary policy began to fail in the European economies as intra-EEC trade increased.

- *The welfare state*: many European economies had developed a strong welfare state through the Golden Age, and therefore entered the recession with rigid labour costs and high levels of unemployment benefits for workers. As firms were forced to lay off workers in order to remain profitable, both unemployment and governmental debt increased.

EEC member states responded to this economic situation in one of two ways: either through strict anti-inflation policy (Germany and the Netherlands) or through increased Keynesianism (France and the UK). The latter led to greater national debt, and did little to relieve the effects of the recession. Eventually, the economic policies of most European countries began to shift towards Monetarism (also known as the 'New Economic Orthodoxy'), which focuses on controlling inflation and deregulation (see *Economic and Monetary Union*). This shift was a crucial factor in the formation of the coalition that would result in the programme to complete the Single Market by 1992 (see *The Single Market*).

However, the differing strategies of member states and the strain that the recession placed on their national governments had profound implications for the further deepening of the Community. Throughout this period, member states consistently reneged on many of their Treaty obligations by creating non-tariff barriers (NTBs) to trade and other measures to protect national industries and employment. Further integration in the areas agreed upon at the 1969 Hague Summit was abandoned, as member states increasingly used the threat of veto (resulting from the Luxembourg Compromise) to block any EEC legislation that might threaten national industries. As a result, very few pieces of legislation were passed, and even fewer were implemented by member states. The apparent disregard for Treaty obligations and the needs of the EEC led both politicians and academics to speculate about the end of the European project.

2 The collapse of the Bretton Woods System and the European Monetary System (EMS)

The Bretton Woods Conference in 1944 created the post-war international monetary system known as the Bretton Woods System (BWS). The BWS was based on all currencies having a fixed exchange rate with the US dollar. In addition, US dollars could be converted into gold at any time, and vice versa. In order to maintain parity with the dollar, central banks across the world kept reserves of US dollars, which they used to intervene in foreign exchange markets. While the BWS worked fairly well initially, strong economic growth in the 1960s and increased US military spending created the need for more paper money in the system. The USA satisfied this demand by printing more US dollars, without securing the paper currency with gold. When other governments began to lose confidence in the system, US President Nixon declared that the dollar was no longer convertible into gold. This declaration, in August 1971, ended the BWS, and destabilized world currencies.

The large fluctuations in currency values in the 1970s and the reluctance of the USA to construct a new international system emphasized the need for a new monetary arrangement. While the first attempt at a new monetary system in 1972 was relatively unsuccessful, it did provide a basis for the launch of the European Monetary System (EMS) in March 1979. The key to the EMS was the exchange rate mechanism (ERM), devised as a means of minimizing currency fluctuations around the European Currency Unit (ECU). In general, the EMS was fairly successful in this regard, partly due to a new agreement on the use of Monetarism through the EEC (see *Economic and Monetary Union*). Moreover, the EMS had a positive macroeconomic impact on the EEC, since it helped fight inflation and created the currency stability needed for economic recovery.

Therefore, while the collapse of the BWS exacerbated the recession, it also acted as a catalyst for deepening, through the development of an independent European monetary system. The EMS not only provided the historical precedent for the launch of Economic and Monetary Union (EMU) in January 1999, it also facilitated the convergence of European economies needed to correct the divergent policy choices made by member states at the onset of the recession. As a result, the EMS helped to reunite the EEC, and offered a rationale for renewed economic co-operation between member states.

3   The first EU enlargement

The first enlargement of the EU was decided upon in December 1969 at the Hague Summit, before the beginning of the recession. The British application for membership, which had been vetoed by French President Charles de Gaulle twice in the 1960s, was crucially important. First, the UK had pushed for the creation of the European Free Trade Association (EFTA), as an alternative form of economic co-operation within Europe. Therefore, as the largest economy in EFTA, the UK's membership in the Community ensured the dominance of the EEC. Secondly, UK membership in the EEC triggered applications from Ireland and Denmark, as both had economies that were strongly dependent upon trade with the UK. Thirdly, the economic differences between the EEC and the applicant countries (the UK in particular) forced some EEC policy reform in order to facilitate successful enlargement.

The first enlargement not only provided a template for future widening of the Community, but also created a connection between EFTA and the EEC (which was a contingency of UK and Danish accession) that aligned the economies and policies of the two economic communities. This alignment greatly facilitated the fourth enlargement of three former EFTA countries into the Community. Widening also facilitated deepening, not only through policy reform, but also through the creation of a new regional policy in 1974 as the inclusion of Ireland created the need for a more comprehensive policy to support poorer member states. At the same time, the UK demanded a policy which would compensate for the lack of economic benefit it received from the CAP (it was paying far more into the budget for this policy than it was receiving in return). The European Regional Development Fund

(ERDF) was therefore created both to compensate the UK for the CAP and to help solve Ireland's economic problems. The ERDF later provided the basis for a more comprehensive European regional policy, initiated in the 1980s.

However, the results of widening were not all positive. The enlargement added three new member states with very different economies, which conflicted with the more homogeneous economies of the original six member states. In this sense, widening created a stumbling block to further deepening. As newer member states with economic preferences that differed from the rest of the Community, the UK and Denmark would become the member states most reluctant to accept further integration in many policy areas.

C   Economic recovery and the launch of the Single Market Programme (SMP) (1980–1992)

The economic recovery in the second half of the 1980s and the SMP created a virtuous circle of integration and economic expansion that facilitated the creation of the European Union (EU). While the shift in the global economy certainly aided this process, it was the political and economic developments at the EU level that fuelled the rapid completion of the common market. The speed of economic integration also resulted in a push for rapid political integration, in the form of the controversial Treaty on European Union (TEU).

I   Cassis de Dijon *and mutual recognition*

Prior to the introduction of the Single Market Programme, European integration had proceeded slowly, due to two factors: product harmonization and unanimity voting in the Council of Ministers. As a result of the Luxembourg Compromise, QMV had not been introduced into the decision-making process within the EEC; moreover, each member state maintained a national veto. Therefore, national barriers to the free movement of goods – in the form of non-tariff barriers (NTBs) – could only be removed through product harmonization, the process whereby all member states would agree on common standards for products (see *The Single Market*). However, because each member state wished to protect its national industries while at the same time promoting national products within other member states, product harmonization proceeded incredibly slowly. As a result, the small amount of legislation that was passed provided for only the lowest levels of integration.

This situation changed due to a concept called 'mutual recognition', which was introduced by the ECJ in the *Cassis de Dijon* ruling of 1979 (see *Law and European Integration*). The principle of mutual recognition states that any product legally manufactured in one member state, in accordance with the regulations of that member state, must be allowed into the market of any other member state in the Community. The key to the success of this proposal was the fact that mutual recognition was both compatible with Monetarism and avoided the problems associated with harmonization. It thus eliminated the need to remove many individual barriers to trade through legislation, thereby also avoiding the problems with unanimity voting in the Council.

Mutual recognition had two other positive attributes that facilitated further deepening and widening within the Community. It did not constrain further widening in the same way that product harmonization might have (namely, by forcing new member states to adopt hundreds of EU product standards before accession). In addition, it provided the motivating principle behind the SMP, thereby facilitating rapid deepening both economically (through the removal of barriers to trade) and politically (in the form of the Single European Act) throughout the late 1980s and early 1990s.

2   The 1985 White Paper and the Single European Act (SEA)

The European Commission used the principle of mutual recognition as the foundation of the Cockfield Report (commonly known as the '1985 White Paper'). The goal of this report was to produce a plan for the revitalization of the European project through the completion of the Single Internal Market. The report identified over 280 remaining barriers to the completion of the internal market. While mutual recognition helped to eliminate most NTBs to trade, the Commission proposal indicated that other legislative tools would be necessary for the completion of the internal market through the SMP (also known as the '1992 project', as 1992 was the deadline for completion). Of primary importance were the introduction of QMV on issues pertaining to the internal market and the establishment of the co-operation procedure for decision making between the European Parliament (EP) and the Council (the first direct election of the EP in 1979 had produced a more pro-active legislative body interested in gaining decision-making power and promoting integration). The Single European Act (SEA), signed in February 1986, served to implement the treaty amendments necessary for the SMP, and corresponded with the Iberian enlargement of the EC. The SEA would also change the title of the Communities from the EEC to the EC (Economic Community). In addition, the SEA introduced a policy on economic and social cohesion that would broaden the scope of European regional policy, and provided a legal basis for the long-term implementation of EMU.

As a result, the 1985 White Paper and the SEA provided the greatest impetus toward deepening since the ratification of the Treaties of Rome, while also creating a platform for the successful widening of the Community to include Greece, Spain and Portugal.

3   The second and third EU enlargements

The second and third enlargements had a profound effect on the character of the EC and on the direction of further integration. Despite the relative poverty of the country, the accession of Greece in 1981 benefited both parties, as it offered the Greeks democratic and economic stability after the years of dictatorship and provided the current member states with an important geopolitical partner in the Aegean during the Cold War. Similarly, the third enlargement (known as the 'Iberian enlargement') concerned the membership of two impoverished countries recovering from decades-long dictatorships. However, the accession of Spain and Portugal was initially opposed by France and Italy, since Iberian agricultural exports would compete with their own products. For this reason, the Iberian enlargement was delayed until CAP and budgetary reforms were agreed upon at the Fontainebleau Summit in June 1984.

The widening of the EEC to include three relatively poor, agriculturally based economies was facilitated by the deepening taking place through mutual recognition and the SMP. At the same time, widening created the need for further deepening through the development of an EU-level regional policy that had not been included in the treaties. The stimulus for the development of this policy was both economic and political. Economically, the SEA (1986) introduced the concept of 'economic and social cohesion' as a counterbalance to increased market pressures caused by the SMP (see *Regional Policy*). Politically, Greece and Italy were able to negotiate a side-payment for their approval of the Iberian enlargement, in the form of the 1985 Integrated Mediterranean Programmes (IMPs). Similar to the ERDF, the IMPs were funding programmes designed to compensate Italy, Greece and southern France for increased competition in agricultural products resulting from the Iberian enlargement. These programmes later led to the development of the Structural Funds, which provide funding to regions suffering from unemployment, industrial decline and below-average GDP.

D   The Treaties of European Union, Amsterdam and Nice (1992–2002)

The 1990s began with a crisis of confidence in the EU, and ended with the introduction of a common currency. The Treaty on European Union (TEU, also known as the Maastricht Treaty) played a crucial role in the development of the EU during this period. The ratification of this treaty, which profoundly changed the nature of European integration, proved surprisingly difficult following the success of the SMP. While this ratification crisis served to slow down the pace of integration, it also assisted the Community in developing a new institutional flexibility, which then allowed for continued deepening throughout the period.

I   The ratification of the TEU

The Treaty on European Union was an ambitious revision of the foundations of the Community:

- It reconfigured the Treaty around three 'Pillars': the Economic Community (EC), Common Foreign and Security Policy (CFSP), and Justice and Home Affairs (JHA).
- It established EU citizenship.
- It provided the framework for the completion of the single market through a single currency.
- It expanded the role of the EU into areas that had traditionally been the preserve of national governments, such as social and monetary policy.
- It increased the use of QMV, and introduced a new legislative procedure (co-decision) that granted more power to the EP.

As a result, Denmark and the UK, member states that had traditionally been most reluctant to delegate any additional sovereignty to the EC, opposed many of the provisions of the TEU. In particular, the Social Charter and the establishment of a common currency were so unacceptable to the British and the Danes that a Danish national referendum held in 1992 rejected the Treaty, and the British Parliament became completely divided in its attempts to ratify the TEU. National referendums held in other member states approved the TEU by slim margins. Uncertainty about the future of the EC was exacerbated by the currency crisis in September 1992, which severely weakened the EMS and signalled the beginning of an economic downturn throughout Europe.

In order to save the TEU, the Edinburgh European Council of December 1992 created several new provisions to increase accountability, transparency and flexibility within the EU. In particular, the principle of subsidiarity reassured member states that decision making would be made at the most appropriate level of government. In addition, the UK and Denmark were allowed to opt out of contentious policy areas, such as participation in the third stage of EMU, defence policy provisions, and aspects of JHA. Once these opt-outs were accepted, the TEU was able to enter into force, in November 1993. The new provisions made the EU more flexible, and allowed for continued deepening, albeit at a slower pace, despite the reservations of some member states (see *Flexible Integration*). Paradoxically, had the rapid deepening prescribed by the TEU taken place, it might have acted as a barrier to further deepening, as it could have undermined the fragile consensus on the future of the Community which existed between the member states and the citizens of those states.

2   The collapse of the EMS and the introduction of the Economic and Monetary Union (EMU)

The factors that led to the success of the EMS throughout the 1980s deteriorated in the early 1990s. The liberalization of capital movements (an element of the SMP) in January 1990 led to large-scale speculation on capital markets. More importantly, the asymmetry of the EMS in favour of the Deutschmark began to undermine the system, as Germany raised interest rates in an effort to offset the inflation caused by reunification (see *Economic and Monetary Union*). Higher interest rates in Germany resulted in higher interest rates throughout the EMS economies, which exacerbated the economic slowdown in the rest of the EC (since these member states were in recession, they needed low interest rates to stimulate their economies). This resulted in the collapse of the EMS in 1992–3, which coincided with the problematic ratification of the TEU.

Ironically, the solutions to the problems which had undermined the EMS were outlined in the TEU: namely, the creation of the EMU with a permanent fixed exchange rate, a European Central Bank, and a single currency. The 1989 Delors Report, which provided the foundation for the Treaty provisions on EMU, recommended a three-stage system for the implementation of the single currency. Of primary importance was the third stage, which introduced the euro (€) as legal tender, and fixed the bilateral exchange rates of the participating currencies. In order to participate in the third stage of EMU, member states had to fulfil the convergence criteria – price and exchange rate stability, in combination with low inflation and restricted national debt. The criteria resulted in the successful nominal convergence of EU economies, and had a very positive effect on those member states with the highest levels of inflation and national debt. By 1998, eleven countries had qualified to take part in the third stage of EMU. Three countries (Denmark, Sweden and the UK) did not wish to proceed; initially, Greece did not qualify to take part in the third stage. The EMU was officially launched in January 1999, and the euro began circulation in January 2002 (see *Economic and Monetary Union*).

The consequences of the EMU are twofold: first, the EMU marked a significant deepening of the Community through the creation of a common currency, and thus the final step in the completion of the common market. Secondly, the method by which the EMU was achieved encouraged the convergence of all EU economies (even those not participating in EMU), which should have positive ramifications for the economic unity of the Union. As a result, EMU has solidified the integration achieved through the SMP, and provides an impetus for further deepening within the fields of tax and fiscal harmonization. At the same time, the stringency of the convergence criteria and the extent to which the EU economies have converged may become barriers to future widening, since the economic demands of participation in the EMU may be too difficult for the new market economies of Central and Eastern Europe.

3 The fourth EU enlargement and future enlargements

The fourth enlargement of the EU, to include three of the seven remaining EFTA member states, was facilitated by the establishment of the European Economic Area (EEA) in May 1992. The EEA replaced the bilateral relationships that the EU had established with individual EFTA members as a condition for the first enlargement. Under the EEA, all EFTA countries were required to adopt most EU legislation under the first Pillar of the TEU, including internal market, social and environmental legislation. Three EFTA applicants – Austria, Sweden and Finland – were easily able to adopt the remaining legislation necessary for accession, and to take up the responsibilities of membership. The fourth enlargement was therefore quick and relatively painless for the EU and the accession countries.

However, future enlargements will not enjoy such favourable circumstances. Following the collapse of the Soviet Union, ten countries from Central and Eastern Europe (as well as Malta, Cyprus and Turkey) have negotiated accession agreements with the EU. Unlike the EFTA countries, the current applicants are significantly poorer than the rest of the EU, and have relatively young, underdeveloped market economies, which will have difficulty surviving the pressures of the more developed market economies in the Union. Moreover, the relatively new democratic governments in the applicant countries are finding it a challenge to adopt and implement the vast amount of EU legislation necessary for membership (see *EU Enlargement*).

At the same time, this next, anticipated enlargement has acted as a catalyst for deepening through the implementation of internal reform of the institutional structure of the EU. In order to accommodate the new member states, the EU has initiated several institutional and policy reforms, which should improve the functioning of the EU as a whole. Should these reforms fail to be successfully implemented by the time of the next enlargement (scheduled for 2004), they could create a barrier to the further deepening of the Union.

4 The Amsterdam and Nice treaties

Compared to the TEU, both the Amsterdam and the Nice treaties initiated much more modest reforms to the Union. However, these reforms were significant in several areas, especially the reconfiguration of EU institutions and policies in preparation for widening. The 1997 Amsterdam Treaty introduced the first measures necessary for the next enlargement, including a limit on the number of members of the European Parliament. More importantly, this Treaty facilitated more rapid integration in several slow-growing policy areas, especially JHA and CFSP. Policies on immigration, asylum and judicial co-operation were transferred from the intergovernmental third Pillar of the Treaty to the more supranational EC Pillar, and the provisions of the Schengen Accords on the free movement of people throughout the Community were fully incorporated into the Treaty structure. In addition, growth in the field of CFSP was encouraged through the creation of a High Commissioner for CFSP and the limited introduction of QMV into this policy area. Formal procedures for flexible integration within the EU were also established by the Amsterdam Treaty, allowing for various rates of integration between member states (see *Justice and Home Affairs*, *Common Foreign and Security Policy*, and *Flexible Integration*).

Yet, the impact of these Treaty revisions was not immediately evident within the Community, and both politicians and academics complained that the Treaty had not gone far enough in preparing the Union for enlargement. As a result, the 2001 Nice Treaty built on and extended the reforms made in 1997, especially with regard to the institutional structure of the EU. In particular, this Treaty established the number of EP seats to be held by each member state following enlargement, reweighted QMV to accommodate additional member states, and established 'reinforced QMV' which requires a double majority (by both member states and population) for QMV. In addition, flexible integration, which is seen by many as the key to continued deepening in light of the next widening, was enhanced by the Treaty. Moreover, the Charter of Fundamental Rights was recognized by the Treaty, although it did not become a binding legal document.

In many ways, these treaties have attempted to correct some of the deficiencies in the Union, which became apparent during the ratification of the TEU. In particular, the democratic deficit and the lack of transparency in the EU had undermined the confidence of EU citizens in the feasibility and wisdom of further integration. The reforms made at Amsterdam and Nice partially addressed these issues, through recognition of the importance of fundamental rights and in some ways through the institutionalization of flexible integration, so that member states can choose their own pace of integration while remaining part of the Union. Perhaps more significantly, the more modest goals of these treaties acknowledge the fact that integration must keep pace with the needs and desires of EU citizens rather than the ambitions of their national governments.

Food for thought

The tension between deepening and widening is perhaps greatest now that the Community is enlarging to almost five times its original size. There is much speculation that continued widening could prevent further deepening, due to lack of consensus among member states with very different agendas. While tools such as flexible integration have been introduced to counteract such difficulties, the deepening of only portions of the Community without those member states which are either unwilling or unable to participate in further integration could destroy the bonds holding the EU together. However, the two main projects that the EU is now embarking upon, eastward enlargement and the Convention on the Future of Europe, seem to demonstrate that the Union will attempt to balance the demands of both widening and deepening in the coming years.

Student-to-student tip

The study of European integration is greatly aided by an accurate chronology of historical events. For this reason, most chapters address the historical background of the policy area under analysis. We recommend augmenting this information by using the Historical Overview at the end of this volume, so that not only the chronology, but also the causality, of events becomes more apparent.

Selected bibliography

Selected chapters

Dinan, D. (1999) *Ever Closer Union*, 2nd edn, London: Macmillan, part I: 9–201.
   Dinan provides a detailed and thorough introduction to the history of the EU, with a focus on political actors.

Tsoukalis, T. (1997) *The New European Economy Revisited*, 3rd edn, Oxford: Oxford University Press, chapters 2–3: 33–79.
  Tsoukalis offers an excellent synthesis of economics and politics in these two historical chapters.

Bulmer, S. (1997) 'History and Institutions of the European Union', in M. Artis and N. Lee (eds), *The Economics of the European Union: Policy and Analysis*, Oxford: Oxford University Press, chapter 1: 5–32.
  This chapter provides a conceptual and historical framework for EU policy and political developments.

Crafts, N. and G. Toniolo (eds) (1996) *Economic Growth in Europe since 1945*, Cambridge: Cambridge University Press, chapters 1–2: 1–72.
  Based on both applied economics and economic history, these chapters emphasize chronological and institutional detail.

General books

Urwin, D. W. (1995) *The Community of Europe: A History of European Integration since 1945*, 2nd edn, London: Longman.
  Widely used in academia, this is the best concise introduction to the history of European integration up through the TEU.

Schulze, M.– S. (1999) *Western Europe: Economic and Social Change since 1945*, London and New York: Longman, chapters 1–9: 1–157.
  This book is excellent not only for its breadth and authority, but also for its accessibility. It offers a wide-ranging introduction to economic and social developments since World War II.

Supportive websites

http://europa.eu.int/abc/history/index_en.htm The Commission provides a year-by-year summary of historical events affecting the EU.

http://www.let.leidenuniv.nl/history/rtg/res1/index.htm Leiden University offers a very rich website with many interesting links to historically related events.

http://www.iue.it/LIB/SISSCO/VL/hist-eur-integration/Index.html The excellent European University Institute at Florence has developed a thorough website with different links and resources of some countries' and European histories.

2

Theories of European Integration

Bjørn Høyland and Mark Schieritz

In the field of integration there are several competing theories that have been used to describe, explain or predict the nature and course of the integration process. The choice of theory used by an individual researcher in any published work not only reflects the personal bias of the author, but also shapes how the researcher forms his or her conclusions about the course of integration. Therefore, the theories of European integration provide a framework for understanding the topic of European integration, as well as several tools for analysing individual European Union (EU) policies and dissecting the work of the academics that write about them.

The facts

A   The need for theories

Theories provide guidelines for empirical investigations by directing attention to some factors while neglecting others. Theories play a critical role in identifying the issues and problems, as well as who wins and who loses as a result of a particular aspect of European integration. As no single theory is capable of taking all factors into account, the selection of factors for analysis is very important, since this determines the relationship between variables. For example, the statement 'The integration project was re-launched with the Single European Act (SEA) in the mid-1980s' is not a theoretically neutral, factual statement; it assumes that particular types of events and actors are more important than others. In this case, it contends that political bargains made between member states were more important to integration than the economic demands of multi-national corporations. The statement also assumes a particular causal relationship: namely, that economic integration follows from political decisions.

An alternative theoretical approach might argue that the SEA was only a political consolidation of the economic developments already taking place. In this counter-argument, the important actors are trans-national business, and the important events are day-to-day decisions. In fact, this statement would reverse the causal relationship proposed by concluding that political decisions are a reaction to economic developments. The conflict between these theories is the result of each theory's choice of primary actors.

There are three primary types of integration theories: orthodox theories, issue-specific theories and critical theories, which are described below.

B   The orthodox theories

The two main theories of European integration are neo-functionalism, developed by E. B. Haas in *The Uniting of Europe* in 1958, and intergovernmentalism, developed by Stanley Hoffman in *Obstinate or Obsolete? The Fate of the Nation State and the Case for Western Europe* in 1966. Based on international relations theory, these two theories are critical to the integration debate.

C   The issue-specific theories

There are several theories that attempt to explain specific aspects of the integration process. Rational choice institutionalism and sociological institutionalism, for example, are based on actor preferences; however, sociological institutionalism uses a wider definition of the idea of 'institution' as its basis of analysis. The principal-agent framework is utilized to examine the relationship between the Commission and the member states. Historical institutionalism analyses integration in relation to other historical events and along a historical continuum. While these theories can be applied to the entire integration process, they are more successful in explaining particular interactions between particular actors.

D   The critical theories

This category is used to describe theories that do not fit into the orthodox inter-national relations theory framework, and tend to focus on the relationship between events and actors. They include constructivism, political economy and the eclectic theories.

The problems/issues

A   Neo-functionalism vs Intergovernmentalism

The orthodox theories stress the importance of different actors in the integration process. While neo-functionalists, such as Haas, propose that supranational institutions, such as the European Commission and the European Court of Justice (ECJ), are the primary engines of EU integration, intergovernmentalists such as Moravcsik maintain that the member states control the pace depth of integration.

I   Neo-functionalism

This theory focuses on the importance of the supranational actors in the integration process, with particular emphasis on trans-national elites who supposedly facilitate integration. However, the most important concept in this theory is spillover. Spillover occurs when integration in one area results in demands for integration in others. Spillover can be either economic or political:

- *Economic (or functional) spillover* occurs when incomplete integration undermines the effectiveness of existing policies and institutions. This, in turn, creates an impetus from these institutions to widen and deepen integration, through the creation of either new institutions or new policies. Economic and Monetary Union (EMU), for example, can be argued to be the result of economic spillover from the Single Market Programme (SMP); in other words, the SMP could not be complete until the EU had a single currency (see *Economic and Monetary Union*).
- *Political spillover* takes place when the existing supranational structures of the EU initiate the development of new political organizations to support their increased power and responsibility. Here, co-operation in one area facilitates pressure for co-operation in neighbouring areas. For example, when agreeing to common rules on competition, it made sense for the Community to agree to common environmental standards as well (see *Environmental and Social Policies*). Thus, this type of spillover widens the scope of EU competences, while deepening integration in specific areas.

Critique: while neo-functionalism is able to identify the conditions for supranational influence and their ability to promote further integration, it cannot explain the inconsistent nature of integration. A good example is the Luxembourg Compromise of 1966, which allowed for a *de facto* national veto on all issues by all member states, and arguably slowed down the integration process during the 1970s. Neo-functionalism is also criticized for exaggerating the capacity of trans-national elites and supranational organizations to guide the pace of integration against the will of the member states.

2 Intergovernmentalism

This theory focuses on the role of the member states in the integration process, and predicts areas of integration by distinguishing between issues of high and low politics. *High politics* concerns issues that affect national sovereignty, while *low politics* concerns issues of a technocratic and generally uncontroversial character. Intergovernmentalists argue that integration occurs as a result of deliberate political decisions taken by heads of state in traditional negotiations. In addition, it assumes that the outcome of these negotiations (and therefore the pace and breadth of integration) is determined by three factors:

- *National preferences*, which are predetermined at the national level before the heads of state begin negotiation at the EU level. These preferences will determine how each member state will vote in the Council of Ministers, and on what issues it may be willing to compromise.
- *Intergovernmental bargaining*, in which each state will try to maximize its individual returns from any EU policy decision. This type of negotiation often results in decisions being taken at the lowest level of compromise or in side-payments being made in exchange for votes.
- *Lowest-common-denominator decisions*, which are created when nations attempt to limit any further yielding of sovereignty. Occasionally, the threat of exclusion (from a policy area or from the Union itself) will result in higher-level compromises.

The creation of the SEA can illustrate the intergovernmentalist argument, by outlining the position of the three main actors: France wanted to use the SMP to pull itself out of recession and to increase the political prestige of the Community; Germany was interested in the SMP because it would create a bigger market for German industry; the UK viewed the SMP as an opportunity to export British neo-liberal ideas to the European continent. Even though each member state had its own set of national preferences, they all agreed that the SMP could maximize their individual returns, despite the fact that such a programme would limit aspects of their sovereignty (see *The Single Market*).

Moravcsik argues that the threat of exclusion often forces reluctant states either to go ahead with integration in some undesirable areas or to leave the EU (either completely or partially through the opt-out option). For example, the UK did not agree to any of the social policy initiatives proposed during the Maastricht negotiations; instead of blocking everyone else from moving ahead, the UK decided to 'opt out' of the Social Protocol (see *Environmental and Social Policies*). Some academics also contend that side-payments are used in the intergovernmental bargaining process in order to buy off potential losers from further integration. For example, EMU created economic challenges for the weaker EU economies (Spain, Ireland, Portugal and Greece). In order to ensure political support for EMU, other member states were willing to establish the Cohesion Fund, which offered these poorer member states financial relief (see *Economic and Monetary Union* and *Regional Policy*).

Note that the traditional intergovernmental approach takes state preferences as given, designed to preserve the sovereignty of the state, while liberal intergovernmentalism maintains that preferences are shaped by different societal interests, mediated through the top bureaucrats and heads of state, who are mainly concerned with economic gains.

Critique: intergovernmentalism has been criticized for focusing on 'history-making' bargains, thereby neglecting the role of day-to-day decisions. Intergovernmentalists also portray the state as a single unilateral actor, ignoring the fact that the state consists of several different actors (such as constituencies and regional governments) with their own goals and agendas. In addition, intergovernmentalism neglects the role of non-state actors, such as interest groups and multi-national corporations. Therefore, the theory has difficulty explaining the expansion of the EU, and especially the creation of new institutions, such as the Court of First Instance (CFI), or the increased competences of the Commission, in areas such as the Structural Funds (see *Regional Policy*).

B Issue-specific theories

Unlike the orthodox theories, issue-specific theories do not attempt to provide an explanation of the whole integration process. Instead, they create general tools for understanding parts of the process. Rational choice institutionalism, the principal-agent framework and historical institutionalism are examples of these kinds of theories or frameworks.

I Rational choice institutionalism

Initially derived from comparative politics, this theory assumes that actors (whether they are member states, interest groups or the Commission) attempt to maximize their preferences in an institutionally and strategically constrained environment. Institutions are defined as formal legal entities that influence actors, either by providing the actors with information or by constraining actor behaviour through decision-making rules. According to rational choice institutionalism, the impact that institutions have on actors is limited; institutions can affect actor strategies, but not actor preferences. Applied to the EU, rational choice institutionalism offers two major insights:

- First, the EU was created based on the utility that it was expected to provide to national governments. Specifically, the EU has been set up to perform four tasks: to interpret the treaties, monitor compliance with Treaty obligations, reduce transaction costs through policy initiation, and produce policy credibility.

- Secondly, policy making in the EU is explained by highlighting the differences in decision-making rules. For instance, under the co-operation or co-decision procedure, policy outcomes are likely to be fairly close to Commission or European Parliament (EP) preferences, so that these institutions become 'conditional agenda-setters'. Under these procedures, it is easier for the Council to accept than to reject a proposal. With the consultation procedure, however, policy outcomes are more likely to be closer to Council preferences, as the EP only has an absolute veto on such policies. Hence, the type of rules under which policy making occurs directly affects policy outcomes (see *Institutional Actors*).

Rational choice is successful in explaining both the interaction between the EU institutions and the policy outcomes in different policy areas. It also helps to explain intergovernmentalist theory, by stressing the constraints that decision-making rules place on powerful actors when they attempt to maximize their interests.

Critique: rational choice has been criticized for focusing too much on formal rules, thereby neglecting the importance of informal negotiations in Brussels. In addition, the definition of institutions is sometimes criticized for being too narrow. Sociological institutionalism, a competing theory, offers a broader definition of both institutions and rules; however, this theory is often criticized for being too inclusive, and therefore too subjective. Other academics question whether actor preferences can be constant and remain unaffected by the interaction with institutions (see the communicative action approach below). In addition, Hix argues that the EU cannot be understood as a political system similar to current nation-states.

2 Principal-agent framework

This framework is used by rational choice institutionalists in order to explain why the principals (i.e. member states) delegate power to agencies (i.e. the EU institutions). The principal-agent framework argues that delegation occurs because member states want to reduce transaction costs in the creation, administration and enforcement of policies. These costs arise because member states do not trust each other to comply with the Treaty. Having a neutral, independent agent (i.e. the Commission) as the administrator of EU policy solves this problem, because all member states agree to abide by the decisions of the agent (this problem is sometimes referred to as the 'prisoner's dilemma').

The relationship between the principals and the agent is characterized by the balance between what the principals consider to be the optimal level of delegation to the agent and the amount of control over policy that they are willing to concede to the agent. However, once the agent is created, it begins to develop its own set of interests and agenda in the integration process – agency officials may wish to maximize their own political power, or the agency may be 'captured' by outside private interests. By anticipating the positions of the different principals, the agent can make policy proposals that are both acceptable to the principals and favour the agency's institutional and policy interests. Alternatively, the agency may 'shirk': in other words, it may pursue policies that are opposed to the principals' interests to further its own political goals. This approach therefore concludes that the agent becomes an autonomous political actor, affecting the balance of power between the principals.

Principals can limit the autonomy of the agent by using their policy discretion to monitor the agent's behaviour. Monitoring can occur by acting on complaints against the agent or by designing rules and procedures that minimize the agent's discretion, as well as by changing key personnel or even revising an institution's mandate. On the other hand, subjecting the agent to excessively strict controls will decrease its efficiency and flexibility, whilst increasing costs associated with monitoring the agency. Excessive constraints could nullify the rationale behind the creation of the agent in the first place.

In the EU, member states (= the principals) fear that the Commission (= the agent) will attempt to promote integration and enhance its own power to a greater extent than is mandated by the Treaty. Through the creation of the COREPER (the Committee of Permanent Representatives), the Council of Ministers has attempted to regain some control over the political process, by designing rules and procedures that limit the power of the Commission. However, the ultimate threat (namely, changing the Commission's mandate) would be very hard to achieve in the EU, as any such changes would require a Treaty revision that would have to be agreed by unanimity (see *Institutional Actors*).

Critique: criticism of this framework is directed against the assumption that the new agency will develop preferences that inevitably conflict with those of the principals. Yet, the member states have developed significant safeguards to prevent the Commission from abusing its delegated powers, including the COREPER and comitology. This could indicate that the member states fear supranational control, as indicated by this theory. However, this theory fails to recognize the different preferences within the agency and between the different member states by treating the principals and the agent as homogeneous entities with set preferences.

3 Historical institutionalism

This theory maintains that the role of a policy or institution may evolve into something that was not originally intended or desired by its creators; in other words, a member state might not have predicted the development of a particular policy when it originally agreed to the contents of the Treaty. However, the creation of policies and institutions leads to 'path dependencies', which make such unintended consequences difficult to correct. For example, the Common Agricultural Policy (CAP) began as an allocative policy intended to boost agricultural efficiency. Over time, it evolved into a redistributive policy, transferring resources from the European consumer and taxpayer to the farming community. Because of strong vested interests, the CAP has proved difficult to reform (see *Common Agricultural Policy*).

Historical institutionalism also draws attention to the rising costs of leaving the Community. Member states often accept unwanted policy outcomes because they have little choice – rejecting unwanted policies is often possible only if a member state decides not to fully participate in the workings of the Community (e.g. through an opt-out clause) or to leave the Community completely. Both options are normally perceived to be against national interests. Therefore, this theory offers a good explanation of why member states accept some unwanted policy outcomes. In addition, historical institutionalism argues that those politicians who originally signed the Treaty might not have been concerned with its future implications for their country, because they themselves would have withdrawn from political life by the time the policy could have negative repercussions. Thus, the importance of different time horizons is also emphasized in the historical institutional explanation.

Critique: critics argue that while historical institutionalism may explain why unexpected developments in integration occur, it neglects the importance of actors' long-term interests and their ability to predict future outcomes. Note also that rational choice institutionalism and historical institutionalism can be very similar, and sometimes differ only in the way they label the phenomena they describe.

C Critical theories

'Critical theories' is the general term for theories that do not support the basic rationalist assumption that actors maximize outcomes. By contrast, the basic assumption of these theories is that the interests of the actors are shaped and reshaped by events. These theories also focus on the interaction between actors rather than the actors themselves, and therefore often take several factors into account. By contrast, orthodox theories have generally been constructed on the basis of the analysis of a few selected phenomena. Accordingly, the task of such theories is not to explain a lot with a lot, as the constructivist does, but instead to explain a lot with a little, as the neo-functionalist does with the concept of spillover. Whereas the orthodox theories benefit from their simplicity and clarity, this does not mean that the critical theories, despite their complexity, cannot further understanding about integration. Below are brief explanations of several critical theories.

I Political economy

This theory uses economic methodology to study political subject matter, or a political science approach to study economic subject matter. Political economy analysis is particularly interested in cases where the aggregate cost–benefit analysis does not necessarily prevail. For example, political economy might focus on circumstances in which special interest groups, which would lose out from some aspect of integration, block the pursuit of maximum overall benefits. Therefore, the motivation of key actors begins with an analysis of the distinction between the overall costs and benefits for society as a whole and those costs and benefits specific to a special interest group – in other words, the asymmetric distribution of costs and benefits. Through the consideration of the interaction between economic and political factors, political economists believe that the problems with the EU system and the determining factors within that system are more easily identified. In each policy chapter in this book, the *Who wins/who loses* section examines the issue from a political economy point of view.

2 Constructivist theories

The primary difference between constructivist theory and the more orthodox rationalist approaches to integration is the emphasis on society and situation. Constructivism argues that the world is shaped by social interaction rather than by individuals. Moreover, actors' interests and identities are not fixed – they are shaped by each situation through a series of complex (and sometimes contradictory) practices. Therefore, whereas rationalism focuses on how actors behave in order to maximize their preferences, constructivism attempts to explain how actors' preferences are shaped or have evolved in a specific situation. Within the context of EU integration, constructivism is primarily interested in explaining the constraints on the behaviour of strategic actors and how the different actors understand the same situation. Thus, constructivism focuses on establishing the parameters of a situation, in order to analyse it. This often leads to a concentration on the role of ideas, and especially on how an idea can become dominant within a certain context.

In *Theory of Communicative Action*, Jürgen Habermas developed a constructivist theory, which emphasizes the role of the 'guiding norms' developed in the negotiation and deliberation process. However, these norms are not interpreted as static, but are instead developed in the process of communicative action – the process by which at least one of the participants in the debate is willing to listen to the argument of other participants. Because of the force of that argument, participants may change their understanding of the context of the issue in question. If the context changes, so will the norms (and therefore the decisions) of the participants in the debate.

3 Eclectic theories

These theories are exemplified by the concepts proposed by Susan Strange in *Mad Money* (1998). Her primary methodology is 'enveloping structures'. These structures might be markets and technology that have an effect on integration and are mutually reinforcing. She embraces a variety of disciplines in her attempt to explain the EU.

Critique: critics argue that while critical theories are helpful (since they take many different factors into account), the volume of factors that are analysed by these theories or frameworks can itself be a barrier to the appropriate use of the theories. Since so many factors are used in the analysis, it becomes difficult to determine which factors play the primary role in determining integration.

Who wins/who loses

Political economy theory often analyses policy in terms of distributional gains and losses (i.e. winners and losers from a particular policy development). As this book demonstrates, the winners and losers from any particular policy or event in EU integration change, depending on which theory one applies to the situation. Therefore, when examining a policy area or an institutional process, the main actors to consider include:

- Member states
- EU institutions (the Commission, the Council, the EP and the ECJ)
- Interest groups, such as business and regions
- EU citizens
- The rest of the world, including international organizations, third-country (non-EU) nationals and developing nations

Food for thought

Theories often present themselves as neutral explanations of EU integration. However, they are created by academics with their own biases and preferences. Therefore, are the theories merely explanatory tools, or are they ideological vehicles for promoting a certain type of European Union?

Student-to-student tip

Reading the seminal works on neo-functionalism and intergovernmentalism is not recommended. The ideas of Haas and Hoffman have developed in such a way that works by Moravcsik and Sandholtz and Stone Sweet will prove much more helpful in developing a working understanding of the theories in their present context. In addition, Susan Strange's articles on the EU offer a good foundation for familiarity with the eclectic theories, which have recently become more popular in academic circles.

Summary

- There are several theoretical approaches to the progress of European integration, ranging from the orthodox theories to the critical theories.
- The primary orthodox theories are neo-functionalism, which focuses on spillover, and intergovernmentalism, which focuses on the negotiation process between member states.
- In addition, the study of different aspects of EU integration has led to the development of more issue-specific theories, such as the principal-agent theory. The benefit of these theories is that they provide a framework for understanding how the EU evolves.

- While often conflicting, all these theories have valid arguments and specific insights, which should be understood in order to gain insight into the integration process.

Selected bibliography

Primary sources on the theories

Intergovernmentalism:

Moravcsik, A. (1999) *The Choice for Europe: Social Purpose and State Power from Messina to Maastricht*, London: UCL Press, chapter 5: 314–78.
The book presents liberal intergovernmentalism in great detail, and is very harsh with its opponents. See in particular the chapter on the SEA.

Neo-functionalism:

Sandholtz, W. and Stone Sweet, A. (eds) (1998) *European Integration and Supranational Governance*, Oxford: Oxford University Press.
Sandholtz and Stone Sweet have edited this book, presenting neo-functionalism in a new, up-to-date style. While complex, it does include Pierson's important explanation of historical institutionalism.

Eclectic theories:

Rumford, C. (2002) *The European Union: A Political Sociology*, Oxford: Blackwell.
Rumford offers the first book-length treatment of the political sociology approach to the EU. It is useful as a supplement or alternative view on most of the current debates, in particular on questions of societal importance, including unemployment, core–periphery relations, enlargement and the democratic deficit.
Strange, S. (1998) *Mad Money*, Manchester: Manchester University Press, chapter 4: 60–77.
Strange's last volume, *Mad Money* examines globalization in several different countries using the eclectic framework, and offers a specific chapter on the EU.

Overviews of the theories

Nugent, N. (1999) *The Government and Politics of the European Union*, 4th edn, London: Macmillan, chapter 18: 491–519.
Nugent provides a good overview of the theoretical approaches without going into too much detail.
Wallace, H. (2000) 'Analysing and Explaining Policies', in H. Wallace and W. Wallace, *Policy-Making in the European Union*, 4th edn, Oxford: Oxford University Press, chapter 3: 65–81.
This is an excellent overview of the theoretical approaches to the EU, and is especially complementary to the one above.
Rosamond, B. (2000) *Theories of European Integration*, London: Macmillan.
Rosamond explains all the theoretical approaches in their historical context; it is perhaps the best book for students who find theorizing about the EU fascinating.
Checkel, J. and Moravcsik, A. (2001) 'A Constructivist Research Program in EU Studies', *European Union Politics*, vol. 2, no. 2: 219–49.
This article discusses the move towards mid-range theories within the constructivist framework. The discussion highlights the difference between constructivism and rationalism, while also identifying common ground between these theories. In particular, Moravcsik questions the added value of constructivism and whether it leads to alternative hypotheses.

Pollack, M. A. (2001) 'International Relations Theory and European Integration', *Journal of Common Market Studies*, vol. 39, no. 2: 221–44.

    Pollack presents a clear overview of the current theoretical debate, by arguing that there is a convergence between the realist, liberal and institutionalist approaches within the dominant rationalist framework.

Jachtenfuchs, M. (2001) 'The Governance Approach to European Integration', *Journal of Common Market Studies*, vol. 39, no. 2: 245–64.

    Jachtenfuchs argues that while other integration theories aim to explain the integration process, the governance approach offers an explanation of how the integration process influences national policies.

Supportive websites

http://www.helsinki.fi/~amkauppi/hablinks.html (English language) and *http://www.uni-magdeburg.de/iphi/aktuelles/Habermas2.html* (German language) These two websites provide information on Jürgen Habermas and the Theory of Communicative Action.

http://www.bham.ac.uk/IGS/course/integ.htm This site currently provides a helpful lecture on the various theories. Unfortunately, there are few similar sites available on integration theories.

http://www.eiop.or.at/eiop This site is a data base of working papers on European integration from several leading research centres. Several of the papers are of a theoretical nature, in particular papers from ARENA, which tend to be of a constructivist or governance nature.

Part II

THE UNION AS A POLITY

3

Institutional Actors

Vincent Coen and Riccardo Maestri

The term 'institutional actors' refers to the primary decision-making institutions in the EU; as such, they influence the way in which policy is formed and integration proceeds. The Treaties of Rome (1957) attempted to create a balance between these institutions by giving them overlapping executive, legislative and judicial powers. This leads to several problems, including a lack of transparency, power struggles between the institutions, and arguably increased tensions between the EU institutions and the member states. For this reason, studying the role and responsibilities of each actor is key to understanding the current status of EU policies and the issues that will present challenges to the Union in the future.

The facts

A The main institutional actors

The four key institutional actors in the European Union are the European Commission (the Commission), the European Council of Ministers (the Council), the European Parliament (EP) and the European Court of Justice (ECJ). In addition to these institutions, there are many secondary institutions, called 'bodies' and 'agencies', which support the activities of the Union (see below).

I   The European Commission

What is the Commission?
The Commission is often considered the central institution of the EU, with both legislative and executive powers. It is headed by a collegiate body (the College of

Commissioners), currently composed of twenty commissioners. Each EU commissioner is elected for a renewable five-year term by the member states, which agree to nominate a Commission President, after consulting the EP. Since the Amsterdam Treaty (1997), the Commission President has been subject to a vote of approval by the EP. Once approved, the President and the member states nominate the other nineteen commissioners. The EP must then approve the Commission as a whole, as it does not have the right to approve individual nominations. Currently, the larger member states (the UK, France, Germany, Italy and Spain) have two commissioners each, while the remaining ten members have one each. As agreed in the Nice Treaty (2001), starting in 2005, the Commission will consist of one commissioner per member state. When the Union reaches twenty-seven member states, the number of commissioners will be smaller than the number of member states, and commissioners will be selected using a rotation system based on national representation.

How does the Commission work?

The Commission must act under the principle of collective responsibility. While decisions are made by a simple majority vote, the Commission is collectively responsible for all decisions taken. Each commissioner is assigned one or several policy areas by the President, and is assisted by his or her own personal cabinet. Each policy portfolio has a different level of political prestige, and policy areas such as competition, agriculture and finance are considered to be most desirable.

Based in Brussels and Luxembourg, the Commission is also composed of a permanent Secretariat of approximately 18,500 officials, divided into twenty-eight Directorates-General (DGs). Each DG is responsible for one policy area, and special units exist for research, translation and legal services. Before the Amsterdam Treaty, the DGs were numbered – for example, the Competition Directorate-General was originally known as DG IV. Each DG also has its own policy preferences and favourite interest groups that it will consult on policy issues. While the DGs are supposed to work in tandem, disagreements between them often arise in conflicting policy areas. A good example of this is the *Danish Bottle case*, where the Energy DG (now known as DG TREN) brought a case against Denmark, despite the protestations of DG Environment (see *Environmental and Social Policies*).

What powers does the Commission have?

- *Legislative powers.* The Commission is the only institution that may formulate new proposals for Community legislation within the policy areas of the first (and to a certain extent, the third) Pillar of the Treaty. These are presented to the Council and the EP, who then accept, amend or reject the proposals. Since in many instances the EP has far less legislative power than the Council, the Council remains the primary law-making body. Even though the Commission is the sole policy-initiator, it must often modify its own proposals in order to facilitate consensus within the Council. It can also formulate policy and set agendas on its own initiative. Examples include the 1985 *Commission White Paper on the Internal Market*, its 1993 paper on deregulation (*Growth,*

Competitiveness and Employment), and *Agenda 2000*, containing proposals for future membership of Central and Eastern European countries within the Union.

- *Other legislative powers.* The Commission has been delegated quasi-legislative powers by the Council, in the fields of competition, external trade, agriculture and fisheries. If delegated special powers, the Commission is normally monitored by a management committee of national representatives.
- *Executive powers.* The Commission's executive tasks include administration of the EU budget, day-to-day management of EC Competition Policy, and representation of the Community on the international stage. To this end, the Commission is charged by the Council to negotiate on behalf of EU member states in several international organizations, such as the World Trade Organization (WTO). It also negotiates the accession treaties with applicant countries.
- *Supervisory powers.* The Commission has primary responsibility for ensuring that EU decisions are adequately implemented, and therefore has authority to bring legal action against persons, companies, states or Community institutions that have violated EU laws and regulations. In this respect, the Commission acts as the 'guardian of the Community treaties'.

Supporting institutions

EU policy is also supervised by over ten independent regulatory agencies, whose work is overseen by the Commission. They include bodies such as the European Environmental Agency and the European Agency for Safety and Health at Work. As these agencies do not have the power to adopt and implement policies, their main role is to monitor policy developments and provide expertise.

2   The Council of Ministers

What is the Council?

The Council of Ministers, composed of a representative from each member state who is authorized to make policy decisions for the government of that state, is the main legislative forum in the European Union. The Presidency of the Council rotates between the member states every six months. Unlike the Commission, the Council does not consist of a fixed group of representatives. There are two forms of the Council:

- The 23 *Specialized Councils*, whose membership changes according to the subject being discussed, such as agriculture or environment. The ministers responsible for these policy areas in each of the different member states come to Brussels to form the Council.
- The *General Council*, which consists of national Foreign Ministers and deals with general questions of co-ordination of the EU and foreign policy.

How does the Council work?
There are three voting procedures within the Council:

- *Simple majority*: used largely for procedural issues; eight votes out of fifteen are needed to pass a measure.
- *Unanimity*: used in those areas of the Treaty which are most politically sensitive and where the exercise of EU competence is most closely scrutinized, such as taxation and enlargement. Under unanimity, each individual member state has the power to block legislative decisions.
- *Qualified Majority Voting (QMV)*: QMV is a weighted form of voting, whereby each member state has a different number of votes, based on population (this will change with enlargement). Of a total of eighty-seven votes, a 'qualified majority' of sixty-two votes is required to approve proposals (for more details, see *Institutional Processes*).

What powers does the Council have?

- *Legislative powers*. The Council must approve Commission proposals in all policy areas, before this legislation can become EU law. While the Council increasingly shares legislative powers with the EP in areas such as Environmental Policy, it remains the primary decision-maker in the EU. As such, the preferences of the member states, which are communicated through the Council, influence not only the ratification of legislation, but also the type of legislation that is returned to the Commission for reconsideration.
- *Powers of delegation*. The Council has chosen to delegate many important tasks to the Commission, in order to increase both efficiency and legitimacy. However, the Council is reluctant to give the Commission more power than necessary, because it fears that the Commission will follow its own agenda, rather than that of the Council (see the principal-agent theory in *Theories of European Integration*). In order to prevent this, the Council has institutionalized a system of supervisory committees, composed of national representatives, called the *comitology system*. The Council can also request that the Commission submit legislative proposals in areas of EU policy which the Council would like to develop.
- *Supervisory powers*. The Council oversees the work of the other EU institutions, and can take them before the ECJ if they fail to uphold Community law.
- *Co-ordination powers*. There are several policy areas which still remain the sole responsibility of the member states, such as general economic policy, foreign and security policy, and aspects of justice and home affairs. The Council serves as a forum for these policy areas, where member states can consult each other and jointly decide on policy developments.

Supporting institutions

- The COREPER consists of member state representatives with ambassadorial rank, and is responsible for preparing Council meetings. The COREPER ensures that the ramifications of each piece of legislation proposed by the Commission are understood and agreed upon by the member states before a vote is taken. There are approximately 150 different COREPER working groups, which review Commission proposals and prepare reports that set the agenda for COREPER meetings. These reports are discussed by either COREPER I, composed of deputy permanent representatives, or COREPER II, composed of ambassadors from each member state. The COREPER presents most legislation to the Council as 'A points', which is legislation that has already been agreed to, but which still needs formal approval. Debatable legislation is presented as 'B points'; this legislation needs to be further discussed by the ministers concerned before a final decision is made. Most Commission proposals are analysed by COREPER I, which is primarily responsible for internal market policy. A smaller percentage of more controversial legislation is analysed by COREPER II.

• The *comitology committees* are also made up of representatives of national governments, who normally have expertise in certain policy areas. Their job is to control measures adopted by the Commission, by approving the implementation of policy measures. Under the Comitology Decision of 1987 (Council Decision 87/373 EEC, revised in 1999), five types of committees are used, which can vary by providing the Council with strong supervisory control or allow the Council only a weak, consultative role.

The difference between COREPER and comitology is that COREPER is responsible for overseeing the adoption of Commission proposals, while the comitology system controls the implementation of these proposals.

3   The European Parliament

What is the EP?
The EP replaced the Assembly established in the European Coal and Steel Community (ECSC, the precursor to the EU) in March 1962. MEPs have been directly elected by EU citizens (rather than appointed by national governments) for five-year terms since 1979. The EP is currently composed of 626 members. According to the Nice Treaty, membership after enlargement will be limited to 732 MEPs, and distribution of MEP seats will be as shown in table 3.1. (For more details on institutional reform, see *Enlargement*.)

As in QMV, smaller states are over-represented in the current system: Germany has one MEP per 808,000 citizens, while Luxembourg has one MEP per 60,000 citizens.

The EP meets one week in each month in plenary sessions in Strasbourg; more frequently, however, EP committees meet in Brussels, and the Secretariat meets in Luxembourg. This geographical fragmentation of the Parliament typifies the compromises often reached at the EU level, in order to satisfy the national interests of member states, who understand the benefit of having EU institutions in their country. The situation is nevertheless far from practical, and is expensive for the Union.

Table 3.1   Distribution of MEP seats

	Present seats		Future seats	
	Number	Percent	Number	Percent
Germany	99	15.8	99	13.5
France	87	13.9	72	9.8
Italy	87	13.9	72	9.8
Netherlands	31	5.0	25	3.4
Belgium	25	4.0	22	3.0
Luxembourg	6	1.0	6	0.8
UK	87	13.9	72	9.8
Ireland	15	2.4	12	1.6
Denmark	16	2.6	13	1.8
Greece	25	4.0	22	3.0
Spain	64	10.2	50	6.8
Portugal	25	4.0	22	3.0
Austria	21	3.4	17	2.3
Sweden	22	3.5	18	2.5
Finland	16	2.6	13	1.8
Poland	–	–	50	6.8
Hungary	–	–	20	2.7
Czech Rep.	–	–	20	2.7
Slovenia	–	–	7	1.0
Estonia	–	–	6	0.8
Cyprus	–	–	6	0.8
Romania	–	–	33	4.5
Bulgaria	–	–	17	2.3
Slovakia	–	–	13	1.8
Lithuania	–	–	12	1.6
Latvia	–	–	8	1.1
Malta	–	–	5	0.7
TOTAL	**626**		**732**	

What powers does the EP have?

- *Legislative powers.* The EP's powers vary according to which of the twenty-two legislative procedures are used. In general, the EP has the most power to affect legislation under the co-operation procedure, established by the SEA, and the co-decision procedure, developed in the Treaty on European Union (TEU, 1992).
- *Budgetary powers.* The EP must approve or reject the entire budget, which the Commission prepares and then negotiates with the Council. The EP has amended or rejected the budget on three occasions. However, the EP has final jurisdiction only over non-compulsory expenditures (such as environmental and regional policies), which constitute about 40 per cent of the EU budget, while the Council maintains control over all compulsory expenditures (such as agriculture).

- *Supervisory powers.* The EP plays a strong advisory role in the Community. It has the power to bring other institutions before the ECJ when they interfere with parliamentary prerogatives; it can investigate acts of misadministration carried out by EU institutions (through the EU Ombudsman or EP Committee of Petitions); it can also formally question both the Commission and the Council on a variety of matters, from human rights to local environmental initiatives. In addition, the EP plays a role in appointing the President of the Commission, and must approve each new Commission. More importantly, the EP can dismiss the Commission on a vote of censure by a two-thirds majority. Although the Parliament has never used this power, the mere threat of censure was sufficient to force the Santer Commission (1995–9) to resign. However, the EP cannot force individual commissioners to resign, which weakens its power. The EP Committee on Budgetary Control is responsible for the internal monitoring of expenditures. In order to strengthen this supervisory role, the other institutions must submit an annual report to the EP, and answer questions put forward by MEPs.

How does the EP work?
The EP has gradually gained more significant powers through the expansion of the legislative procedures. The Treaties of Rome only required the Council to consult the Parliament before accepting or rejecting the Commission's proposals. This legislative procedure is known as the *consultation procedure*, and is still used in areas such as the Common Agricultural Policy (CAP).

The SEA significantly increased the EP's legislative role, by granting it some agenda-setting powers, and by allowing it to accept, reject or amend some legislative proposals in a limited number of areas (such as research, environment and development). Known as the *co-operation procedure*, it is currently used only for issues pertaining to EMU. The SEA also gave the EP the right to ratify international agreements concluded by the Council and to ratify the admission of new members to the EU, under the *assent procedure*.

Most recently, the TEU gave the EP the right of veto in some EU legislation, such as that pertaining to free movement of workers and consumer protection. The Treaty of Amsterdam extended this procedure to areas such as employment, freedom of establishment, and equal pay for men and women. Known as the *co-decision procedure*, the Commission can still accept or reject any amendment requested by the EP, but in the end, both the Council and the EP have to agree on issues for them to become law (these procedures are explained in more detail in *Institutional Processes*).

Supporting institutions
The committees in the EP propose changes to legislation, usually in the form of a report, paper or draft resolution, which is then submitted to the full Parliament for approval during the plenary sessions in Strasbourg. Because alterations to committee proposals are unlikely to succeed in plenary sessions without the support of the committee in charge, the committees have a great deal of power over the legislative agenda of the EP. There are currently seventeen committees that

carry out preparatory work for the plenary sessions. The allocation of committee positions is determined by the size of the representation of each party, while the agenda of the plenary sessions and other important parliamentary activities are determined by the leaders of the political parties. So that the EP can monitor the Commission effectively, commissioners must appear regularly before the relevant EP committee, in order to explain Commission decisions.

There are currently around 100 EU political parties, organized into eight official political groups. The two largest political parties are the Party of European Socialists (PES, centre-left) and the European People's Party (EPP, centre-right). However, neither of these two parties is large enough to constitute even a simple majority without forming a coalition with one or more of several smaller parties, such as the Greens or the Liberals. Coalitions are often necessary under the co-operation and co-decision procedures, as the Treaty currently requires a vote by an absolute majority of all sitting MEPs for final resolutions. In many ways, European political parties in the EP act like national political groups; the key difference is that the MEPs form parties based on political convictions rather than nationality. In order to encourage multi-national parties, the number of MEPs needed to form a new party declines as the number of member states represented by the MEPs increases. Below is a description of the current major parties and the number of members in the fifth parliamentary term (1999–2004):

- European People's Party (EEP): Christian Democrats from all member states, numbering 233.
- Party of European Socialists (PES): Social Democrats from all member states, numbering 175.
- European Liberal, Democratic and Reformist Group (ELDR): Liberals (primarily Dutch Liberals) from several member states, numbering 53.
- Confederal Group of the European United Left/Nordic Green Left (EUL): a radical-left group composed of fringe environmental and ex-Communist parties from several member states, numbering 50.
- Green Party: Green Party members from nine member states, numbering 45.
- Union for Europe (UFE): a group of conservatives primarily composed of French Gaullists and members of Ireland's Fianna Fáil, numbering 22.
- Europe of Democracies and Diversity (EDD): a Euro-sceptic group that includes members of the UK Independence Party, numbering 16.
- Independents: MEPs not affiliated with a European political group, numbering 32.

4   The European Court of Justice

What is the ECJ?
The European Court of Justice (ECJ) is the institution in charge of ensuring that EU law is applied uniformly and of resolving disputes over EU law. The ECJ is located in Luxembourg, and consists of fifteen judges – one from each member state, appointed for six-year renewable terms. The judges are chosen by the national

governments from the judiciary in the upper national courts or jurists of recognized competence. The president of the Court is elected by his or her colleagues in the ECJ, for a three-year renewable term. In addition to the judges, the ECJ has nine Advocates-General. With legal backgrounds similar to the judges, they prepare opinions on cases in order to assist the Court in making a ruling. While these opinions can be rejected by the ECJ, they are most often accepted, and are often cited amongst the legal literature surrounding a case.

It is important to point out that the ECJ differs from two other bodies: the International Court of Justice, the judicial body of the United Nations (UN), which meets in The Hague (the World Court), and the European Court of Human Rights (ECHR), which was established by the Council of Europe in Strasbourg. EU member states must accept the final decisions and judgments of the ECJ, but have no legal obligation to accept those of the other two courts, which are not part of the EU.

What powers does the ECJ have?
The ECJ can be described as a European version of the US Supreme Court. Its decisions are final, apply to both member states and individuals, and are not subject to appeal. Unlike the US Supreme Court, the decisions of the judges are reached under the principle of collegiality, and no dissenting opinions are published. While the Court originally did not have the right of judicial review in the majority of the provisions contained in the second and third Pillars of the Treaties (in the areas of CFSP and JHA), the Treaty of Amsterdam extended the Court's power, and the ECJ can now rule on all aspects of Pillar III (JHA) except the validity or proportionality of police services and measures taken to maintain law and order.

While the powers of the ECJ were established by the treaties of Paris and Rome, a number of landmark cases have allowed the Court to gain significant power beyond the framework of the original treaties. These powers include supremacy of EU law over national law on issues related to the economic prerogatives of the Union. The member states have generally accepted the ECJ's competence in these areas (see *Law and European Integration*).

How does the ECJ work?
The ECJ can only affect EU legislation by ruling on cases submitted to it. Cases can be brought before the ECJ in four ways:

- *Preliminary rulings from national courts* (Article 234 (ex-Article 177)). National courts can request a preliminary ruling on issues of EC law that affect national rulings (approximately 90 per cent of the opinions issued by the ECJ on these references are accepted by the national courts).
- *Actions brought by the Commission/member states against member states* (*Commission* vs *Member State*, Article 226; *Member State* vs *Member State*, Article 227). As a guardian of the Treaties, the Commission often finds it necessary to bring a member state to Court due to failure to apply a directive or other legislative act. However, member states can also bring cases against each other.

- *Actions brought by other institutions/member states against EC institutions* (Articles 230 and 232). If the Council, the Commission or the EP fails to act, and, in so doing, infringes upon a requirement laid down in the Treaties, it can be brought to Court by another institution or member state.
- *Appeals against judgments made by the Court of First Instance* (see below).

Once a case has been brought before the ECJ, it will be decided either in chambers (by three to five judges) or before the full Court. Advocates-General give their opinion on the case during the oral procedure (when the case is being discussed), but are not involved in any deliberations or voting on the judgment. Rather than acting as legal representatives of one of the parties, the Advocates-General are the legal representatives of the public interest. While not binding, the opinions of the Advocates-General are published in advance of the judgment, so that the Court has enough time to consider them.

Requests for preliminary rulings are usually given precedence over other types of cases, such as cases brought by the Commission against a member state. Despite efforts to streamline procedures by allowing more cases to be heard in chambers, the ECJ still faces a backlog of cases, with many requests taking up to 21 months to be processed.

Supporting institutions

The Court of First Instance (CFI) was established in 1986 by the SEA, in order to reduce the backlog of ECJ cases, and became operational in November 1989. Initially, the member states were only willing to allow the CFI to review EU staff cases; however, its jurisdiction currently includes Competition Policy cases and those involving damages. In general, cases of a technical nature, involving detailed questions of fact, will be referred to the CFI, while cases involving points of law proceed to the ECJ. Similarly to the ECJ, the CFI is composed of fifteen judges, one from each member state; however, there are no Advocates-General in the CFI. CFI judgments can be appealed against to the ECJ, but only on the basis of a point of law. According to Nugent, approximately 20 per cent of cases are heard by the ECJ on appeal. The waiting period for the CFI (an average of 30 months) is even longer than that for the ECJ.

B   Other bodies

I   The European Council

The European Council (not to be confused with the Council of Ministers or the Strasbourg-based Council of Europe) consists of the fifteen heads of state or government (HOSG) assisted by their Foreign Ministers and the President of the Commission. This Council meets in ordinary session twice a year, primarily to define general policy guidelines. While not established by the Treaties of Rome, it was informally introduced at the Paris Summit of December 1974. The European

Council was formally recognized as an official body of the EU in the TEU. The European Council takes place in the country that holds the Presidency at that time. It has three main tasks:

- To provide a forum for discussing topics and policies that fall outside of the Treaty, usually relating to the future development of the Union.
- To facilitate the legislative process, by removing barriers in the Council of Ministers. The HOSG have the authority to resolve problematic issues that have been blocked by a lack of consensus; they are also able to construct package deals covering several policy areas.
- To create policy and guidelines for the Common Foreign and Security Policy for (CFSP).

As of 2004, the European Council will always take place, regardless of the member state that holds the Union Presidency, in Brussels.

2   The European Central Bank (ECB)

Established in the TEU, the Frankfurt-based ECB came into existence in June 1998. The ECB has its own legal personality, and is responsible for independently conducting monetary policy in the euro-zone (such as setting short-term interest rates). The ECB's primary task is to maintain price stability. It is composed of two bodies: the Executive Board and the Governing Council. The ECB is governed by the six-member Executive Board under the leadership of a president and a vice-president appointed by the HOSG. Members are elected for a non-renewable eight-year term, and their duties include the implementation of the guidelines set by the Governing Council. The Governing Council consists of the Executive Board and the central bank governors of the countries fully participating in monetary union (currently all member states except for the UK, Denmark and Sweden). The duty of the Governing Council is to define the guidelines of monetary policy. The European System of Central Banks (ESCB) includes the ECB and the central banks of all EU member states (see *Economic and Monetary Union*).

3   The Court of Auditors

Set up by the Treaty on Budgetary and Financial Provisions in July 1975, the Court of Auditors began work in 1977. However, it only received formal recognition as an institution within the TEU, which allowed the Court of Auditors to bring cases before the ECJ. The Court's main activity is auditing EU accounts and monitoring the implementation of the EU budget. In this capacity, it must affirm that the revenue and expenditure of the EU have been handled appropriately. The audit is published in an annual report. The Luxembourg-based Court consists of fifteen members, who are appointed by the Council for six-year terms (see *The EU Budget*).

4   The Economic and Social Committee (ESC)

Created by the Treaties of Rome, the Brussels-based ESC consists of 222 members representing employers, trade unionists and other groups engaged in economic and social activity, and its members are appointed by the Council for four-year renewable terms. The ESC develops opinions on issues that affect the Union. Despite its long history, the ESC has remained an advisory committee to the Council and the EP. While it is mandatory for the ESC to be consulted in a number of fields before a legal act can be passed, its role is limited, and its opinions do not carry much weight with the other institutions. However, it has the right to issue opinions on its own initiative on any matter of Community interest.

5   The Committee of the Regions (CoR)

Established by the TEU and based in Brussels, the CoR is an advisory body similar to the ESC. The CoR's main role is to discuss regional issues and develop joint opinions on policies affecting EU regions. While the Council and the Commission can consult the CoR on any issue, they are only obliged to do so in a limited number of areas (such as Education and Culture Policy decisions). However, the CoR has the right to issue opinions on its own initiative on any matter of Community interest. The CoR consists of 222 representatives from regions and localities across the fifteen member states, appointed by the Council on the basis of proposals from the member states for four-year renewable terms (see *Regional Policy*).

6   The European Ombudsman

Established by the TEU and seated in Strasbourg, the EU Ombudsman is appointed by the EP for a five-year term, to receive complaints regarding misadministration (incompetence or deliberate wrongdoing) by EU institutions from any EU citizen. Upon receiving a complaint, the Ombudsman submits a report on the investigation of the charges to the EP and the institution accused of misconduct. However, it cannot sanction or compel another EU institution to correct acts of misadministration.

7   The European Investment Bank (EIB)

Set up by the Treaties of Rome and seated in Luxembourg, the main task of the EIB is to fund projects that promote balanced development as well as economic and social cohesion within the EU. To this end, it raises substantial funding, which it directs into long-term, low-interest loans for financing capital projects in the member states and in certain non-member states (for example, the CEECs, Mediterranean and Lomé Convention countries). The EIB focuses on regions that are lagging behind or facing industrial decline, with particular emphasis on cross-frontier projects.

The problems/issues

A The Commission as regulator

The existence of institutions such as COREPER and comitology indicates that the member states are concerned about delegating power to the Commission. If such elaborate structures are necessary to keep the Commission in check, why do the member states delegate to the Commission at all? There are several responses to this question.

- An independent body can attain a higher level of policy credibility than any single member state. This is because none of the member states trust each other to act consistently in the interest of the common good. Therefore, they prefer to delegate powers to an intermediary – supposedly neutral – organization. As such, the Commission acts as a referee between the member states, ensuring that everyone is following the 'rules' outlined in the Treaty. This concept is known as the principal-agent framework (in which the principals are the member state and the Commission is the agent – see *Theories of European Integration*).
- Majone contends that this interpretation is too simplistic, arguing that the principal-agent framework cannot satisfactorily explain the subsequent behaviour of the Commission. The Commission now has competence in many policy areas which member states did not originally intend to delegate to the supra-national level (such as Environmental Policy). Majone argues that the Commission is a policy entrepreneur with its own agenda, which it can sometimes impose on the member states. Because the Treaty acts as an incomplete contract, the Commission can use its discretion to develop EU policy for its own benefit. In doing so, it has sometimes imposed its own agenda on unwilling member states. This is known as the 'relational contract' theory.

B Democratic deficit

Within the EU, there is a great deal of concern, especially among citizens, about the lack of connection between EU citizens and the EU as an institution. Because of the complex institutional structure, the technical nature of most EU regulations, and the complicated way in which legislation is created, many politicians and academics feel that the EU lacks transparency – in other words, it is not understandable to EU citizens. More importantly, some politicians contend that the EU does not have a democratic basis for its legislation. This criticism is often focused on the COREPER and comitology system. Both institutions consist of civil servants and technical experts, who do not run for election, and are therefore not accountable to the EU citizens. Since the COREPER pre-approves legislation for the Council, many (especially in the EP) argue that bureaucrats rather than elected politicians are determining EU legislation. However, member states often argue that these monitoring bodies do necessary preliminary work on legislation, despite the fact that they contribute to the democratic deficit and lack of transparency.

The EU might become more democratic if the EP, as the only directly elected EU body, were given more powers. Critics argue that most citizens vote for MEPs not on the basis of European politics but instead on the basis of national politics. Since EP elections are viewed by voters as being of secondary importance, MEPs arguably do not have a true democratic mandate. In addition, Eurobarometer surveys demonstrate that EU citizens are largely indifferent to the EU. This was demonstrated most recently by the initial failure of the Irish referendum ratifying the Treaty of Nice in June 2001, despite general government and establishment support.

Who wins/who loses

In the case of **institutional actors**, the distribution of power between political entities determines the winners and losers. The extension of QMV and the co-decision procedure have limited the absolute veto power previously enjoyed by the Council. These changes have increased the power of the Commission and the EP, with QMV allowing the Commission to propose more legislation promoting European integration, and co-decision providing the EP with final veto power over some legislation.

However, loss of power by the **member states** is not complete: all these supranational advances have taken place over long periods of time, and primarily in the first Pillar of the Treaty. In the case of the TEU, the ECJ lost power when it was denied the right to review cases in the second Pillar (CFSP) and third Pillar (JHA), although it later gained a limited role over JHA issues in the Amsterdam Treaty (see *Justice and Home Affairs*). In addition, as Garrett and Tsebelis point out, the EP and the Commission might not be absolute winners from the use of the co-decision procedure (see *Institutional Processes*).

Since the EP is a directly elected body, the **EU citizen** might be considered a winner from the increase in the EP's legislative power. However, the EU citizen also elects the national politicians who sit on the European Council and appoint their representatives to the Council of Ministers. While indirect, this is also a form of democratic control. Therefore, while the extension of QMV may increase the pace of integration, this does not necessarily make the EU citizen a winner.

Food for thought

Can the Commission increase its power without control over the EU budget? Political theory indicates that most governmental bodies attempt to maximize power by being 'budget-maximizers', i.e. by increasing their budgets. But the Commission has relatively little control over the EU budget, whose size is fixed by law. Given this constraint, scholars like Majone argue that the Commission has chosen instead to increase the scope of its powers through regulation, the costs of which are borne by member states and companies rather than by the EU budget.

Student-to-student tip

When studying a particular policy, it is very helpful to know which procedure is used in that area, and whether decisions are taken by QMV or unanimity, as this can have a profound effect on how the legislation develops. In addition, while it is not necessary to memorize the sequence of review in the co-decision procedure or the exact method through which the COREPER works, it is essential to know which institution is performing which role (agenda-setter, final decision-maker, etc.) for any policy you are exploring. For an insider perspective on how these theories affect actual legislation, visit http://europa.eu.int/eur-lex/en/index.html to see 'Legislation in preparation' in the *Official Journal* (where all EU legislation is published). In addition, the *Official Journal* publishes EP positions and Council comments on most directives under construction.

Summary

Governmental powers are shared between four main institutional actors, with varying degrees of power over legislative, executive and judicial tasks, depending on the policy area concerned. The four main bodies are the Commission, the Council, the EP and the ECJ.

- The *Commission*'s main role is to propose legislation, supervise the execution of EU policies, and bring violations of EU law to the attention of the ECJ.
- The *Council* is the principal decision-making body, and ensures that the interests of the member states are protected. It supervises the work of the Commission, both in the creation of legislation (assisted by the COREPER) and in the execution of EU policies (assisted by comitology).
- The *EP*'s role is to represent the EU citizen. Its powers in the legislative process have increased over time, and it is now the junior partner in policy making within the first Pillar. The EP also has executive powers in the form of budgetary oversight and approval of the Commission.
- The *ECJ* is responsible for the universal application of EC law, and therefore resolves all issues of EU law.

The main problems associated with EU institutions include the effects of the EU's legislative procedures, the role of the Commission, and the democratic deficit within the policy-making process.

Selected bibliography

Institutional structure

Dinan, D. (1999) *Ever Closer Union*, 2nd edn, London: Macmillan, chapters 8–11: 205–332.
  Dinan presents the EU institutions in a very detailed, but fairly descriptive way.
Nugent, N. (1999) *The Government and Politics of the European Union*, 4th edn, London:
  Macmillan, Part II: 99–378.
  The second section of this volume is extensively devoted to the institutions and political actors of the
  EU.

Institutional issues

Majone, G. (1996) 'The European Commission as Regulator', in *Regulating Europe*,
  London: Routledge, chapter 4: 61–79.
  This chapter describes the role of the Commission and the theory behind delegation.
Pollack, M. (1997) 'Delegation, Agency and Agenda Setting in the European Community',
  International Organization, vol. 51, no. 1: 99–134.
  Pollack examines the theoretical justifications for delegating power to a supranational institution,
  focusing on the neo-functionalist and intergovernmentalist approaches to the development and
  functioning of the Commission.
Wessels, W. (1998) 'Comitology: Fusion in Action. Politico-administrative Trends in the EU
  System', *Journal of European Public Policy*, vol. 5, no. 2: 209–34.
  Wessels provides a fairly straightforward account of the issues surrounding comitology, while also
  explaining the technicalities of the committees.

Supportive websites

http://europa.eu.int/inst-en.htm A comprehensive overview of the European institutions.
http://europa.eu.int/comm/ The European Commission.
http://ue.eu.int/ The Council of Ministers.
http://www.europarl.eu.int The European Parliament.
http://www.curia.eu.int/ The European Court of Justice.
http://www.eca.eu.int/ The Court of Auditors.
http://www.ecb.int/ The European Central Bank.
http://www.esc.eu.int/ The Economic and Social Committee.
http://www.cor.eu.int/ The Committee of the Regions.
http://eib.eu.int/ The European Investment Bank.
http://www.euro-ombudsman.eu.int/ The European ombudsman.
http://europa.eu.int/agencies/carte1_en.htm A site for all EU agencies.
http://www.europarl.eu.int/groups/ A site describing the political groups in the EP.

4

Institutional Processes

Alexis Xydias and Riccardo Maestri

The term 'institutional processes' refers to the primary methods through which EU law is created. These processes include not only the procedures used in the creation of EU legislation, but also the use of unanimity or majority voting in the approval of legislation and the creation of new EU treaties. Since they have developed over time and through compromises between member states, these processes are complex and often appear convoluted. However, the institutional processes also shape the development of legislation in fundamental ways that reflect the balance of power between institutional actors and member states. For that reason, a clear understanding of these institutional processes is key to a comprehensive analysis of the EU.

The facts

A   Types of legislation

There are two legal sources of Community law:

- *Primary legislation*, which refers to the treaties as well as to amendments and supplements to the treaties that create the constitutional framework for the Union. Primary legislation includes the treaties establishing the European Communities (such as the Treaty of Paris and the Treaties of Rome), and later treaties, such as those that consolidated Community policies and those that led to the accession of additional countries.
- *Secondary legislation*, which consists of the laws made by the Community institutions in exercising the powers conferred on them by the Treaties. The instruments

of secondary legislation are *regulations, decisions, directives, recommendations* and *opinions*.

B   The Union Presidencies and intergovernmental conferences (IGCs)

The Presidency of the EU is held by one member state on a six-monthly, rotating basis, and normally alternates between larger and smaller member states. The country that holds the Presidency plays an important role in influencing the Council's policy agenda for that half-year. The president country also hosts and chairs the European Council summits. As a result, important Treaty revisions, such as the Treaty of Nice (which was debated at the European Council summit), give the Presidency (in this case, France) the power to set the agenda, propose the first draft treaty, and mediate differences between member states.

IGCs are held to revise the founding treaties of the EU, and therefore affect the creation of primary legislation. There have been seven IGCs so far; the most important ones have led to the SEA, the TEU, the Amsterdam Treaty and the Nice Treaty. The IGCs are intergovernmental processes, with final agreements taken by the HOSG; the roles of the Commission and the EP are mainly consultative. The next IGC is planned for 2004, for the purpose of clarifying the division of powers between the EU institutions, the countries belonging to the Union, and the regions within these countries.

C   Legal instruments in secondary legislation

While the EU Treaties create the framework for EU law, the secondary EU legislation provides the concrete policy details necessary to the proper functioning of the Community. In order to provide flexibility to the institutional actors, this legislation can take several forms. Article 249 (ex-Article 189) of the Treaty defines these instruments as follows:

- *Regulations* are directly applicable to all member states (i.e. they do not require the passing of additional legislation in the individual states), and are binding in their entirety. Most regulations relate to detailed aspects of the operation of the work of the Union, such as the Common Agricultural Policy (CAP) or the Single Market.
- *Decisions* are binding in their entirety on those whom they address (they usually relate to particular matters of concern, and only to certain countries).
- *Directives* are the most common form of EU legislation. They require member states to achieve a particular objective within a stated time limit. Therefore, directives are binding insofar as they require a certain result, but allow individ-

ual states the flexibility to decide how to achieve the desired policy outcome. This means that for every directive that is passed by the EU, there must be a corresponding legislative process within each member state (unless that state can already satisfy the requirement without the need for new legislation – see *Judicial Processes*).

- *Recommendations and opinions* are statements made by the EU with no binding force. The Committee of the Regions (CoR) and the Economic and Social Committee (ESC) issue opinions on most preliminary legislation.

D Legislative procedures

There are twenty-two types of legislative procedures which can be used to produce new EU legislation. However, these procedures fall into four main categories: assent, consultation, co-operation and co-decision. The Treaty determines the legislative procedure to be used within each policy area. The procedures work in the following way: legislation is proposed by the Commission, and is generally passed to the ESC as well as the CoR for comment. The legislation is then presented to the Council and the EP simultaneously, and the EP gives its opinion. In both the assent and the consultation procedures, the legislative process ends at this point, with a final vote by the Council on whether or not to accept the legislation. In the two remaining procedures, the legislation is amended by the Commission after the first reading, in accordance with suggestions from the EP and the Council. The Commission resubmits the modified legislation to both the EP and the Council for a second reading. The procedures can be concluded after any stage if the two legislative authorities have reached agreement. The functioning of the four procedures is illustrated in figure 4.1.

E Qualified Majority Voting (QMV)

QMV is a weighted form of voting, whereby each member state has a different number of votes, based on population (which will change with enlargement). It is primarily used for internal market policy, and therefore also in conjunction with the co-decision procedure. Of a total of eighty-seven votes, a 'qualified majority' of sixty-two votes is required to approve proposals. This means that coalitions of twenty-six or more votes can block decisions. While QMV was designed to prevent larger states from imposing their decisions on smaller members as well as to prevent smaller states from systematically blocking decisions, the system currently favours small states to a disproportionate degree (e.g. Belgium has a population one-eighth the size of Germany's, yet has five votes under QMV compared with Germany's ten). In light of enlargement, the Nice Treaty (2001) has established a new distribution of votes (see table 4.1).

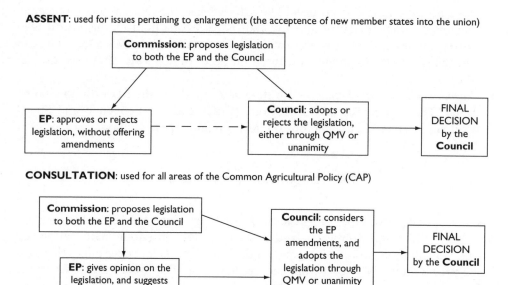

ASSENT: used for issues pertaining to enlargement (the accepence of new member states into the union)

CONSULTATION: used for all areas of the Common Agricultural Policy (CAP)

Figure 4.1 The four categories of procedures that can be used to produce new EU legislation.

While most international organizations require unanimity for decision making, the Treaties of Rome (1957) included a provision for the gradual use of QMV. However, the implementation of QMV was delayed by President de Gaulle of France, who demanded that each member state have the right to veto any Council proposals that conflicted with its national interest. The resulting French walk-out of the Council in 1965 (known as the 'Empty Chair Crisis') led to the Luxembourg Compromise of 1966, which allowed for such a national veto. Although this veto power was very rarely used, it acted as a barrier to progressive policies and forced the Council to act by consensus. The Single European Act (SEA, 1986) instituted the use of QMV for many issues within the first Pillar of the Treaty (especially those dealing with the Single Market), for the first time following the Luxembourg Compromise. Use of QMV has been extended in all the EU treaty revisions since the SEA, including the treaties of Maastricht, Amsterdam and Nice.

F Models of EU governance

The governance structures in the EU are strongly influenced by the institutional processes currently being used to create EU legislation. However, there is no current consensus on the future shape of the EU polity, as some member states not only wish to integrate faster than others but also envision integration developing in different directions. There are four main competing visions:

CO-OPERATION: used for Economic and Monetary Union (EMU)

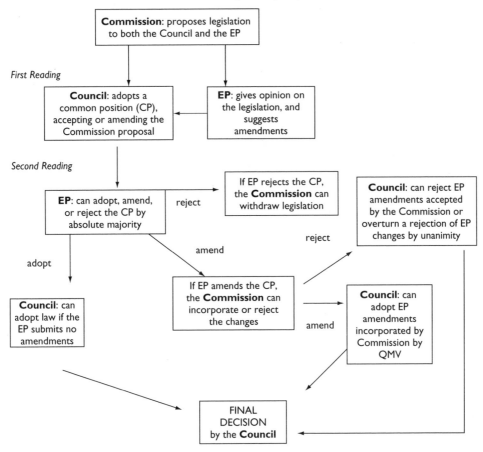

Figure 4.1 continued

- The *Westphalian model/federalism* portrays the EU as a political system in the making, which should eventually encompass all activities traditionally associated with the nation-state (including provision of security and welfare). In this model, the Commission and the EP are the main institutions.
- The *intergovernmentalist model* considers the EU project as a means of strengthening the powers of participating nation-states. From this perspective, European competence should not develop unless there is a 'compelling and compatible substantive national interest'. Therefore, the Commission and the EP remain minor institutions in such a system, in comparison to the Council.

CO-DECISION: used for Environmental Policy and some areas of Education and Culture Policy

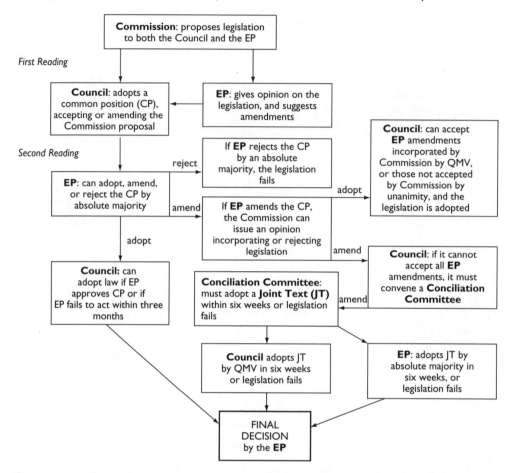

Figure 4.1 continued

*In the co-decision procedure, the Conciliation Committee is convened only following the second reading of proposed legislation, and only if the Council is unable to accept the amendments proposed by the EP. It is comprised of fifteen members each of the Council and the EP and one Commission member, who cannot vote. The Council members must approve the Joint Text (JT) by qualified majority voting (QMV), and the EP members must approve the JT by an absolute majority, in order for the legislation to be approved.

- The *regulatory model* considers the EU to be an international organization, which should not be responsible for national policies, but only those that are more efficiently dealt with at the European level (such as market integration). In this model, the Commission and the EP have more powers in some policy areas and fewer in others.
- The *multi-level governance (MLG) model* argues that supra- and sub-national authorities will gain and share decision-making powers at the expense of the member states (see *Regional Policy*).

Table 4.1 Distribution of votes

	Present votes		Future votes	
	Number	*Per cent*	*Number*	*Per cent*
Germany	10	11.5	29	8.4
France	10	11.5	29	8.4
Italy	10	11.5	29	8.4
Netherlands	5	5.7	13	3.8
Belgium	5	5.7	12	3.5
Luxembourg	2	2.3	4	1.2
UK	10	11.5	29	8.4
Ireland	3	3.4	7	2.0
Denmark	3	3.4	7	2.0
Greece	5	5.7	12	3.5
Spain	8	9.2	27	7.8
Portugal	5	5.7	12	3.5
Austria	4	4.6	10	2.9
Sweden	4	4.6	10	2.9
Finland	3	3.4	7	2.0
Poland	–	–	27	7.8
Hungary	–	–	12	3.5
Czech Rep.	–	–	12	3.5
Slovenia	–	–	4	1.2
Estonia	–	–	4	1.2
Cyprus	–	–	4	1.2
Romania	–	–	14	4.1
Bulgaria	–	–	10	2.9
Slovakia	–	–	7	2.0
Lithuania	–	–	7	2.0
Latvia	–	–	4	1.2
Malta	–	–	3	0.9
TOTAL	**87**		**345**	

The problems/issues

A The choice of legislative procedure

The twenty-two EU legislative procedures involve the EP, the Commission and the Council to varying degrees. As illustrated above, they fall into four general categories: assent, consultation, co-operation and co-decision. The rarely used assent procedure grants the least power to the EP, and co-decision grants the most.

The procedure used in each policy area, as well as the use of QMV or unanimity, is determined by the Treaty. For the most sensitive issues in the first Pillar (such as enlargement), *assent* and unanimity are the rule. Some areas, such as the Common Commercial Policy (CCP), allow for no EP involvement. Currently, the most common procedures in the first Pillar are consultation and co-decision. *Consultation* is used for sensitive but inherently practical areas, such as agriculture, while *co-decision* (and formerly *co-operation*) is used for Single Market Programme (SMP) policies (see *The Single Market*).

Therefore, the choice of procedure has a profound effect on the balance of power between the EP, the Council and the Commission in the decision-making process. Under the assent procedure, for example, it is only by giving its opinion that the EP can influence legislation. The Council then makes the final decision on the legislation. Consultation, by comparison, allows the EP to accept, reject or propose changes to a piece of legislation, which the Council either accepts or rejects.

By comparison, the co-operation and co-decision procedures shift the balance of power, providing more equity between the EP and the Council. While both co-operation and co-decision procedures are very complex (with time limits and Commission approval dictating the course of decision making), the main difference between the co-operation procedure and the co-decision procedure is who takes the final decision on the legislation. In the co-operation procedure, the Council has the veto power; but with co-decision, the EP has the final veto on legislation. In addition, the co-decision procedure allows for the creation of a Conciliation Committee after the second reading, should the EP and the Council fail to agree on the legislation.

In all these procedures, the Commission maintains the right of initiative, but in the co-decision procedure, the Commission's role is somewhat taken over by the EP in the later stages of decision making. This causes tension between these two institutions, which are traditionally allied against the intergovernmental forces of the Council. The complexity of these procedures and the way in which they affect the balance of power among the EU institutions also contribute to the lack of transparency in EU politics.

B   The power index argument

In an attempt to understand the distribution of power among the different policy actors, Garrett and Tsebelis – both rational choice theorists (see *Theories of European Integration*) – developed the 'power index argument'. This argument attempts to quantify the balance of power under each legislative procedure. Under the consultation procedure, for example, the approved policy will not be particularly integrationist, since unanimity voting (primarily used in this procedure) usually equals lowest-common-denominator decisions favouring the position of states least in favour of integration. Therefore, the Council is the key decision-maker under this procedure. The co-operation procedure allows the EP more power, as it becomes a 'conditional agenda-setter', because EP amendments can be accepted in the Council by QMV. As a result, the views of the somewhat more integrationist states may prevail, even though the Council retains veto power. In the co-decision procedure, the EP appears to have more power since it has final veto power.

However, the Council plays an agenda-setting role under co-decision, as it can convene a Conciliation Committee to form a Joint Text.

As a result of these assumptions, Garrett and Tsebelis have come to the interesting conclusion that the EP has more power under the co-operation procedure than under the co-decision procedure. Since the treaties of Maastricht and Amsterdam have almost completely eliminated the co-operation procedure in favour of the co-decision procedure, such a conclusion implies that the EP has lost power during recent Treaty revisions.

However, these conclusions are highly controversial. Many scholars, notably Mosey and Sculley, argue that Garrett and Tsebelis do not take account of the Commission as policy-initiator, and fail to accurately predict the position of the Council if conciliation breaks down under co-decision. Therefore, the basic assumption regarding which actor has the final say under each procedure is undermined. Notably, the EP itself does not seem to agree with Garrett and Tsebelis, believing instead that it has gained power through the co-decision procedure. Despite these criticisms, the power index model offers an interesting insight into the dynamics of EU legislative politics.

C Federalism as an institutional process

When the term 'federalism' is applied to the EU, it is frequently understood as the creation of a superstate at the European level – often referred to as 'the United States of Europe'. However, federalism at the EU level can also be understood as a description of the process whereby the EU is developing a more 'state-like' structure. In many respects, the degree of federalism in the EU can be assessed through an analysis of the shift of decision-making capacities from the national to the EU level and the institutional processes applied to these new capacities. Since supranational institutions are likely to benefit from this increase in legislative power, both the Commission and the EP have historically argued in favour of federalism. However, many member states (most particularly the UK) have resisted the creation of a federal system in the EU. Anti-federalist politicians and academics maintain that any movement towards a federal system in the EU undermines the sovereignty of member states by subordinating national legislative powers to those of the Community. For this reason, the extension of QMV to and the use of co-decision in new policy areas are often fiercely contested issues between member states during the IGC process, since these institutional processes are understood to increase the decision-making power of the EU, and thereby lead to increased EU federalism.

Who wins/who loses

While the existence of institutional processes *per se* does not produce winners and losers, the choice of certain processes over others can inherently favour some actors over others. For example, the expanded use of QMV and co-decision in the most recent Treaty revisions generally benefits pro-integrationist actors and institutions. For the **European Parliament**, the expanded application of the co-decision procedure results in more legislative power for this institution. Since the EP is the only EU legislative body that is directly elected by **EU citizens**, the increased use of co-decision can be understood to help moderate the democratic deficit within the EU (see *Institutional Actors*). However, the increased use of QMV by the **Council of Ministers** may not represent a similar benefit for the EU citizen. This is because QMV eliminates the national veto available under unanimity, thereby minimizing the ability of member states to protect their citizens from legislation that may negatively affect them. At the same time, the use of QMV accelerates the development of a policy area, by allowing more integrationist legislation to be passed. Therefore, **member states** that favour federalism or the development of a particular policy area may push for the use of QMV during Treaty negotiations. For these reasons, much of the recent debate over the use of QMV and co-decision has focused on decision making in sensitive policy areas, such as CFSP and JHA.

Food for thought

How would the extension of QMV affect the power balance between the various EU institutions? In the Nice Treaty, QMV and co-decision were extended to just a few additional policy areas. Would the further extension of QMV within the first Pillar (taxes, social security systems) and into the third Pillar of the Treaty (joint police action) undermine the sovereignty of the member states, or could it facilitate the reform and development of policies necessary for enlargement? Would the further extension of co-decision help to eliminate the democratic deficit by increasing the involvement of the EP, or just create greater transparency problems?

Student-to-student tip

Institutional processes are more easily understood through practical examples. The EU offers easy access to the most recent legislation, as well as proposed legislation, through the publication of the *Official Journal* on the website. *The Official Journal of the European Communities (OJ)* is the official gazette of the European Communities. It contains the texts of all secondary legislation, draft legislation and official announcements and information about the activities of Community institutions. The *Official Journal* is divided into three sections: Legislation (L series), Information and Notices (C series, from the French title *Communications et Notices*) and the Supplement (S series). The best place to search for older legislation is CELEX, which – while accessible only by subscription – is often available to students at university libraries.

Summary

- There are two types of legislation in the EU:

- *Primary legislation* refers to the EU treaties created at intergovernmental conferences.
- *Secondary legislation* refers to the directives, regulations and decisions created by the institutional actors to facilitate the proper functioning of the Community.

- There are four main legislative procedures used in the creation of secondary legislation:
  - *Assent* – used for the most sensitive issues decided under Pillar I, and which does not involve the EP.
  - *Consultation* – allows the EP to accept, reject or propose changes to legislation, but the final decision on the legislation is made by the Council.
  - *Co-operation* – used only for certain issues associated with the EMU.
  - *Co-decision* – allows for the equal participation of the EP and the Council in the legislative process.
- Qualified majority voting (QMV), the voting procedure used in the Council for many issues within the Community Pillar of the Treaty (especially those related to the Single Market), has been expanded in every treaty revision since the SEA.
- The choice of legislative procedure used in each policy area affects the pace at which that policy area is developing at the EU level, and has a significant impact on the shape of EU governance in the future.

Selected bibliography

Chalmers, D. (1998) *European Union Law*, volume 1: *Law and EU Government*, Aldershot: Ashgate.

While primarily conceived as a legal volume, this book gives a very comprehensive introduction to the basic legislative structure of the EU, with a particular focus on the EP (see pp. 116–35, and 164–81).

Garrett, G. and G. Tsebelis (1996) 'An Institutional Critique of Intergovernmentalism', *International Organization*, vol. 50, no. 2: 269–99.

This classic article outlines the power index argument. The response to this article by Mosey and Scully is also very interesting.

Pollack, M. (2000) 'The End of Creeping Competence? EU Policy-Making since Maastricht', *Journal of Common Market Policy*, vol. 38, no. 3: 519–38.

Pollack discusses the nature of policy making in the 1990s, exploring the capabilities of the institutional actors to solve issues of both a budgetary and a regulatory nature. In particular, he contends that while the institutions have run into some difficulties in solving budgetary and enlargement issues, they have generally performed better in the area of regulating the internal market.

Tsebelis, G. (2002) 'Veto Players' Analysis of the European Union', in *Veto Players: How Political Institutions Work*, Princeton, NJ: Princeton University Press and Russell Sage Foundation, chapter 11: 248–82.

Tsebelis presents his perspective on agenda-setters and veto-players in terms of an analysis of the interaction between the political institutions of the EU. The volume offers a clear explanation of the many different aspects of EU politics: in particular, the degree of policy stability likely to occur in different policy areas according to decision-making rules, policy preferences and the number of actors involved.

Supportive websites

http://europa.eu.int/institutions/decision-making/index_en.htm This index on the *Europa* website provides information about all the different legislative procedures and the areas of application for each procedure, as well as graphic depictions of the procedures.

http://europa.eu.int/eur-lex/en/index.html Eur-Lex is a free data base of adopted legislation and includes the *Official Journal* (*OJ*), which now has a searchable data base and consolidated versions of the Treaties.

http://europa.eu.int/celex/htm/celex_en.htm CELEX includes primary and secondary legislation, reports of cases before the ECJ, national implementation measures, and European parliamentary questions. However, access to CELEX is by subscription only.

http://europa.eu.int/scad/en-warn.html SCAD Plus is a bibliographic data base, listing Community documents, legislative texts and periodical articles on Community topics by broad subject headings.

http://europa.eu.int/cj/en/act/index.htm For information on current cases, summaries of judgments, Advocate-General opinions, and full text of judgments of the ECJ.

Official treaty sites

http://europa.eu.int/eur-lex/en/dat/2002/c_325/c_32520021224en00010184.pdf The consolidated EU Treaty as of 2002, available as a single PDF file.

http://europa.eu.int/abc/obj/treaties/en/entoc.htm The consolidated EU Treaty, available in HTML format.

http://europa.eu.int/eur-lex/en/treaties/index.html The Amsterdam and Nice treaties, available on the web.

Non-official sites

http://www.jeanmonnetprogram.org For essays and papers on the decisions of the ECJ from the Harvard Law School.

http://eiop.or.at/eiop/ The European Integration online Papers (EIoP) has an archive of legal papers dealing with a variety of subjects, from constitutionalism and fundamental rights to the legal aspects of Environmental Policy.

5

Interest Groups

Jean-Charles Pascoli

In terms of EU integration, interest groups are defined as formal political organizations which represent the policy preferences of certain sectors of the EU population. As policy decisions shift from the national to the supra-national level, European interest groups have correspondingly expanded their lobbying effort to the EU level, in order to capitalize on the changing locus of decision making. As a result, EU interest groups have become strategic actors who contribute to the integration process. They do so both by providing information to Brussels and by acting as an EU electorate. This situation creates an important dynamic between the institutional actors and non-governmental organizations (NGOs), thereby affecting the shape of EU integration. (Note that this chapter focuses on the role played by formal organized interest groups (in particular, business, public interest and regional interest groups) in EU policy making, rather than informal interest groups composed of like-minded citizens.)

The facts

A   Objectives and rationale for interest groups

Interest groups in Brussels attempt to influence the EU policy- and decision-making processes by gathering information for their constituencies and by providing information to EU institutions that could favourably influence policy. This implies both a reactive and a pro-active role:

- First, the interest group office will gather EU data and information about new directives or Commission initiatives in the initial stages of the process (reactive function).
- Secondly, the office will use its own information to design strategies, create position papers, and develop programmes that correspond to the policy being discussed, and then submit these to the supranational institutions and their constituents (pro-active function).

In both functions, the interest group attempts to protect its constituents. By collecting information about new policies, it can get a head start in adapting new legislation (this can be especially valuable for business interests, where an early start means a competitive advantage). By creating position papers, it can present data supporting its interests, which could influence the creation of new EU legislation.

B Types of EU-level interest groups

EU-level interest groups generally fall into the following categories: business, re-gional/territorial, public, professional and labour interests. Private companies (busi-ness lobbies), public interest groups and sub-national authorities (regional lobbies) are currently the most numerous and important lobbyists in the EU. Professional lobbyists and labour interests also have a presence in Brussels, but such groups currently do not play a significant role in policy-making processes, for several reasons. In particular, most companies and non-governmental organizations find that they can be more effective lobbyists than the professional lobbying organizations, especially because most EU institutions prefer to deal directly with businesses or with the public. In addition, despite the presence of the European Trade Union Confederation (ETUC) and the existence of the Social Charter, labour groups from different countries find it difficult to form a united front in EU politics. This may be because each labour group has its own national agenda, or because of the reduced importance of organized labour in some EU countries (see *Environmental and Social Policies*).

C Business and public interest groups

Business and public interest groups increased their representation in Brussels in response to the creation and implementation of the Single European Act (SEA) and the Single Market Programme (SMP) during the 1980s. Because the SEA and the SMP shifted the competences from the national level to the supranational level in many areas, these groups were forced to diversify their lobbying efforts in order to maintain influence over the policies that affect them (see *The Single Market*).

D   Regional interest groups

Regional interest groups have expanded their presence at the EU level in response to changes in EU Regional Policy, such as the 1988 reform of the EU Structural Funds. As a result of the SEA and the SMP, areas of shared competence/legislative responsibility between the regions and the EU have grown. The reforms in 1988, which gave the sub-national actors a role in the creation of EU Regional Policy, provided the regions with a reason to establish interest offices in Brussels (see *Regional Policy*).

E   Functioning of the system

It is often said that Brussels is run on the exchange of information rather than the exchange of money. This is because the EU has a small budget and governs through regulations rather than redistributive policies. Therefore, interest groups come to Brussels not only to gain access to grants (even the Structural Funds are tiny compared to national budgets), but also to influence legislation with economic ramifications in their area of interest. For example, if the pharmaceutical lobby can persuade the Commission that time-sensitive patents on some types of drugs must be extended to cover research costs, the entire industry benefits financially from the new regulation. In order to persuade the Commission to accept their position, the pharmaceutical companies need to provide the EU with information which demonstrates that the importance of continued research outweighs EU consumer interests.

F   The provision of information

Because of limited financial resources, both the Commission and the European Parliament (EP) often rely on interest groups to provide the information necessary to create EU policies. This can be seen as a mutually beneficial relationship for both parties:

- The interest groups that provide the information have the opportunity to affect policy to their own advantage, by having their opinions heard by decision-makers.
- The Commission and the EP benefit not only by having access to expertise and detailed information, but also by utilizing interest groups as a constituency. In this way, the Commission and the EP attempt to reduce the democratic deficit in the EU decision-making process. In order to build up this constituency, the

Commission provides funding to many under-represented interests, especially public interest groups, which have difficulty competing with the better-funded business lobbies. This funding has allowed a greater presence of environmental, consumer and social interest groups in Brussels.

Allowing the naturally biased information provided by interest groups to form the basis for EU legislation may not be the optimal way to create policy. In order to do their own research and to hire their own independent experts, however, the Commission and the EP would need much larger budgets than the member states are willing to provide (see *EU Budget*).

G   The relationship between interest groups and institutional actors

Since the Commission is the agenda-setter and policy-initiator in most areas of EU policy, interest groups have traditionally focused on forming relationships with the Directorates-General (DGs) that deal with their particular policy area. However, with the expansion of EP influence through creation of the co-operation and co-decision procedures, interest groups have begun to focus some of their lobbying efforts on members of the European Parliament (MEPs), especially those on influential EP committees, in fields such as Environmental Policy.

The problems/issues

A   Theories explaining interest group mobilization

There are a number of traditional theories that explain interest group interaction (or intermediation) within a political structure. Although based on the nation-state structure, these theories have also been used to explain the formation of lobbies in the EU capital. Two are outlined below:

- *Neo-corporatism* proposes that intermediation is dominated by the three main economic actors in the state: business, labour and government. Therefore, it is useful in explaining development such as the Social Charter in the EU, but cannot explain the presence of other types of interest groups in the post-industrial era, such as consumer and environmental groups.
- *Neo-pluralism* maintains that all interest groups are in competition for the attention of decision-makers. Therefore, it is a useful theory for understanding the development of Environmental Policy, where several interest groups are fighting for the attention of the Commission, but cannot explain why some lobbies receive more attention than others.

Because the structure of the EU as a political entity is different from that of most nation-states, a number of theories on EU-level intermediation have developed. These theories explain how interest groups take advantage of the structure of the EU polity and how they develop relationships with the key supranational actors, namely the Commission and the EP.

- According to *neo-functionalism*, the mobilization of interests at the EU level demonstrates the fact that interest groups have made a significant contribution to the integration process. In theoretical terms, neo-functionalism assumes that lobbies are strategic actors in this process, who, by pursuing their own interests, will create pressure for further integration. By building alliances with the supra-national institutions of the EU, interest groups strengthen the position of the Commission and the EP *vis-à-vis* the member states. This implies that interest groups also contribute to the weakening of the position of the nation-state as the primary decision-maker in EU politics.
- *Multi-level governance* (MLG), a theory developed by Gary Marks, was initially used to explain the relationship between the European regions, member states and the Community, and has been extended to describe the role played by interest groups in EU policy and decision making. It focuses on the ability of supranational institutions and lobbies to share control of EU policy making with the member states. While this theory maintains that the member states control the integration process through the treaties and their leading role in high politics, it also argues that this control is not complete; the EU institutions and interest groups take advantage of all opportunities to influence the bargaining process, whether through policy initiation or the provision of information. Hence, member states do not fully direct the integration process, as is main-tained by intergovernmentalist theory. Yet multi-level governance also argues against neo-functionalism, contending that the current situation is permanent, and not simply a transitional stage in the elimination of the nation-state.

B   The shift from a national to a supranational strategy

As a result of the development of new EU policy areas and the strengthening of the Commission's competences in these areas, interest groups have strategically chosen to move some of their lobbying effort to Brussels. In addition, because of the primacy of EU law over national legislation, a decision taken at the supranational level may undermine the interests of a particular group in its home country.

An example of this is Environmental Policy, which is now primarily the compe-tence of the EU. Environmental regulations affect not only public interest groups such as Greenpeace but also the regional authorities, which must enforce them, and multi-national/European corporations, which must abide by EU-level environmen-tal regulations. Hence, a presence in Brussels allows interest groups to be alerted to new policy developments earlier in the decision-making process, thereby defending their interests more effectively.

Representation in Brussels also allows interest groups to develop relationships with DGs and EP committees. Through these relationships, interest groups are more likely to be asked to provide the EU institutions with information for use in creating policy. It is through this provision of information to the EU institutions that interest groups can remain influential in the development of the policies which affect them.

C The strategic rationales behind interest group representation

I Business groups

Firms have several reasons for EU-level representation. The process of globalization created the need for multi-national companies (MNCs) to have their interests represented on a larger, more international platform. More specifically, the fragmentation of the European economy, in comparison with the USA and Japan in the early 1980s, created enthusiasm among MNCs for the Single Market Programme (SMP), since the SMP was synonymous with bigger markets. Centralized EU-level regulations also reduce transaction costs for EU firms and MNCs, by providing one set of standards and one forum for the negotiation of these standards.

The SMP and the Single European Act (SEA) also had a significant impact on business representation. The SMP destroyed the previous system of 'national champions', because it demanded that governments stop providing large national firms with state aid. The SEA introduced Qualified Majority Voting (QMV) for the Council in many areas of economic policy, which meant the loss of the national veto. This increased the risk that member states could be outvoted in important policy areas. Hence, multi-nationals could no longer rely on their interests being secured at the national level (see *The Single Market*).

2 Regional groups

Within the last twenty years, there has been an increase in both devolution and regionalism within many member states. As a result, competences that were originally held at the national level are now the responsibility of the regions within a state. Devolution in Scotland, for example, means that the Scottish Parliament now has control over certain legislative areas. Regionalism in Spain has led some regions to demand more autonomy over policies which directly affect them.

Consequently, regional responsibility for enacting policies created by the EU has increased dramatically, leading to vertical links between the regions and the Commission. These links have been reinforced by the establishment of the Committee of the Regions (CoR) in 1994 and the reforms of the Structural Funds in 1988 and

1993, and have encouraged regions to look to the Union, rather than solely to their national governments, for favourable legislation and funding (see *Regional Policy*). In the area of the Structural Funds, the process by which EU decisions are reached, for example, favours better-organized, better-informed regions, which are able to provide the Commission with the information it needs to make new policies. Through the provision of this information, regions have new opportunities and are able to design programmes which are both compatible with the relevant EU regional policies and benefit their region.

3 Public interest groups

NGOs have been drawn to Brussels by two factors: increased EU legislative competences and competition from business interests. As a result of the SEA, the EU now has expanded responsibilities in areas such as consumer, environmental and social policies. Public interest groups, especially those with trans-European constituencies (such as Friends of the Earth), understand that their ability to provide information to the Commission and the EP on issues of public interest is crucial to their attempts to influence EU-wide policy. These groups also know that they will be well received by the EU institutions, which are concerned with the unequal representation of business interests versus public interests in Brussels.

Because business interests are almost always better funded, the Commission and, more recently, the Council have begun providing funding to NGOs, especially environmental and consumer groups, in order to counterbalance the strong representation of business. Rapid expansion in the number of public interest groups in Brussels has also led to increased competition among groups for the attention of the EU institutions. In order to have a voice in Brussels, these groups must be able to provide the Commission with high-quality information.

D Why some interest groups are more influential than others

If the EU is based on an exchange of information rather than money, why are business groups still more successful at influencing EU politics? Olson's theory of collective action provides a theoretical framework that explains the varying levels of influence between different interest groups. He argues that business interest groups are more influential than public interest groups because of the way in which costs and benefits from regulation are distributed. He divides these costs and benefits into two categories:

- concentrated (which affect a small group of individuals significantly), and
- diffuse (which affect a large group of individuals slightly).

For instance, environmental regulations usually have a concentrated (or high) cost for the producers of products that pollute but a relatively diffuse (or small) benefit for everyone in the community when levels of pollution drop. Because the costs are concentrated on the small group of producers, these individuals have a strong incentive to co-ordinate their lobbying efforts in order to prevent unfavourable legislation. On the other hand, the EU public as individuals only benefits to a small degree from the improved environmental conditions, and therefore has considerably less incentive to mobilize in order to fight for higher levels of protection (see *The Common Agricultural Policy*). This situation makes lobbying by public interest groups more difficult, as most people are interested in clean air and water, but don't have a large vested interest in it – unlike the producers, who might have to pay a high price in order to comply with new, stricter regulations. As a result, business lobbies (with concentrated costs and benefits) are usually more organized and therefore more effective at lobbying than public and regional interest groups (with diffuse costs and benefits).

However, there are some issues that have enjoyed overwhelming public support, and resulted in strong public mobilization, such as food safety after the BSE/British beef crisis in the late 1990s, or the concern over genetically modified organisms (GMOs). When the EU public becomes very aware of a policy issue, legislators are likely to respond to the demands of the greatest number of constituents, rather than the concentrated lobbying efforts of a particular industry.

Who wins/who loses

EU institutions have benefited greatly from the increased presence of interest groups in Brussels. The exchange of information for influence has allowed these actors to gain prestige and power. This is especially true of the Commission, which is able to create more effective policy with the expertise provided by interest groups than would otherwise be possible, given its limited resources. The Commission in particular gains legitimacy from interest group support when it confronts opposition to its policy proposals in the Council. The 1990 Structural Fund Campaign led by the World Wildlife Fund, which highlighted the environmental harm caused by the application of this policy, demonstrates how the Commission uses interest groups to persuade the Council to make changes to EU policies.

Interest groups can also be perceived as winners, as the concentration of decision making in Brussels reduces the transaction costs for these organizations. It is far easier for interest groups to focus their lobbying efforts on one location and on institutions that make policy for all member states than to lobby in each individual member state, each of which has different regulations and institutional frameworks. For regional interest groups in particular, lobbying in Brussels is appealing because it gives these groups an additional venue for emphasizing the needs of their region and an opportunity to circumvent their national governments.

Some neo-functionalists contend that **member states** have lost influence as interest groups have shifted the focus of their lobbying efforts away from the national to the supranational level. Yet, most interest groups continue to lobby at several levels simultaneously, understanding that member states still control the majority of decision making in the EU.

More important, perhaps, is the fact that the EU institutions, especially the Commission, have begun to use interest groups as a pseudo-constituency. However, it is questionable whether interest groups really represent the will of **EU citizens** accurately. This problem is especially apparent in the area of labour representation, which lacks influence on the EU level, despite the Social Charter and support from the Commission.

Food for thought

How democratic is the EU policy process if the primary policy-makers are dependent on information provided by interest groups? The Commission attempts to balance the information it receives from different interest groups when it creates EU policies, by financially supporting public interest groups and by inviting various groups to Committee discussions on policy issues. However, the bias inherent in the information provided by these groups may affect the legislation in such a way that it no longer benefits the majority of the EU population. If this is the case, does it justify an increase in Commission resources, so that the institution would not be so dependent on interest groups?

Will the recent rapid increase in interest group representation in Brussels mean that only the best-funded interest groups have their voice heard by EU institutions? Until recently, it was relatively easy for interest groups to have their opinions heard by relevant members of the Commission. However, with the explosion in the number of interest groups now lobbying in Brussels, the Commission has tried to limit the number of interest groups it consults. This means that smaller, newer interest groups will have a much more difficult time voicing their opinions to decision-makers. As a result, the problem of unequal representation, and therefore the democratic deficit, may increase rather than decrease.

Student-to-student tip

EU interest groups themselves provide an excellent, if sometimes biased, resource for information about EU policy issues, and are usually very responsive when contacted. The *European Public Affairs Directory* lists contact details for the majority of these organizations, and can be found in most university libraries.

Summary

- The increase in interest group representation in Brussels is the result of the shifting policy competences between the national and the EU level.
- The three primary types of interest groups in Brussels – business, public interest and regional – all have unique reasons for maintaining a presence at the centre of EU decision making.
- Because the EU specializes much more in regulatory than redistributive policies, the EU political engine can be said to run on the exchange of information, rather than the exchange of money.

- For most groups, there are two main reasons to have an office near the centre of EU decision making: to gather information about policy developments as they develop, and to provide information to EU institutions that might influence EU policy.
- The EU institutions, which have limited resources, welcome this exchange of information, as it provides them with needed data and helps relieve, in some ways, the democratic deficit in the Union.

Selected bibliography

Greenwood, J. (1997) *Representing Interests in the European Union*, London: Macmillan.
  Well-structured and concise, this book provides excellent information on the reasoning behind interest group mobilization. The conclusion offers useful arguments in the neo-functionalist/ intergovernmentalist debate.

Pollack, M. (1997) 'Representing Diffuse Interests in EC Policy Making', *Journal of European Public Policy*, vol. 4, no. 4: 572–90.
  Pollack explores the different aspects of interest group intermediation in the EU, in particular how interest groups relate to the EU institutions.

Coen, D. (1997) 'The Evolution of the Large Firm as a Political Actor in the European Union', *Journal of European Public Policy*, vol. 4, no. 1: 91–108.
  Working out of the London Business School, Coen provides significant statistical data to back up his pluralistic thesis.

Kohler-Koch, B. (1997) 'Organised Interests in the EC and the European Parliament', *European Integration online Papers (EIoP)*, vol. 1, no. 9. Available via website: http:// eiop.or.at/eiop/texte/1997_009a.htm.
  This article is very helpful in explaining the growing role of the EP in interest group mobilization.

Marks, G. (1993) 'Structural Policy and Multi-Level Governance in the EC', in A. Cafruny and G. Rosenthal (eds), *The State of the European Community*, volume 2: *The Maastricht Debates and Beyond*, London: Longman, chapter 23: 391–410.
  Marks outlines the major arguments and counter-arguments for multi-level governance theory.

Weber, K. and M. Hallerberg (2001) 'Explaining Variation in Institutional Integration in the European Union: Why Firms May Prefer European Solutions', *Journal of European Public Policy*, vol. 8, no. 2: 171–91.
  Using a transaction-cost framework, this article offers a theoretical explanation for why European firms in different industrial sectors have pressed for different degrees of European integration. The authors explain their framework with examples from the aerospace, pharmaceutical and automobile industries.

European Public Affairs Directory (2002) Brussels: Landmark Press.
  This annually revised directory contains the names and addresses of all registered interest groups in the European political landscape, and is very useful for original research.

Supportive websites

http://europa.eu.int/comm/secretariat_general/sgc/lobbies/index_en.htm This site comprises more than 800 non-profit organizations working at the Community level and covering approximately 100 branches of activity.

http://www.unice.org The Union of Industrial and Employers' Confederation of Europe (UNICE) is the largest organization of business interests in Europe.

http://www.aer-regions-europe.org/ The Assembly of European Regions (AER) represents almost 300 regions from both EU and non-EU countries.

http://www.etuc.org The European Trade Union Confederation (ETUC) is the labour equivalent to UNICE in the Social Charter.

http://www.eeb.org The European Environmental Bureau (EEB) focuses on influencing the Commission on environmental issues, and has more than 120 members.

http://www.europages.com The *European Business Directory* contains an exhaustive list of businesses in Europe.

http://www.eurochambers.be The European Chamber of Commerce represents the views of 14,000 businesses at the EU level.

http://www.copa.be The COPA–COGECA website represents the position of the largest European agricultural lobby group. The site provides very good fact sheets and position papers on CAP issues.

6

The EU Budget

Patrycja Sawicz

The EU is a unique political entity, and this is reflected in its budget. In terms of size and expenditure, the EU budget resembles neither that of an international organization nor that of a conventional state. Since it is by controlling the flow of revenues and expenditure that governments express their policy preferences, the small EU budget acts as a limitation on the EU's redistributive programmes and as a constraint on Commission activism. Therefore the structure and scope of the budget are directly related to the nature of the EU and the competences of its institutions.

The facts

A   The history of the EU budget

The Treaties of Rome (1957) established only a very limited budget for the Community. The European Economic Community (EEC) was financed solely through contributions from the member states. However, in April 1970, national contributions were abolished in the Treaty of Luxembourg (the first budgetary treaty). Revenues for the budget were to be raised through the introduction of 'own resources', consisting of monies collected from customs duties, agricultural levies and VAT. Because of rapidly increasing Common Agricultural Policy (CAP) expenditures and decreasing revenues from import levies in the 1980s, the budget became too small to finance the activities of the Community. At the same time, member states (the UK in particular) began to question the way in which the budget was spent. This led to a series of budget reforms.

- The *1975 Second Budgetary Treaty* established a Court of Auditors, and expanded the role of the European Parliament (EP) in budgetary decisions.
- The *1984 Fontainebleau Summit* allowed the UK to receive some budgetary compensation (called the 'budget rebate'), in return for an increase in its VAT contribution and limits on CAP expenditures.
- The *1988 Delors I Package* responded to the need for more money to finance the new policy competences introduced in the Single European Act (SEA). Delors I increased the 1988–92 budget by 7.6 per cent in exchange for limiting the size of the EU budget to 1.15 per cent of EU GNP. Delors I also reintroduced direct contributions from member states, should the Community's own resources not cover expenditures.
- The *1992 Delors II Package* substantially increased the 1999 budget by 22 per cent, and raised the budget limit to 1.2 per cent of EU GNP, in order to facilitate changes that would result from the Treaty on European Union (TEU).
- The *Inter-institutional Agreement of 1999* increased the 2000–6 budget by 15.9 per cent and raised the budget ceiling to its current level of 1.27 per cent of EU GNP. The next review of the budget will occur in 2006.

B EU revenues

I Characteristics of the budget

The EU's budget is unusual, in that it is too large to be that of an international organization, while displaying several features that distinguish it from the budgets of conventional states.

- Unlike a national government, the EU cannot incur any debt. Therefore, EU expenditures must equal revenues, and cannot run a deficit.
- As EU revenues are capped, the EU budget currently cannot exceed 1.27 per cent of EU GNP, which constrains the ability of the EU to take on new policy competences or expand current policy areas.
- The size of the EU's budget is small when compared with national budgets, relative to GNP: the EU budget for 2001 amounts to just over €93.78 billion, or 1.27 per cent of EU GNP, whereas the US budget for 2001 amounted to around €1,991 billion, or 20.0 per cent of US GNP.

2 Financing the budget

Unlike conventional states, the EU does not have the authority to impose taxes, but instead finances the budget through its four 'own resources'.

- *Agricultural levies.* Under the CAP, the EU imposes tariffs on less expensive agricultural goods produced outside the EU, in order to ensure that the more

expensive EU agricultural goods remain competitive. It also penalizes overproduction of certain EU agricultural products through fines. In 2002, this
amounted to €1.7 billion, approximately 1.8 per cent of the budget.
- *Customs duties*. These are revenues raised from tariffs imposed on imported non-
agricultural goods. In 2002, this amounted to €14.2 billion, approximately 14.8
per cent of the budget.
- *Value added tax (VAT)*. The EU collects 0.75 per cent of all VAT revenues (also
known as sales tax) from all member states. This amounted to €36.6 billion in
2002, or 38.3 per cent of the budget.
- *Percentage of member state GNP*. The EU collects a set amount of money
annually from member states, which varies from state to state according to the
size of its economy (measured as a percentage of GNP). This contributed €41.1
billion, or 43.0 per cent, to the budget in 2002.

(Miscellaneous sources and surpluses from the previous year amounted to €2.0
billion, or 2.1 per cent of the 2002 budget.)

C   EU expenditures

I   Breakdown by structure

Another feature that distinguishes the EU's budget is the way in which money is
spent. For example, the 2001 US budget is represented in figure 6.1. Conventional
states' spending therefore concentrates heavily on areas such as social security,
housing, education, health and defence. These areas of spending are entirely missing
from the EU budget (see figure. 6.2). The EU budget is divided as shown in table 6.1.

2   Change in EU budget

Changes in EU budgetary expenditure have been most apparent in the two EU
redistributive instruments: namely, the CAP and the EU Regional Policy. In 1988,
the CAP received almost 70 per cent of the EU budget, leaving EU Regional Policy
with less than 20 per cent. In 2002, by contrast, CAP expenditures had dropped to
46.3 per cent, whilst spending on the Structural and Cohesion funds had risen to
33.4 per cent (see *Common Agricultural Policy*).

3   Breakdown by member state

The largest net contributors to the EU budget are Germany, France, Italy and the
UK, whilst the largest recipients are Greece, Ireland, Portugal and Spain. This
breakdown reflects the fact that most of the EU budget goes towards Regional

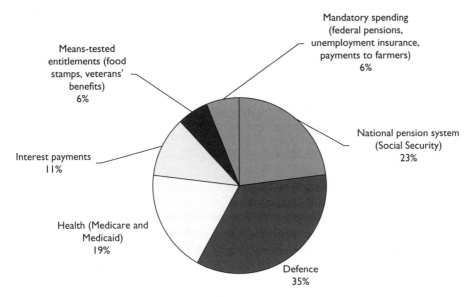

Figure 6.1   The 2001 US Federal Budget. Source: *Citizen's Guide to the Federal Budget 2001*, at *www.access.gpo.gov/usbudget*.

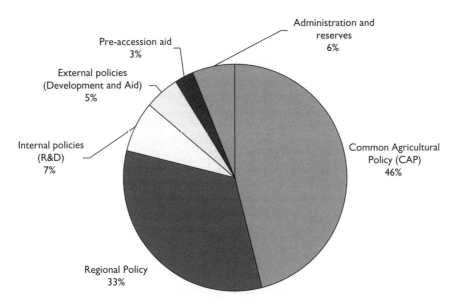

Figure 6.2   The 2002 EU Budget. Source: European Commission.

Table 6.1   The EU Budget

Area of expenditure	Amount (million €)	Per cent
Common Agricultural Policy (CAP)	46,587	46
Structural and Cohesion Funds	33,638	33
Internal policies (i.e. R&D)	6,558	7
External actions (i.e. humanitarian and development aid)	4,873	5
Administration costs of EU institutions	5,012	6
Pre-accession aid	3,120	3
Reserves	676	<1
Total	**100,672**	**100**

Policy and agriculture, which in theory aim to assist poorer regions and poor farmers. However, due to political pressures, some richer countries are also net beneficiaries of the EU budget, such as Denmark, Belgium and Luxembourg.

D   How the budget works

The budget is agreed upon in two stages.

1   Stage 1: the financial perspective

This decides the main budgetary priorities, the maximum budget size, and the highest spending ceilings for each EU programme area. Each financial perspective lasts for a seven-year period, and the current one extends from 2000 to 2006. The financial perspective is proposed by the Commission and agreed upon by the unanimous vote of the Council; the European Parliament (EP) has only advisory status at this stage.

2   Stage 2: the annual budgetary procedure

The Commission proposes the annual budget, after which the Council and the EP decide precisely how revenues will be spent. This procedure is subject to the ceilings already agreed upon in the financial perspective and depends on whether compulsory or non-compulsory expenditures are being discussed. *Compulsory expenditures* are those incurred through the EU's legal obligations towards third parties, such as non-EU countries and farmers; final decisions on these expenditures are the prerogative of the Council. Thus the EP has little direct say over CAP spending. All other EU expenditure, including Regional Policy funding, is defined as *non-compulsory expenditures*, over which the EP has final jurisdiction. Once the spending for compulsory and non-compulsory expenditures has been decided, the budget is adopted or rejected in a final vote by the EP.

E Power over the budget

As the Commission proposes both the financial perspective and the annual budget, it wields a large amount of influence over the shape of the budget. In addition, the Commission has the formal responsibility for implementing the budget; however, member states have *de facto* responsibility for implementing around 85 per cent of the budget, primarily because they execute the day-to-day running of the CAP and the Structural Funds. As the EP and the Council can amend Commission proposals, these institutions exert the largest influence on the budget, depending on the budgetary procedure used.

The financial perspective is of key importance, as it provides the financial frame-work of the EU for the next seven years. As the EP can only advise the Council on the content of the financial perspective in this procedure, the Council has the most power in the creation of the financial perspective. By contrast, the Council's control over the annual budgetary procedure is weaker, given that the EP has authority over non-compulsory expenditures. This situation is reversed for compulsory expen-ditures, where the Council has the authority. Therefore, it would appear that power is shared fairly equally between the two institutions.

Yet, the Council's control over compulsory expenditures is not complete, as the EP must approve the budget as a whole. In the past, the EP has threatened to reject the budget in order to win concessions from the Council over compulsory expen-ditures (in fact, the EP did reject the budget in 1982). Consequently, the balance of power in the annual budgetary procedure lies largely with the Parliament.

The EP plays another important role in supervising the budget, since it must discharge past budgets – in other words, the EP must pass a motion indicating that it is satisfied with the implementation of the past budget (based on annual reports submitted by the Court of Auditors). Refusal to discharge the budget is viewed as a vote of no confidence in the Commission. This gives the EP enormous political power. In 1999, following sharply critical reports from the Court of Auditors on the 1996 budget, the EP debated whether to refuse the discharge. Although the budget was passed, the EP subsequently set up a Committee of Independent Experts to investigate; this in turn produced such a damning report on the Commission's management of the budget that the Santer Commission felt obliged to resign. Consequently, substantial parts of the current Commission reform proposals aim to improve budgetary implementation.

The problems/issues

A The EU budget and economic theory

According to Musgrave, public policy has three distinct functions: allocation, stabilization and redistribution.

- *Allocation of resources.* Public policy is directed at improving the efficient use of resources. The EU budget targets groups such as those representing agriculture and innovation, thereby significantly altering their use of resources.
- *Stabilization.* While macroeconomic and monetary policies attempt to achieve certain economic objectives (such as strong growth, low inflation or low unemployment), national budgets also contribute to economic stability through progressive taxation and social security systems. In addition to the EU budget being too small to perform this function, taxation and social security systems remain under the control of the member states, thereby preventing the EU budget from having a stabilization effect.
- *Redistribution.* Public policy also aims at ensuring that different social and regional constituents receive fair shares of overall welfare. The EU budgetary role in this arena is mixed, as some target groups (primarily farmers and poorer regions) are strongly affected by the EU budget, while the average EU citizen remains relatively untouched by EU redistribution.

B   The size and structure of the EU budget

Political scientists use the EU budget to investigate how the EU political system works. In particular, they are interested in why the budget is so small, and why it remains so firmly linked to agriculture and Regional Policy. Academics, such as Hix, propose five explanations:

I   Intergovernmental bargaining

The structure and size of the budget are a direct consequence of negotiation between EU member states on European integration. The budget is used as a 'side-payment' to buy support from poorer member states for EU policies that would otherwise primarily benefit richer member states. Examples of this include the CAP (used to buy French support for opening markets to German industrial products in the Treaties of Rome) and the Structural Funds (used to buy the support of the weaker regions, who feared the effects of market liberalization, for the SEA).

2   Private interest groups

Groups such as farmers and regions benefit greatly from EU policies, and use their organizational power to lobby member governments and the EU institutions for the continuation of such redistributive programmes. At the same time, the costs of these programmes are spread across a large number of people; as a result, taxpayers and consumers have relatively little incentive to lobby for change. Unequal lobbying representation has made policy reform of programmes such as the CAP very difficult (see Olson's theory of collective action in *Interest Groups*).

3 Commission entrepreneurship

As an independent actor, the Commission uses its agenda-setting powers to further its own interests. In particular, it exploits the budget in order to promote further European integration, since this will increase its own powers. While the Commission has considerable influence over the budget through its role as policy-initiator, it also exerts indirect control over the budget through its day-to-day running of programmes co-ordinated at the EU level (such as some regional and environmental programmes).

4 Institutional rules

Because the financial perspective is agreed by unanimity in the Council, all member states must perceive that they have received a national benefit from the budget or they would exercise their national veto power. However, the annual budgetary procedure is decided by Qualified Majority Voting (QMV), making it easier for outside institutions (namely, the Commission and the EP) to influence the yearly budgetary outcomes.

5 Parliamentary activism

The EP plays a substantial role in shaping the budget, which it has used to strengthen its position in the policy-making process. The ability to adopt or reject the budget, jurisdiction over non-compulsory expenditure (which now forms the largest portion of the budget), and control over the discharge of past budgets gives the EP significant influence, as witnessed by the resignation of the Santer Commission. Consequently, it is unsurprising that the EP has been attempting to increase the size of the budget, by calling for the creation of a fifth 'own resource', and by opposing the division between compulsory and non-compulsory expenditure.

C The need for a bigger EU budget

In consideration of the growing importance of the EU as a political entity, many academics and politicians have argued that a larger EU budget could benefit the Community in several ways.

- The *ideological* argument contends that a larger budget would further European integration, thereby strengthening the relative importance of the Community and enhancing the roles of the EU institutions. Conversely, this would weaken the power of the member states. Therefore, a budgetary increase (like EU influence on taxation) is often opposed as a threat to sovereignty by member states, such as the UK.

- The *redistributional* argument is based on concerns about the effects of EU enlargement. With the accession of a number of significantly poorer countries to the EU, efforts to combat regional inequalities will need to be dramatically increased. However, the main beneficiaries of Regional Policy (namely, the Cohesion countries) have fiercely resisted attempts to cut their share of EU funds. A compromise may therefore lead to an increased future budget for the 2007–12 financial perspective.
- The *stabilization* argument is based on two possible adverse scenarios resulting from EMU. In the EMU, countries no longer have an independent monetary policy with which to adapt to economic crises. The alternative methods of managing such economic crises (labour mobility and wage/price flexibility) are very limited within the EU. In addition, national fiscal spending is constrained by the Growth and Stability Pact (restricting budget deficits to less than 3 per cent of GDP). In the case of asymmetric shocks, the argument for an increased EU budget is strong, as a larger budget would allow for inter-country fiscal transfers, in order to maintain economic stability (see *Economic and Monetary Union*).

Despite these arguments and the growing political and economic obligations of the EU, the Berlin European Council modified the 'own resources' system to reduce the budgetary burden on member states. The new system, which came into effect on 1 January 2002, not only freezes the ceiling on the EU budget at 1.27 per cent of the combined EU GDP, but allows the member states to retain up to 25 per cent of EU 'own resources' as a collection cost (up from 10 per cent) and reduces the amount of VAT contributed to the EU budget from 1 per cent to 0.75 per cent in 2002 and 0.5 per cent in 2004. In addition, the Berlin European Council decided that no new 'own resource' would be introduced until the Commission presents a report on the issue by the end of 2005.

Who wins/who loses

Individual member states are both winners and losers from the EU budget. Measured in terms of financial compensation, the winners are the net beneficiaries from the budget (the Cohesion countries), whilst the losers are the net contributors to the budget (Germany, the UK, France and Italy). On the other hand, the richer member states are arguably those that benefit more from market liberalization, which, in turn, has been made possible through budgetary side-payments to the Cohesion countries. As a group, however, member states have lost power, as increases in the EU budget are directly linked with the growth of EU competences.

By comparison, **EU institutions** are winners, as the budget has helped finance some of their most ambitious programmes. In particular, the EP has gained considerable influence over the budget, especially for an institution accused of lacking real political power.

The average **EU citizen** has not been directly affected to a significant extent by the EU budget. In some ways, citizens are losers, because they have suffered from higher food prices incurred through the CAP regime. Conversely, regions and farmers received significant support from growth of the EU budget.

Food for thought

Does the EU need a bigger budget? Economists argue that the possibility of an asymmetric shock to the EU economy under the EMU regime could be counterbalanced by the centralization and expansion of the EU budget. Others argue that enlargement could destabilize the Union if the budget is not increased. In addition, if the EU is to evolve into a conventional state-like structure with a conventional budget, including responsibility for policies like taxation and social security systems, a larger budget will be necessary. However, a larger budget could indicate that the EU is taking over the duties of the member states, and thereby threatening national sovereignty.

Student-to-student tip

The most accessible sources for understanding the budget are produced by the EU institutions themselves. The DG Budget website and the EP Fact Sheets are simple and very user-friendly. They are worth reading before moving on to the more academic articles.

Summary

- The EU budget is financed through four different revenue streams, known as its 'own resources':
  - agricultural levies
  - customs duties
  - VAT
  - member state contributions, calculated as a percentage of GNP.
- The biggest contributors are Germany, the UK, France and Italy; the biggest beneficiaries are Portugal, Spain, Ireland and Greece.
- Over 80 per cent of the budget is spent on agriculture (the CAP) and Regional Policy (the Structural and Cohesion funds). However, except for farmers and the regions, the EU's budget does not have a significant impact on most EU citizens when compared with the effect of national budgets. This is because national budgets are comparatively larger (measured in terms of percentage of GNP) than the EU budget.
- The budgetary policy-making procedure involves the Commission, the Council and the EP. The Council has the most power in setting the financial perspective, which is the seven-year framework within which the budget is decided. The EP

has more power in the annual budgetary process. The EP also has the important political responsibility of discharging the budget.

- Pressure to increase the size of the budget comes from enlargement, EMU, and concerns about the future of the EU. Due to both the money involved and differing political ideologies, any such proposals cause controversy between the EU institutions and among member states.

Selected bibliography

Comprehensive books

Laffan, B. (1997) *The Finances of the European Union*, London: Macmillan.
> This 300-page book is an excellent in-depth study of the finances of the Union.

Begg, I. and N. Grimwade (1998) *Paying for Europe*, Sheffield: Sheffield Academic Press.
> This concise volume outlines the possible options for reforming the EU budget. It proposes an agenda for gradual reform which takes into account the political and economic constraints of the Union.

Overviews

Bladen-Hovell, R. and E. Symons (1997) 'The EU Budget', in M. Artis and N. Lee (eds), *The Economics of the European Union: Policy and Analysis*, Oxford: Oxford University Press, chapter 14: 372–94.
> This is an excellent resource, which also contains a helpful chronology of major financial reforms.

Hitiris, T. (1998) *European Union Economics*, New York: Prentice-Hall Europe, chapter 4: 88–115.
> Explaining the basic economic theory behind the budget, Hitiris outlines the arguments for and against fiscal federalism and the creation of a federal budget for the EU.

Tsoukalis, L. (1997) *The New European Economy Revisited*, 3rd edn, Oxford: Oxford University Press, 209–22.
> Tsoukalis combines economic theory with a historical perspective which thoroughly explains how the budget has evolved over time.

Nugent, N. (1999) *The Government and Politics of the European Union*, 4th edn, London: Macmillan, chapter 14: 389–412.
> Nugent offers an excellent account of the process of making the budget.

Ackrill, R. (2000) 'The European Union Budget, the Balanced Budget Rule and the Development of Common European Policies', *Journal of Public Policy*, vol. 20, no. 1: 1–19.
> This article presents the role of the budgetary rules, particularly in relation to the development of the Common Agricultural Policy.

Supportive websites

http://europa.eu.int/comm/budget/index.htm DG Budget provides a good introduction to this field, along with data on the current budget.

http://www.europarl.eu.int/factsheets/default_en.htm The European Parliament Fact Sheets are particularly good for understanding the role of the EP in the budget-making process.

http://www.cec.org.uk/info/pubs/bbriefs/index.htm This site offers Background Briefings from the EU Commission representation in the UK.

Part III

EU Law

7

Constitutionalism

Christopher Hobley

The Treaties of Rome (1957) created the European Community as an organization controlled by the member states and based on international law. Over time, the EU has evolved into an economic and political entity governed by a form of constitutional law, possessing its own form of sovereignty. The process that transformed the EU from an international organization into a sovereign body is known as 'constitutionalism'. Constitutionalism defines the rules whereby the EU functions, and gives the EU some of the political features traditionally associated with nation-states, including citizens and binding legislation. However, as the national sovereignty of the member states comes into conflict with the growing sovereignty of the EU, the way in which EU constitutionalism develops has gained increased importance for the future of the Community.

The facts

The Treaties of Rome left the exact legal status of the European Community unclear and open to interpretation by both the member states and EU institutions. A series of rulings by the European Court of Justice (ECJ) gave the Community increased power *vis-à-vis* the member states, and created a constitutional basis for the EU. The key cases in this process are summarized below.

A   Case 26/62, *Van Gend en Loos* (1963) and a new legal order

In Case 26/62, *Van Gend en Loos* vs *Nederlandse Administratie der Belastingen* (*VGeL*) (1963), a Dutch chemical importer was taken to court by the Dutch authorities for refusing to pay extra duty resulting from a change in the tariff classification of urea formaldehyde. The importer argued that this duty breached Article 25 (ex-Article 12) of the Treaty of Rome, which prohibits tariff increases between member states. International law allows member states to invoke provisions of a treaty, but does not require national courts to allow citizens the right to invoke international treaties in domestic courts. The case was referred to the ECJ, which decided it had jurisdiction to rule on the matter. In order to do so, it created a new distinction between EC law and other types of international law, arguing that 'the Community constitutes a new legal order of international law for the benefit of which the states have limited their sovereign rights, albeit within limited fields, and the subjects of which comprise not just the Member States but also their nationals' (*VGeL*, 1963). This conclusion was a radical change from previous rulings under international law, especially because there is nothing in the Treaty that states that the Community constitutes a new legal order. In practice, EU integration has been furthered substantially by the ability of individual citizens, and not just member states, to bring cases before the ECJ for judgment under EU law.

B   Case 6/64, *Costa* vs *ENEL* (1964) and the doctrine of supremacy

The ECJ justified the creation of a 'new legal order' in the *Van Gend en Loos* case by arguing that the EU legal order contains certain areas in which the Community has sovereign power (such as trade between member states). This means that in areas where the EU has sovereignty, individual member states cannot overrule Community decisions. However, the EU legal order and national legal orders often overlap, especially since those subject to EU law and national law are both member nations and the citizens of these states. Therefore, in order for the Community to be sovereign, it must have the competence to overrule national laws that conflict with EU laws. This competence is called the 'doctrine of supremacy'. The ECJ laid the foundations for the doctrine of supremacy in the *Costa* case, when it ruled that in conflicts between EU law and national law, EU law should prevail. As in *Van Gend en Loos*, it was recognized that the Treaties of Rome had not explicitly stated that EU law was supreme to national legal orders, but the ECJ interpreted the Treaty to imply the supremacy of EU law. Critics of the ECJ have argued that in this case (as well as many others), the ECJ overstepped the limits of its authority by creating law rather than merely interpreting it (this is known as judicial activism).

C   Challenges to supremacy: Case 11/70, *Internationale Handelsgesellschaft GmbH* vs *Einfuhr- und Vorratsstelle für Getreide und Futtermittel* (1972) and *Brunner* vs *European Union Treaty* (1994)

The creation of a new legal system by the ECJ made the national governments of many member states uneasy about the development of EU legal structure, as this system threatened the sovereignty of member states. Consequently, member states have issued several direct challenges to the doctrine of supremacy, especially in the area of fundamental rights. The Treaties of Rome explicitly protect the economic rights of EU citizens, but not other fundamental rights, such as social and human rights. Therefore, the doctrine of supremacy created a critical problem: it demands that Community law (which doesn't protect human rights) overrule national law (which does). As a result, accepting the doctrine of supremacy means accepting instances in which human rights are not protected. This problem first arose in the *Internationale Handelsgesellschaft* case, where the ECJ ruling on the case caused the German constitutional court to raise concerns over the inadequacy of the Community's protection of fundamental rights (see *Fundamental Rights*). The German court consequently issued the *Solange* judgment, whereby the constitutional court reserved the power to protect the basic rights of its citizens against violations by the Community until the EU provided protection for fundamental rights. The *Solange* judgment thus weakened the doctrine of supremacy by making it contingent on the review of national constitutional courts.

As the ECJ gradually increased its protection of fundamental rights, many legal scholars argued that the *Solange* judgment no longer presented a threat to the supremacy of EU law, and it was assumed that the ECJ had become the *de facto* 'supreme court' of the EU legal system. This assumption was challenged in *Brunner*, when a German citizen asked the German constitutional court to rule on whether the Treaty on European Union (TEU, 1992) violated the German Basic Law. Although the German constitutional court ruled against Brunner, the court emphasized that the EU is a federation of states that 'remain sovereign'. This ruling implied that the existence of the EU as a sovereign entity does not undermine the judicial status of the member states, and that the doctrine of supremacy is still subject to the review of national constitutional courts.

The problems/issues

A The doctrine of conferred powers, *Kompetenz-Kompetenz*, and subsidiarity

The discussion of EU constitutionalism relies on three important concepts.

I The doctrine of conferred powers

Initially, the Community was thought to be similar to other international and intergovernmental bodies, having powers determined by a legal concept called the 'doctrine of conferred powers'. This doctrine argues that the only powers that international bodies have are those conferred on them by member states. It maintains that these powers can be reclaimed by member states at any time, even if this violates the international treaty. Therefore, the doctrine argues that member states always remain masters of the international bodies they created (otherwise known as *Herren der Verträge*). The ECJ undermined this doctrine through the *Van Gend en Loos* ruling, and later strengthened the argument against the doctrine in the *Costa* case, stating that the transfer of powers designated by the Treaty is permanent. In other words, the delegation of certain national competences to the EU level cannot be revoked by a member state if that member state wishes to remain in the Community.

2   The Kompetenz-Kompetenz

Every legal system has a high court, such as a supreme court or a court of appeal, whose decisions are recognized as being final. These courts possess the *Kompetenz-Kompetenz* within that legal system. In the EU legal system, the ECJ formally possesses the *Kompetenz-Kompetenz*, based on powers conferred in the Treaties of Rome. The ECJ explicitly supports its *Kompetenz-Kompetenz* in *Opinion 1/91, Re: Draft Treaty on a European Economic Area (EEA)* (1991), by claiming supremacy over all EU treaties, including those with associated nations.

3   The principle of subsidiarity

As the EU extended its legal powers and policy competences, member states became increasingly uneasy about EU encroachment on national sovereignty. In an attempt both to minimize unnecessary EU involvement in national policy areas and to increase the efficiency of the EU, the principle of subsidiarity was developed as part of the negotiations prior to the ratification of the Treaty on European Union (TEU) in 1993. As defined by Article 5 of the EU Treaty, the EU only has the competence to act if 'the objectives of the proposed action cannot be sufficiently achieved by the Member States and . . . can be better achieved by the Community'. While it is difficult to judge the effectiveness of the principle in preventing further extension of Community competences, member states can use subsidiarity to remind the Commission and other EU institutions of their ability to block EU legislation by evoking Article 5 or Protocol 30 (based on the principle of subsidiarity and proportionality) of the Amsterdam Treaty. The Convention on the Future of Europe has been charged with developing detailed proposals that would improve the effectiveness of subsidiarity within the EU legal structure.

B   Theories of sovereignty

The contention over the development of constitutionalism in the EU is focused on the issue of sovereignty. Theories of sovereignty attempt to clarify whether the member states have relinquished their sovereignty by conferring powers on the Community, or have merely outsourced duties to an external institution.

I Traditional theories of sovereignty

These theories envision sovereignty as a power that exists in set quantities; therefore, if a member state gives away some of its powers to the EU, it will have lost some of its sovereignty. If sovereignty is shared, there is always a hierarchy that establishes who has the final authority to make decisions; in other words, one entity always has the *Kompetenz-Kompetenz*. Without this hierarchy, disagreements between the member states would be very difficult to resolve. Lack of agreement on key legal issues could also threaten the entire system of pooled sovereignty. Traditional theories of sovereignty therefore argue that member states have largely accepted a limited loss of sovereignty to the EU as the price they pay for the economic benefits of EU integration.

2 Sovereignty and the Kompetenz-Kompetenz

Although member states may have accepted that the Community has gained sovereignty, it is unclear to what extent they have actually suffered a corresponding loss of sovereignty. In both *Van Gend en Loos* and *Costa*, the ECJ argued that the member states have permanently transferred sovereignty to the EU in certain policy areas. Thus, if a key element of sovereignty is the ability to act independently, this is now constrained by the ECJ's *Kompetenz-Kompetenz*.

However, the reasoning in *Brunner* demonstrated that some constitutional courts would accept the ECJ's rulings only if they corresponded with their own constitutionally determined priorities. The German constitutional court upheld its own independence by unilaterally threatening to disapply EU law if it conflicted with the fundamental rights protection guaranteed under the German Constitution, thereby denying that it had permanently lost any sovereignty to the EU. However, the implications of *Brunner* are more far-reaching, as this ruling implies that the constitutional courts have the sole power to decide whether aspects of EU law violate constitutional priorities; it also argues that under such circumstances, constitutional courts are the final arbiter of EU law. In other words, the national constitutional courts may also have the *Kompetenz-Kompetenz*.

It is important to note that although the German constitutional court threatened to disapply EU law, it did not actually do so. Therefore, it appears that the EU has a system in which the national and EU legal orders overlap, and in which both constitutional courts and the ECJ seem to have ultimate authority. This is problematic for traditional theories of sovereignty, which argue that such a situation should not be possible, given that sovereignty is viewed in the form of hierarchies where there is no ambiguity about who has the ultimate authority.

3 Constructivist approaches to European constitutionalism

Constructivists argue that traditional theories of sovereignty are inappropriate for the study of the EU. Shaw and Wiener note that the theories outlined above assume that the EU is a state-like body, which it is not. They contend that the EU should be viewed as a political system, based on evolving norms. Since these norms are in flux, they often contradict each other. This, in turn, leads to contradictory legal positions. As a result, the EU legal order sometimes resembles a single hierarchical structure led by the ECJ, while at other times, it appears to be a differentiated and disintegrative legal order, not based on a clear legal hierarchy.

4 New theories of sovereignty

Scholars such as MacCormick have created new theories of sovereignty, which accept that autonomous but still overlapping spheres of law can coexist without one body possessing the *Kompetenz-Kompetenz*. In the absence of an ultimate arbiter, the systems proposed would depend on mutual co-operation in order to avoid conflicts. Member states are already trying to achieve this sort of co-operation through political means. For example, the Maastricht Treaty kept the definition of subsidiarity deliberately ambiguous, so that all member states could interpret the principle any way they chose. In the legal sphere, such co-operation has also emerged in the ECJ's growing protection of fundamental rights. The ECJ co-operates with constitutional courts, in order to prevent challenges to ECJ supremacy. At the same time, national constitutional courts are reluctant to declare Community law to be unconstitutional (see *Law and European Integration*).

However, while ambiguous forms of power sharing based on mutual goodwill may function in the current *status quo*, the development of the EU into a more conventional state-like structure could make such purposely ambiguous forms of power sharing redundant. Therefore, this period of autonomous yet overlapping legal spheres could be transitory rather than permanent. Alternatively, it may be impossible to resolve some conflicts through mutual co-operation. For instance, a constitutional court may decide that a measure is illegal, and, by challenging the ECJ's authority, force a resolution of the *Kompetenz-Kompetenz* problem. The eastern enlargement of the EU raises the possibility of such a challenge to the ECJ's authority; the inclusion of more constitutional courts in the EU legal system makes it increasingly likely that one of them will decide to challenge the ECJ's authority. Such a challenge could threaten the uniform application of law in the Community, thereby potentially undermining the entire EU legal system.

C Constitutionalism and problems with democracy

The absence of an EU constitution can be seen as a threat to the democratic character of the Community. For example, without a constitution, individual rights lack the comprehensive protection they receive under national law. However, many question whether a constitution created without consulting the EU citizenry can be democratically valid.

I   Inadequate individual rights

In traditional political theory, only nation-states can have sovereignty, and this sovereignty is usually formalized through a constitution. By arguing that the Community constitutes a sovereign 'new legal order', the ECJ is implying that the EU is a state-like entity with a founding constitution. However, constitutions traditionally outline the rights and duties of both the state and its citizens, and the Treaties of Rome do not address the citizen or most of the political and civil rights associated with a constitution. Thus, it could be argued that citizens have been made subjects of EU law without having been given adequate rights (see *Fundamental Rights*).

2   No demos

It can also be argued that EU constitutionalism is illegitimate, since a constitution can only be considered legitimate if a political group – called a *demos* – exists; moreover, individuals must accept that they belong to such a group in order for the *demos* to be valid. Since EU citizens generally do not perceive themselves as being part of an EU *demos* (at least not in the same way as they perceive themselves to be French or Greek, for example), constitutionalism at the EU level cannot be valid. Consequently, any laws that affect all EU citizens cannot be considered legitimate. Such an argument may be too extreme, considering the political arrangements in countries like Switzerland, where four different ethnic groups coexist in a system that all view as legitimate. Such situations demonstrate that power-sharing agreements between different *demoi* are possible. Yet the *demos* argument does raise serious concerns about the role of the EU citizen in the European integration process.

3   Lack of citizen involvement

Constitutionalism may also be undemocratic because EU citizens are rarely involved in the development of the EU. European integration has been led primarily by politicians and bureaucrats, and EU citizens have only occasionally been consulted (mainly via referendums) on how they wish European integration to proceed. Through the TEU, citizens of member states became EU citizens. However, in bypassing the normal legislative process, one can argue that the evolutionary process of constitutionalism has robbed EU citizens of a voice in the creation of the EU. The EU has recently tried to remedy this situation through high-profile public discussions of constitutionalism, such as the Convention on the Future of Europe, begun in 2002.

D Does the EU need a 'proper' constitution?

I Arguments in favour

As a result of the concerns outlined above, many theorists have concluded that the EU system needs a proper constitution, not only outlining the powers of the Union, but also stating the limits of its powers. A constitution would also determine the powers of the member states, the regions and the individual. Some academics, such as Weiler, have suggested an interim measure through the creation of a constitutional court (to be composed of judges of the various member states plus a president chosen from the ECJ) to oversee the judgments of the ECJ. Such a system would increase legal certainty by clarifying the claims on *Kompetenz-Kompetenz*. Walker suggests that this would force the Community to strengthen its democratic credentials as well as create a European *demos*, thereby furthering European integration. Such a court might, however, transform the Community from an ambiguous political entity into a much more recognizably state-like structure – a development not favoured by many member states.

2 Arguments against

Academics such as Clapham point out that the advantage of the present situation is that it allows everyone to interpret the Community in the way they want. Should member states be forced to articulate in precise detail how they want the Community to develop, the disagreements between member states could upset the current balance of power within the Community. Conflicts concerning the European Charter of Fundamental Rights and the reforms that need to be enacted in the Community prior to enlargement (such as extension of Qualified Majority Voting) illustrate the problems that arise when the member states attempt to clarify such constitutional issues. In addition, opponents of an EU constitution argue that a constitution would both consolidate power at the EU level and erode national sovereignty, which they believe would work to the disadvantage of the EU citizen.

E The Convention on the Future of Europe

Anxiety about these types of issues led EU policy-makers to organize a Convention on the Future of Europe, which opened in February 2002. The aim of the convention was to hold a public debate on the EU's institutional structure in order to reach a consensus on how the EU should develop, especially in light of eastern enlargement. As a result, the convention was divided into four areas of concern:

- establishing a clear division of responsibilities between the EU and member states;
- simplifying the existing legal instruments of the EU;
- making the EU more democratic, transparent and efficient;
- restructuring and simplifying the EU treaties.

If the conclusions reached during the convention become a reality, many of the outstanding issues surrounding constitutionalism (such as the *Kompetenz-Kompetenz* and EU-level fundamental rights) could be resolved. However, unless such conclusions are reached through a broad consensus of national governments, EU institutions and EU citizens, the findings of the convention are unlikely to lead to the Treaty changes necessary to improve EU constitutionalism.

Who wins/who loses

The constitutionalism debate has made the **ECJ** a winner, primarily because it has become the main court in the EU legal system. However, in achieving this status, the ECJ has also politicized EU law, leading to accusations of legal activism as well as to serious challenges to ECJ authority.

National constitutional courts have lost, in the sense that the ECJ now has the ability to rule on matters over which these courts previously had sole authority. However, the politicization of EU law has also strengthened the position of constitutional courts, since they are increasingly seen as a last legitimate defence against European encroachment, as demonstrated in *Brunner*.

According to traditional theories of sovereignty, **member states** are losers, because constitutionalism means relinquishing powers that previously belonged solely to the nation-state. However, member states may have initially pooled sovereignty in the EU because they were too weak to function as autonomous political actors in an increasingly interdependent world. If this is the case, then EU constitutionalism has allowed member states to regain autonomy, albeit as a group, on the world stage.

The **EU** has certainly profited from the process of constitutionalism, which has allowed it to change from an ordinary intergovernmental body to a political body with state-like features, such as citizens and sovereignty. However, as Weiler argues, the EU has enjoyed a 'constitution without constitutionalism', meaning that the EU has been built without the participation of its citizens. This situation leads to questions about the legitimacy of the European project.

For the **EU citizen**, constitutionalism can be viewed either positively or negatively. If the EU adopts a constitution which both involves EU citizens in its creation and extends the protection of fundamental rights, then constitutionalism will work to their advantage. However, a constitution that is not based on the will of the citizens would lack legitimacy, and could further alienate EU citizens.

Food for thought

While the ECJ has argued that challenges to its authority threaten to undermine the EU legal system, this argument can be viewed as an excuse for the ECJ to acquire more power. However, is it likely that any constitutional court would behave in a way that would fundamentally threaten the EU legal system? Should situations like *Brunner* – in which an outright rebellion was threatened but not carried out – be avoided in the future, or should they be accepted as part of the legitimate judicial process?

How can the process of constitutionalism be made more democratic? While the ECJ has been responsible for many developments in EU constitutionalism, the recent debate has increasingly centred on the need to adopt a formal EU constitution. Would such a constitution resolve the democratic deficit within the EU, and increase the legitimacy of the EU for its citizens? Is the Convention on the Future of Europe the most effective way to engage EU citizens in the debate over constitutionalism?

Student-to-student tip

Traditionally, most information associated with EU constitutionalism was found in legal journals and textbooks. However, with the commencement of the Convention on the Future of Europe, the concept of constitutionalism has moved beyond a philosophical discussion of constitutional ideals to become a major political issue for the national governments of member states. As a result, national media sources offer excellent sources of information on the political side of the debate. Many of them (including the BBC, the *Financial Times*, *Le Monde*, and *Frankfurt Allgemeine*, to name just a few) have archives of articles on these subjects on their websites.

Summary

- The term 'constitutionalism' describes the development of the EU from an international treaty into a semi-autonomous political entity. In particular, the ECJ has developed EU constitutionalism through the *Van Gend en Loos* and *Costa* cases.
- To a large extent, member states have accepted EU constitutionalism, including the consequences of the doctrine of supremacy. However, challenges to the EU legal order (such as the *Solange* ruling and the *Brunner* case) have underlined that such acceptance is conditional. Given the implications of constitutionalism on areas such as sovereignty, democratic governance and the future shape of the European polity, such challenges are unsurprising.
- Of primary importance to the debate on constitutionalism is the issue of who possesses the *Kompetenz-Kompetenz* over EU law. While the ECJ currently claims to be the supreme court of the EU, these claims have been undermined by conflicts over issues such as fundamental rights.
- Scholars and politicians also debate whether the EU needs a proper constitution to solve the problems that threaten EU law. Those in favour of a constitution argue that it would clarify issues such as the *Kompetenz-Kompetenz*; those opposed contend that a constitution constructed without the participation of citizens would lack the legitimacy necessary for it to be effective.

Selected bibliography

Seminal articles on constitutionalism

Grimm, D. (1995) 'Does Europe Need a Constitution?', *European Law Journal*, vol. 1, no. 3: 282–302.

> This article started the debate on European constitutionalism following the *Brunner* case, which Grimm himself ruled on in Germany. The reply to this article by Jürgen Habermas is also well worth reading:

Habermas, J. (1995) 'Remarks on Dieter Grimm's "Does Europe Need a Constitution?"', *European Law Journal*, vol. 1, no. 3: 303–7.

Mancini, G. (1989) 'The Making of a Constitution for Europe', *Common Market Law Review*, vol. 26: 594–614.

> A simplified and strongly pro-European account of constitutionalism, Mancini (a former ECJ judge) provides a useful starting point for newcomers to the subject.

Weiler, J. H. H. (1997) 'The Reformation of European Constitutionalism', *Journal of Common Market Studies*, vol. 35, no. 1: 97–131.

> This very intelligent article offers a thought-provoking overview of constitutionalism with some novel insights and suggestions. However, be warned that many don't find Weiler user-friendly.

MacCormick, N. (1995) 'The Maastricht-Urteil: Sovereignty Now', *European Law Journal*, vol. 1: 259–66.

> MacCormick, a Scottish MEP and social philosopher, presents his theory of overlapping spheres of sovereignty. He discusses other issues pertinent to constitutionalism in:

MacCormick, N. (2000) 'Problems of Democracy and Subsidiarity', *European Public Law*, vol. 6, no. 4: 531–42.

Clapham, A. (1991) *Human Rights and the European Community*, vol. 1: *A Critical Overview*, Baden-Baden: Nomos, and Walker, N. (1998) 'Sovereignty and Differentiated Integration in the European Union', *European Law Journal*, vol. 4, no. 4: 355–88.

> These two authors offer contrasting perspectives on whether the EU needs a constitution.

http://www.les1.man.ac.uk/conweb Constitutionalism Web-Papers (ConWEB).

> This collection of papers is a good starting point for up-to-date articles on constitutionalism and governance. The site is maintained by Jo Shaw and Antje Wiener, legal scholars specializing in constructivist approaches to constitutionalism.

Overviews of constitutionalism

Chalmers, D. (1998) *European Union Law*, volume 1: *Law and EU Government*, Dartmouth: Ashgate, chapter 5: 271–335.

> Chalmers provides an excellent, if complicated, overview of constitutionalism, and offers a good explanation of the facts in the *Van Gend en Loos* case.

De Búrca, G. and P. Craig (1998) *EU Law: Text, Cases and Materials*, New York: Oxford University Press, chapter 6: 255–95.

> This volume presents very good insight into aspects of conditional supremacy not outlined by Chalmers.

8

Fundamental Rights

Amanda Gilman

'Fundamental rights' is an umbrella term for human, economic, social and political rights. Each member state protects these rights to varying degrees, depending on the preferences of its citizens. Since these rights make up a 'contract' between the state and the citizens of that state, the creation of fundamental rights sets parameters on the exercise of state power. Therefore, when national governments create new legislation, they must do so in consideration of these rights. However, while the member states have transferred many of their legislative powers to the European Union, the EU has not provided a comparable level of fundamental rights protection for EU citizens. This has left a gap in fundamental rights protection of EU citizens. The slow process of filling that gap has resulted in increased judicial activism by the European Court of Justice (ECJ) and the development of EU-level rights that mirror those of a traditional nation-state. The effect of these developments on the sovereignty of the EU member states and on the creation of an EU identity underlines the importance of the issue of fundamental rights to the future of the EU.

The facts

A Judicial history of fundamental rights

The Community was founded as an economic organization based on international law. Because of its economic nature, the member states did not include fundamental rights protection in the Treaties of Rome (1957). This does not mean that fundamental rights do not exist at the EU level: EU citizens enjoy several rights related to economic aspects of the Community, such as the right to reside and work in any EU country. Some social and political rights, such as the ability to vote in local elections in one's place of residence, regardless of nationality, have developed to support these economic rights. However, the EU does not provide for the equal protection of other fundamental rights. Increased legislative and policy competence at the EU level has heightened the need for the EU to consolidate the protection of all fundamental rights. So far, the greatest progress in EU-level protection of these rights has been realized through the rulings of the European Court of Justice (ECJ).

Initially, the ECJ did not rule on issues regarding fundamental rights precisely because the Treaty provides no legal basis for judgments in this area. Yet, because of the doctrine of supremacy (see *Constitutionalism*), EU law overrules national law, regardless of whether it protects rights provided for in national constitutions. As Chalmers points out, member states would have eventually been forced to reject EU law as legally binding, if the ECJ had not recognized nationally protected fundamental rights. Therefore, the ECJ needed to include fundamental rights in the Community's legal system in order to protect the supremacy of EU law.

The ECJ's first attempts to include fundamental rights in the scope of EU law occurred in Case 35/67, *Van Eick* vs *Commission* (1968) and in Case 29/69, *Stauder* vs *City of Ulm* (1969). While the Court established the need to protect the fundamental rights recognized by national constitutions through these cases, *Internationale Handelsgesellschaft* was the first case to demonstrate the importance of the issue at the EU level.

B   EU legal supremacy vs fundamental rights: Case 11/70, *Internationale Handelsgesellschaft* vs *Einfuhr- und Vorratstelle für Gertreide und Futtermittel* (1972)

In the *Internationale Handelsgesellschaft* case, a financial deposit made by a German company was confiscated under the terms of an EC regulation. A German court, however, considered that this regulation violated the German constitutionally protected right of freedom to trade. In a preliminary ruling, the ECJ decided that the Community had an obligation to take the fundamental rights traditions of the member states into account when making legislation. As this was the first time that the ECJ was forced to rule on a conflict between EU law and the fundamental rights provisions of a national constitution, *Internationale Handelsgesellschaft* also provides one of the first challenges to the ECJ's doctrine of supremacy. The ECJ reacted to this threat by recognizing the need to protect fundamental rights.

The sensitive nature of the supremacy issue in this case was later confirmed by the *Solange* ruling. After the ECJ's ruling, the *Internationale* case returned to the German courts, where it was eventually appealed to the German constitutional court. Ruling on this case in 1974, the German constitutional court agreed with the ECJ that no breach of fundamental rights had taken place. However, the German court explicitly stated that it would disapply EC law if fundamental rights were not protected by the ECJ (see *Constitutionalism*).

C ECJ review of fundamental rights in the EU: Joint Cases 60 and 61/84, *Cinéthèque vs Fédération Nationale des Cinémas Français* (1985 & 1986) Case 5/88, *Wachauf* vs Germany (1989) and Case 260/89, *Elliniki Radiophonia Tileorassi* (ERT) vs *Dimitiki* (DEP) (1991)

Internationale Handelsgesellschaft established the protection of fundamental rights only for acts of the EU institutions. When non-EU institutions were acting under Community law – such as when national governments implemented directives – the ECJ could not review them for compliance with fundamental rights. The ECJ reinforced this position in *Cinéthèque*. In this case, a French video vendor claimed that a French law forbidding the sale and rental of recent films in video format was contrary to the free movement of goods and constrained the freedom of expression. The ECJ ruled that it did not have competence to review member state compliance in areas that fell under the jurisdiction of national law.

The Court's position on non-institutional judicial review changed in *Wachauf*, in which a tenant farmer's request for compensation was refused by the German authorities, on the basis of their interpretation of an EU regulation. Ruling on this case, the German court argued that this regulation conflicted with the right to own property as protected by German constitutional law, and that the farmer should therefore have received compensation. The ECJ agreed. However, the main development in *Wachauf* was the conclusion that when member states apply Community law, their actions can be reviewed, *on occasion*, by the ECJ for fundamental rights violations. This allowed the ECJ a very narrow window of judicial review (related primarily to directives). However, as it gave the ECJ some judicial review over member states' actions, *Wachauf* was a step towards a fuller protection of fundamental rights for EU citizens.

In the *ERT* case, the Greek government had given ERT (a broadcasting company) exclusive broadcasting rights in Greece. The plaintiffs (a rival broadcasting company) argued that the Greek government had infringed upon their rights, under both the EU free movement of goods and competition principles as well as Article 10 of the European Convention of Human Rights. The ECJ extended the *Wachauf* ruling in *ERT* by stating that *whenever* member states acted under Community law, the ECJ could review their actions in light of the need to protect fundamental rights.

D The balance between the ECJ and member states: Case C-2/92, *R vs Ministry of Agriculture, Fisheries and Food, ex parte Bostock* (1994) and Case C-159/90, *SPUC vs Grogan* (1991)

As in the *Wachauf* case, in *Bostock*, a tenant farmer had increased the milk production on the farm he had leased and had won a milk quota, but did not receive compensation for these improvements when his lease expired. He protested, arguing that the right to property was a fundamental right, which required landlords to compensate tenants under such circumstances. The main difference between the two cases was the role of the member state. In *Wachauf*, the German government refused the tenant's request for compensation because it initially believed that an EU regulation prohibited compensation. In *Bostock*, the issue was whether national authorities had the discretion to refuse the tenant's request for compensation without violating his fundamental right to own property. In this instance, the ECJ ruled that the member state had acted lawfully in refusing Bostock compensation.

In *SPUC* vs *Grogan*, several Irish student unions were distributing free information about abortion services in the UK. As abortion is illegal in Ireland, the student unions (represented by Stephan Grogan and fourteen other student union officers) were taken to court by the Society for the Protection of Unborn Children (SPUC) for promoting an illegal act. The student unions defended themselves, arguing that attempts to stop such activities violated the EU-protected right to provide services. On referral, the ECJ ruled that a service is generally defined as an activity for which one is paid. In this particular case, the provision of information about abortion could not be considered a service, since the information about abortion clinics was not distributed by the student unions on behalf of the abortion clinics, but was instead provided independently of them. The ECJ defined the students' activities as a 'manifestation' of the freedom of expression and the freedom to impart and receive information, rather than as an economic service. Consequently, the ECJ ruled that EU provisions on the freedom to provide services could not prevent the Irish Constitution from prohibiting the student unions from providing information about abortion.

The student unions then argued that the Irish Constitution was prohibiting the freedom of expression and the freedom to receive and impart information. However, the ECJ ruled that it had no jurisdiction over national legislation, which fell outside the scope of EU law. Since the ECJ had ruled that the Irish prohibition did not constitute a violation of the freedom to provide services, the student unions lost the case. Critics have argued that with this controversial judgment, the ECJ purposely avoided ruling on which rights should take precedence: the economic right to provide services, as protected by the Treaty, or the right to life for the unborn, as protected by the Irish Constitution.

E Legislative history of human rights

I Role of the European Parliament (EP)

The EP was the first Community institution to press actively for the inclusion of fundamental rights in the EU mandate. As early as 1977, the Parliament made a Joint Declaration on the need for fundamental rights to be recognized at the EU level. In 1989, the EP called for the adoption of a charter of fundamental rights, and subsequently has been an advocate of incorporating strong human rights language into the Treaty, producing an annual human rights report and establishing honoraria for human rights activists.

2   The treaties of Maastricht (1992), Amsterdam (1997) and Nice (2001)

The Maastricht and Amsterdam treaties established the first legislation in the areas of social and economic rights. The Maastricht Treaty set out provisions regarding discrimination in the workplace, whilst the Amsterdam Treaties supplemented those provisions and added explicit enforcement mechanisms, thereby supplying the ECJ with legislation upon which fundamental rights judgments could be made. These provisions were recently strengthened in the Nice Treaty; now action can be taken against member states that persistently violate fundamental rights (Article 7). Amsterdam also introduced stronger rhetoric on the principle of fundamental rights, linking the EU with non-EU authorities – namely, the European Convention on Human Rights (ECHR) and the constitutional traditions of the member states (Article 6). By moving visas, asylum and immigration from Pillar III to Pillar I, the Amsterdam Treaty also extended the ECJ's competence to scrutinize the EU's activities for fundamental rights protection in these areas.

3   A Charter of Fundamental Rights

After years of social and political pressure, a Charter of Fundamental Rights for EU citizens was drawn up in 1999 by a convention composed of members of national governments, the EP and civil society. This Charter is very similar in content to the ECHR, with the addition of several social rights. Proponents argue that the Charter is necessary to resolve the existing inconsistencies and gaps in human rights coverage within the EU legal system. This is why both the 'Comité des Sages' Report in 1996 and the Commission Report on Fundamental Rights in 1999 declared themselves in favour of such a bill of rights. However, at the Nice Summit (2000), member states decided that the Charter should be only a political declaration rather than a legally binding document. Since it is non-binding, the ECJ may not be in a position of sufficient strength *vis-à-vis* the member states to use the Charter as the foundation for the development of EU fundamental rights case law. However, the Convention on the Future of Europe could recommend that the Charter become legally binding and be incorporated in the EU Treaty (for more on this Convention, see *Constitutionalism*).

The problems/issues

A   The inconsistencies in fundamental rights protection

Until the Maastricht Treaty, the EU did not have a legislative basis for protecting fundamental rights. Thus, the fundamental rights protection that did exist was the result of rulings made by the ECJ in cases such as *Wachauf* and *Internationale*

Handelsgesellschaft. Yet many academics and human rights activists argue that the principles that the ECJ established were inadequately protected by the ECJ. In particular, critics of the Community's human rights record point to the different conclusions reached in *Bostock* and *Wachauf*, contending that the ECJ was motivated by the need to grant member states some national autonomy (in order to prevent outright challenges to its authority), rather than by the desire to protect fundamental rights. Consequently, whenever the ECJ is confronted with controversial cases that threaten sovereignty, it prefers not to intervene. The ECJ's handling of *Grogan* appears to reinforce the perception that the ECJ is not 'serious' about fundamental rights protection, especially as the *Grogan* case dealt with the politically sensitive issue of abortion.

B The EU's over-reliance on judicial remedies

Academics such as Weiler argue that these inconsistencies are mainly due to the EU's over-reliance on judicial remedies to solve fundamental rights problems. The ECJ has failed to provide a clear policy on fundamental rights, because the Court's ability to construct case law in this area can be exercised only when cases are brought before it. More importantly, Weiler argues that a group of judicial rulings cannot replace legislative action. Therefore, the problems with the EU's fundamental rights policy are ultimately due to the EU's failure to legislate, rather than the ECJ's inability to make consistent judgments.

C The legitimacy of ECJ rulings on fundamental rights

Inconsistencies in ECJ rulings can also be attributed to the fact that the ECJ has avoided ruling on human rights disputes in controversial cases because it is afraid of infringing on member states' sovereignty. Since the ECJ lacks a clear mandate to make rulings in these areas, it also lacks the legitimacy to impose its rulings. As the laws of a nation-state effectively represent an internal agreement between the citizens of a nation and its government, its laws are a reflection of that society's particular value system. Academics question whether an outside body has the right to overrule such agreements, thereby imposing its own value system on that of another state. Proponents of this argument refer to *Grogan*, claiming that the ECJ was right to avoid ruling on the legality of abortion, because of its significance to the Irish population.

D Legislative solutions

As the EU's legislative responsibilities increased, it became clear that the EU would be forced to address the issue of fundamental rights protection in a more substantial way. The treaties of Maastricht and Amsterdam attempted to provide a legal basis for fundamental rights protection. However, from a legislative point of view, the legal status of fundamental rights in both treaties is weak and inconsistent. First, current fundamental rights legislation requires secondary legislation to be implemented by the member states; otherwise individuals are unable to claim recourse when their EU-based fundamental rights are violated. Secondly, fundamental rights are not incorporated into all policy areas. The ECJ's power of judicial review in the second (CFSP) and third (JHA) Pillars is still limited to such an extent that the ECJ is not allowed to adjudicate on many issues pertaining to fundamental rights. For example, the right to privacy may be jeopardized by the increased exchange of criminal information by EUROPOL (the European police organization). The Treaty leaves the exchange of this type of information vulnerable to governmental abuse, in ways not protected by either national or EU legislation.

E   The European Convention on Human Rights (ECHR)

While all the member states have signed the ECHR as individual nations, some scholars argued that by signing the ECHR itself, the EU would give the Community a structure in which to develop fundamental rights at the EU level. This possibility has become less probable since the ECJ stated in *Opinion 2/94* that the EU did not have the competence to join an international convention on human rights without an amendment to the Treaty. If the member states are willing to make the necessary changes to the Treaty, the benefits would include bringing the EU into line with a strong tradition of fundamental rights in Europe, as well as adding a second legal system to coexist with and support the ECJ (in the same way that the ECHR currently coexists with and supports constitutional courts).

F   The Charter of Fundamental Rights

Another proposed solution is for the EU to adopt a bill of rights. The EU adopted a Charter of Fundamental Rights at Nice in 2000. This Charter, which grants rights to individuals when the Community and nation-states act under EU law, is not legally binding, and is very similar to the ECHR. Importantly, the Charter places social, political and civil rights on an equal footing with economic rights for the first time. This is arguably a major step in the development of the EU as a political entity, since the rights contained in the Charter are similar to those protected by the ECHR (with the partial exception of some social rights). At the same time, scholars such as Weiler believe that this provides a level of protection far below that which is required by modern society.

   The importance of this document is overshadowed by the fact that it is not legally binding. Therefore, much of the recent debate over fundamental rights has centred on whether the Charter should become law. However, conflicts may arise if the EU attempts to harmonize the fundamental rights traditions of all member states, for the following reasons:

- Attempting to find common ground on social values among nations is very problematic, and there are certain issues (such as abortion) on which no European-wide consensus exists. A legally binding charter may therefore face further difficulties if it does not command enough legitimacy.
- A symbolic link exists between bills of rights and nation-states. The existence of a Charter of Fundamental Rights moves the EU closer to a traditional state-like structure, arousing concerns about national sovereignty.
- It will be very difficult to monitor a legally binding charter of this nature, and will require increased financial and institutional resources to ensure that it is fully enforced.

G The Convention on the Future of Europe

The legal status of the Charter of Fundamental Rights is one of the key issues addressed by the Convention on the Future of Europe, which began in February 2002. The Convention delegates appear to favour the incorporation of the Charter into the EU Treaty, and many member states also seem to be ready to accept the establishment of concrete EU-level fundamental rights. If the Charter becomes law at the Intergovernmental Conference planned for 2004, the EU will have taken a significant step in creating a substantial bond between the EU as a political institution and the citizens of Europe. If the Charter can be considered an EU 'bill of rights', then the Community will also have gained one of the elements necessary for the creation of a constitution similar to those of the member states. For these reasons, many integrationists have supported the creation of a legally binding charter. However, some of those critical of EU constitutionalism also support the incorporation of the Charter into the Treaty, since they believe that defining fundamental rights at the EU level is the only way to correct the gaps in protection currently found in the EU legal system.

Who wins/who loses

The **EU institutions** can be considered winners from the expansion of fundamental rights legislation, as the inclusion of a 'bill of rights' may well be a step towards a formal constitution, similar to those possessed by the member states. This results in more power, accountability and legitimacy for the EU, and especially the ECJ. Through the inclusion of fundamental rights at the EU level, the ECJ can now hold member states accountable for their actions under EU law. However, fundamental rights have also been used by national constitutional courts to challenge the authority of the ECJ (see the *Brunner* case in *Constitutionalism*). It seems unlikely that the

Charter, in its current form, will be able to command enough legitimacy to free the ECJ from the scrutiny of national constitutional courts.

EU citizens have gained protection at the EU level, and therefore should be considered winners. However, fundamental rights protection at the EU level is currently much less comprehensive than national protection or even the protection offered by the ECHR. Even with the inclusion of the Charter in the EU Treaty, it remains unclear as to whether EU citizens will be better protected at the EU level than they currently are at the national level.

Food for thought

What rights should be considered 'fundamental rights'? Many legal scholars argue that labour rights should be elevated to the status of fundamental rights. Should economic rights be considered as important as social or political rights? To what extent should the EU have a common set of fundamental rights, and which rights should be left to the discretion of the member states?

How should conflicting rights be balanced? Grogan demonstrated how the ECJ faces difficulties in deciding which rights should take precedence in cases dealing with EU law versus national law. Can the ECJ be expected to decide between the conflicting fundamental rights in different member states? And which fundamental rights from which nation-states should take precedence over others? Will the ECJ ever have the competence to decide controversial issues such as abortion and euthanasia in a way that affects all member states equally?

Student-to-student tip

Be aware that academics such as Weiler present a deeply philosophical and often complicated view of fundamental rights. However, the issue of fundamental rights is not isolated: legal developments in this area have an impact on the protection of third-country nationals within Schengenland, the power of directly elected representation in the EU decision-making process, and the need for an EU constitution, for example. Information on this issue can be gathered from a variety of political as well as legal sources. National reports tend to be quite biased, so we recommend looking at those published by the EU institutions, which (surprisingly) seem to present a more balanced view.

Summary

- The term 'fundamental rights' refers to the human, social, economic and political rights of citizens. While these rights are protected by each individual member state, the EU provides very uneven protection of these rights under the Treaty. Due to the supremacy of EU law and the growing areas of EU policy competence, establishing EU-level fundamental rights protection has become increasingly important.

- The ECJ has developed EU fundamental rights policy through its case law, such as its decision to review member states' implementation of EU legislation for fundamental rights violations in *Wachauf* and *ERT*. However, other cases, such as *Bostock* and *Grogan*, demonstrate that ECJ rulings have not been consistent in their protection of the fundamental rights of EU citizens. This may be due to several factors, including the lack of a strong legislative base upon which to make rulings and the difficulty in balancing member states' sovereignty with the desire of the member states for ECJ protection of fundamental rights, as demonstrated in the *Solange* ruling.
- The EU has recently developed more legislation to address the issue of fundamental rights at the EU level. Both the Maastricht and Amsterdam treaties expanded social and political rights within the EU. In addition, a Charter of Fundamental Rights was signed at the Nice Summit in 2000. However, in both treaties, fundamental rights remain loosely defined, and the Charter is currently non-binding. This may not provide enough of a basis for the ECJ to legitimately make rulings on fundamental rights protection.
- Two solutions to the current fundamental rights problem in the EU have been suggested:
  - The EU could join the ECHR as a single entity, thereby providing the ECJ with a structure upon which to develop EU fundamental rights protection.
  - The Charter of Fundamental Rights could be developed into a 'bill of rights' for the EU citizen, thereby creating a contract between the citizen and the Community.
- However, both these suggestions face problems, such as issues of final competence, sovereignty, and the harmonization of the fundamental rights of all member states.

Selected bibliography

Background on fundamental rights

Alston, P. (ed.) (1999) *The European Union and Human Rights*, Oxford: Oxford University Press.
  The chapters by Alston and Weiler offer good insight into the development of the fundamental rights debate in the EU. Maduro's chapter does a good job exploring the importance of economic and social rights.

Weiler, J. H. H. (1995) 'Fundamental Rights and Fundamental Boundaries: On Standards and Values in the Protection of Human Rights', in N. Neuwahl and A. Rosas (eds), *The European Union and Human Rights*, The Hague: Martijnus Nijhoff, 56–66.
  This article demonstrates the importance of fundamental rights to democracy and to supranational governance.

Articles on fundamental rights issues

Miller, V. (2000) 'Human Rights in the EU: The Charter of Fundamental Rights', Research Paper 00/32, House of Commons Library, 20 March 2000.

The Research Papers from the House of Commons are very concise, and offer a fair perspective of limited supranational governance. This is a good place to get the views of those opposed to the expansion of EU competences in the field of human rights.

Weiler, J. H. H. and S. C. Fries (1999) 'A Human Rights Policy for the European Community and Union: The Question of Competences', Harvard Jean Monnet Working Paper 4/99.

In this paper, Weiler and Fries present the reasons why the EU should consider signing the ECHR.

De Búrca, G. (1993) 'Fundamental Rights and the Reach of EC Law', *Oxford Journal of Legal Studies*, vol. 13: 283–319.

This article by de Búrca is very enlightening, and provides a contrasting perspective to that of Weiler.

Von Bogdandy, A. (2000) 'The European Union as a Human Rights Organization', *Common Market Law Review*, vol. 37, no. 6: 1307–38.

Von Bogdandy discusses the role of human rights in relation to the development of European integration.

9

Judicial Processes

Jess Clayton

National governments have transferred many legislative responsibilities to the EU. As a result, most laws in some fields, such as Competition Policy, are no longer made at the member state level. However, citizens are only responsible for following national laws, and they can protect their rights only through national courts. This causes a problem, since the rights of EU citizens rely on laws made at the EU as well as the national level. Therefore, the judicial processes of the EU, which allow EU citizens to invoke their rights under EU law, have growing importance. Through direct effect, indirect effect and state liability, EU citizens should be able to maintain the same legal protection of their rights through EU law as through national law. However, there are gaps in protection provided by judicial processes, and it is unclear whether these processes provide an effective safeguard of citizens' rights.

The facts

There are three main types of judicial processes: direct effect, indirect effect and state liability.

A Direct effect

Initially outlined in Case 26/62, *Van Gend en Loos* (1963), direct effect gives EU citizens the right to invoke EU law before national courts. Direct effect therefore ensures that EU citizens can rely on EU law as well as national law in order to protect their rights. There are two types of direct effect:

- *Vertical direct effect* – a provision that can be invoked by an individual against the state for failure to enact, or properly enact, EU law.
- *Horizontal direct effect* – a provision that can be invoked by an individual against another individual for failing to comply with EU law.

Direct effect applies to Treaty provisions as well as regulations, decisions and directives issued by the Commission to the member states. In theory, Treaty provisions become part of the national law in member states. In addition, regulations automatically become part of national law. However, the member states must first transpose directives before they become national law. This is because directives give member states more discretion in their interpretation of EU legislation.

The fact that EU citizens must wait for the member states to transpose EU directives into national law before they can invoke that legislation causes a problem: it means that while Treaty provisions and regulations have both vertical and horizontal direct effect, directives do not have horizontal direct effect until they are transposed into national law. This is because citizens are only responsible for following their national laws, and cannot be held responsible for breaking EU laws that have not been transposed. Because so much EU legislation is issued in the form of directives, the fact that directives have no horizontal direct effect (or, in other words, cannot be invoked by one individual against another) means that EU citizens lose the right to litigate against each other regarding untransposed EU directives. Because much of the legislative responsibility for economic issues has been transferred from the member state governments to the EU, areas where citizens were previously ensured rights may now fall into doubt.

I   Direct effect and Treaty provisions

Direct effect was developed initially through Case 26/62, *Van Gend en Loos* (1963) (see *Constitutionalism*). In *Van Gend en Loos*, a Dutch importer of German chemicals sued the Dutch authority for levying customs at its borders. Since the Treaties of Rome (1957) ensure the free movement of goods across borders, it grants importers/exporters the right *not* to pay customs duties. However, member states had failed to enforce this Treaty provision prior to the *Van Gend en Loos* case. The European Court of Justice (ECJ) ruled that direct effect was necessary in order to safeguard the effectiveness of EU law, as well as the rights of EU citizens (see also *Constitutionalism*).

Case 43/75, *Defrenne* vs *SABENA* (1976), is based on Article 141 (ex-Article 119) of the Treaty, guaranteeing equal pay for equal work (thereby eliminating sex discrimination in the workplace). Since this is a Treaty article, it automatically becomes part of national law; therefore, it has direct effect and must be upheld by the national courts. *Defrenne* is the first case in which the ECJ enforced the horizontal direct effect of Treaty provisions (see also *Law and European Integration*).

2   Direct effect and directives

- Case 41/74, *Van Duyn* (1974). Based on the UK's failure to respect Directive 64/221/EEC on the free movement of workers, this case established that directives also have direct effect under Article 249 (ex-Article 189).
- Case 91/92, *Dori* vs *Recreb* (1994). *Dori* established that directives have vertical direct effect, but not horizontal direct effect. Therefore, *Dori* could not sue a private company which had failed to respect a directive that had not been transposed into national law.
- Case 152/84, *Marshall, no. 1* (1986) and Case 188/89, *Foster* (1990). These two cases defined what is considered the 'state' in cases of direct effect. This is important, as, according to direct effect, a citizen can litigate against the 'state' (but not a private body) if it breaches a directive and the directive has not been transposed into national law by the end of its time limit.

B   Indirect effect

Indirect effect helps to solve the problem caused by the lack of horizontal direct effect for directives. Indirect effect requires national courts to interpret and apply national legislation in conformity with EU law. This means that both the EU law and national law affecting national cases must be considered before the judge decides on a verdict. While this creates a very strong interpretative obligation for national judges, it also creates a problem with legal certainty, because national judges cannot always be certain when they should apply EU law to national cases. This uncertainty arises in two situations:

- when there is no national law through which EU law can be interpreted;
- when national and EU law clearly contradict each other (see Case 334/92, *Wagner-Miret* (1993)).

As a result of this uncertainty, indirect effect also leaves a gap in the protection of EU citizens' rights.

I   Case law for indirect effect

Indirect effect was developed through three important cases:

- Case 14/83, *Van Colson* (1986). A sex discrimination case in Germany, *Van Colson* is the first indirect effect case. The ECJ ruled that the national courts have a 'duty of co-operation' with EU law under Article 10 (ex-Article 5).

- Case 106/89, *Marleasing* (1990). In this Spanish bankruptcy case, the ECJ ruled that even though the Spanish solvency law had been written after the EU solvency law, national courts needed to reference their decisions on all national legislation in consideration of EU law, *regardless* of when the national law was created. *Marleasing* means that more recent national legislation cannot legally undermine EU law, and that EU law should be used not only in cases where national law is unclear (as assumed in *Van Colson*), but in all circumstances, except when there is no national legislation to interpret.
- Case 334/92, *Wagner-Miret* (1993). Whereas *Marleasing* indicated that the interpretative obligation of national courts was extremely strong, *Wagner-Miret* limited this decision to some extent, by establishing that the interpretative obligation indicated by indirect effect should not be so strong as to require national courts to issue rulings that clearly contradict national legislation.

C State liability

State liability allows individuals to sue member states for compensation if they fail to (properly) implement EU law at the national level. State liability should therefore protect EU citizens from the gaps in protection created by direct effect and indirect effect. However, state liability has its own problems: for example, if national governments are too vulnerable to liability, they may be less willing to create potentially liable legislation and may therefore be less effective legislators. Through several liability cases, the ECJ has tried to strike a balance between the rights of the state and the rights of the citizen. First, the state can only be liable for actions under certain conditions. These conditions were established by the ECJ in the *Francovich* case:

- the directive must confer rights on individual citizens.
- those rights must be identifiable.
- there must be a causal link between the violation by the state and the loss to the individual.

However, in the *Factortame* cases, the ECJ decided that a member state cannot be liable unless it is proved that the member state has severely disregarded EU law, and that the breach of EU law is sufficiently serious. This is determined by taking the following factors into account:

- the clarity and precision of the directive;
- the level of discretion left to the member state in applying the directive;
- whether damages caused were intentional;

   – whether the error by the member state was understandable, due to other factors.

I   Case law for State liability

- Joint Cases 6/90 and 9/90, *Francovich and Bonifaci* vs *Italy* (1991). In this case, Italy had failed to implement Directive 80/987/EEC that protects employees in cases of insolvency, despite repeated warnings from the Commission. A worker named Francovich therefore sued the Italian government for his lost pension when his company became insolvent. In response, the ECJ established the three conditions for state liability (outlined above).
- Case 48/93, *R* vs *Secretary of State, ex parte Factortame Ltd, no. 3* (of four suits) (1996). This case was brought by Spanish fishermen against the UK. The British government had required boats fishing in UK waters to have UK ownership. However, a UK Act of Parliament had prevented Spanish fishermen from registering their boats as British. The ECJ awarded compensation to the Spanish fishermen because the national ownership system in the UK was contrary to the economic freedoms established in the Treaties of Rome. This case, along with *Brasserie du Pêcheur*, established that national governments must allow individuals to receive compensation if EU laws are not (properly) implemented, should the violation of EU law be sufficiently serious, using the criteria outlined above.
- Case 46/93, *Brasserie du Pêcheur SA* vs *Germany* (1996). The *Cassis de Dijon* case (see *Law and European Integration*) and Article 28 (ex-Article 30) established the mutual recognition of EU products. However, the German government continued to block the sale of beer from Brasserie, a French beer exporter, based on the German Beer Purity Law. Brasserie therefore sued for compensation, due to loss of sales. On referral, the ECJ followed the criteria for state liability first established in *Francovich* and *Factortame*, and ruled that:
   – the German state failed to properly implement EU law;
   – the breach was sufficiently serious, especially after *Cassis de Dijon*;
   – *however*, the ECJ failed to agree that there was a causal link between the failure of the state and the damages claimed.

Thus, the suit failed.
- Case 392/93, *British Telecom* (1996). This is a complicated case in which BT took the British government to court for having implemented an EU directive incorrectly. The British government argued that this breach was unintentional, because it had misunderstood the directive. In this instance, the ECJ ruled that the mistake made by the British government was excusable because the directive was unclear, and therefore the violation was not sufficiently serious. Hence, no liability was found.

The problems/issues

A   Lack of horizontal direct effect on directives

The inability of individuals to rely on EU directives to protect their rights against other individuals raises concerns about the safeguarding of citizens' rights under EU law. However, simply giving directives horizontal direct effect creates as many problems as it solves. Directives allow member states some discretion in the way they are incorporated into national legislation. This ensures that EU laws are compatible with the individual requirements of national laws and the legal cultures in each member state. Therefore, if directives are given horizontal direct effect, member states lose the discretion they currently enjoy when transposing directives, with possible detrimental effects. On the other hand, without horizontal direct effect, the individual must then rely on the incomplete protection of indirect effect and state liability.

B   Direct effect and member states

Direct effect constitutes a double attack on member states, as failure to properly implement EU legislation could result in the Commission bringing a case before the ECJ against that state and also lead to litigation by individual citizens at the national level. Yet, without the threat of these sanctions, some legal scholars (such as Steiner) claim that the member states have very weak incentives to transpose EU directives and decisions.

C   Legitimacy of EU law

Legal scholars often argue that the legitimacy of EU law is linked to its effectiveness; if the judicial processes established by the ECJ are unable to protect the rights of EU citizens adequately, then the legitimacy of the entire system is undermined. At the same time, the ECJ is dependent on the goodwill of the national courts to enforce its rulings, and therefore cannot be seen to undermine the position of the member states (see *Law and European Integration*). This makes it difficult for the ECJ to balance the needs of EU citizens against the needs of the member states.

D   Discretion of national judges

As a result of indirect effect, national courts must balance their judgments between national legislation and EU law. This raises the question of how the national courts should rule when there is a direct conflict between national and EU law. While EU law is supreme (see *Constitutionalism*, Case 6/64, *Costa* vs *ENEL* (1964)), it is still dependent on the national courts for its enforcement. Most scholars believe that the constitutional position of national courts must be respected, even in the face of EU law; this causes tension between upper courts and lower courts (see *Law and European Integration*). In addition, since *Wagner-Miret*, the system could be understood to favour national law over EU law. The combination of these two factors could undermine the ability of indirect effect to protect individual rights created by EU law. The judicial flexibility created by indirect effect also leads to a situation of legal uncertainty, which can result in an unequal application of EU law across the Community, thereby undermining the legitimacy of EU law.

E   Financial burden of state liability

A major problem with state liability is the possible financial burden placed on national governments. Harlow argues that state liability allows the courts to have an unjustified influence over national budgets, which are usually the strict domain of the legislative and executive branches of government.

Who wins/who loses

In the debate over judicial processes, academics are trying to determine to what extent the individual should be protected at the expense of the national governments of member states. Therefore, the **EU citizen** can be considered both a winner and a loser from this process. If EU law is understood to give additional rights to the individual, then EU citizens are winners, as they now have more protection and they can invoke this protection through their national courts. However, under national law, the individual has the right to litigate against another individual if they break a civil law. EU citizens do not have this right under EU law if an individual fails to comply with an EU directive which has not been transposed into national law. If the responsibility for certain rights, such as economic rights, is transferred from the national to the EU level, then EU citizens are losers, as they lose the right to litigate against each other in some circumstances.

   Member states are often viewed as losers in the debate over judicial processes, especially in the area of state liability. Some academics, such as Harlow, argue that state liability hinders the ability of national governments to legislate, because they can become paralysed by the fear of litigation. She accuses the ECJ of judicial activism in *Francovich*, and maintains that state liability infringes on national sovereignty. However, there is little evidence to support her claims. Other academics, such as Steiner, contend that only through state liability will reluctant national governments be persuaded to transpose EU directives quickly and correctly.

Academics who favour state liability claim that liability allows EU citizens to safeguard the implementation of EU regulation (i.e. citizen enforcement of EU law through litigation) – a job that the Commission, with its small staff and limited resources, cannot perform adequately. In response, Harlow questions whether the citizen should be responsible for the enforcement of EU regulation. In addition, she claims that the majority of cases in which directives are not properly implemented by member states are inadvertent, and that state 'disobedience' is the result of the large volume of EU legislation and problems with interpreting this legislation.

The implications of the development of judicial processes, in particular state liability, can be seen to have more to do with ensuring the effectiveness of EU law than with granting rights to EU citizens. In such a process, **the ECJ** is a clear winner. Through direct effect, indirect effect and state liability, the ECJ has increased its interaction with both the member states and EU citizens. In addition, judicial processes can be seen to strengthen other key elements of EU law, such as supremacy. This, in turn, strengthens the position of the ECJ in the EU.

Food for thought

When should member states be liable for failure to (properly) implement a directive? The BT case suggests that state disobedience is often inadvertent. If this is the case, has the ECJ made the member states too vulnerable to unwarranted litigation through such cases as *Francovich* and Case 312/93, *Peterbroeck* vs *Belgium* (1995) (on time limits for appeals)? Or has the ECJ developed criteria which are just flexible enough to allow case-by-case judgments and to provide the member states with a motivation for properly implementing EU legislation?

Student-to-student tip

One of the problems with studying judicial processes is that some case law is 'bad' case law. In other words, an ECJ ruling may be considered at one time to be a critical turning point for EU law, only to be overruled or considered to be a weak decision at a later date (as with the ruling on *Emmot*). It is important, therefore, to use recent academic articles for your research, and to question any case that appears to be a radical departure from previous rulings.

Summary

The three judicial processes are meant to work together to ensure citizens' rights under EU law. The logic is as follows:

- *Direct effect* ensures that EU laws grant rights to EU citizens by making EU legislation directly applicable to them. However, directives, which make up the majority of EU legislation, do not have horizontal direct effect until transposed into national law.

- This problem is partly resolved by *indirect effect*, which forces all national legislation to be interpreted through EU law, even if the EU law has not been transposed into national law. However, this can only be effective if there is a national law through which EU law can be interpreted, and/or if the national law doesn't directly contradict EU law.
- Even if indirect effect fails, EU citizens have the right to sue the state for failure to (properly) transpose EU law into national law (*state liability*), as long as the criteria for liability are fulfilled.

The main problems surrounding the application of judicial processes are striking the balance between the protection of EU citizens' rights and the protection of the state from excessive liability. Judicial processes also form the practical basis of EU law, and therefore affect issues such as legal certainty and the legitimacy of the EU legal system.

Selected bibliography

General references

Chalmers, D. (1998) *European Union Law*, volume 1: *Law and EU Government*, Aldershot: Ashgate; direct effect: 364–92, indirect effect: 392–8, state liability: 398–433.
  This is a great overview of the subject, and cites much of the relevant literature in this field.
De Búrca, G. and P. Craig (1998) *EU Law: Text, Cases and Materials*, New York: Oxford University Press, chapter 4: 163–213.
  A very thorough, detailed account of judicial processes in which the authors offer both extracts from the actual judgments and commentary from academics.
Hartley, T. C. (1998) *The Foundations of European Community Law*, 4th edn, Oxford: Oxford University Press, chapter 7: 187–215.
  Although more of a text for lawyers, this volume provides a nice contrast to Chalmers and de Búrca and Craig in the way in which cases are explained. The author is particularly good in the fields of indirect effect and state liability.
Regueiro, P. (2002) 'Invocability of Substitution: Invocability of Exclusion', Jean Monnet Working Paper 7/02.
  This paper explains the rationale behind the current status of EU law.

Specifically on state liability

Craig, P. (1997) 'Once More into the Breach: The Community, the State and Damages Liability', *Law Quarterly Review*, vol. 113: 67–94.
  This article gives an accurate description of the logic behind the *Brasserie* decision. The author also discusses the balance of liability between the EU and the member states.
Harlow, C. (1996) 'Francovich and the Problem of the Disobedient State', *European Law Journal*, vol. 2, no. 3: 199–225.
  Harlow is an important critic of state liability, and offers a balanced perspective on the subject. However, she is very biased in favour of the member states and against the extension of the ECJ into areas of national sovereignty.
Steiner, J. (1993) 'From Direct Effect to Francovich: Shifting Measures of Enforcement', *European Law Review*, vol. 18: 3–22.
  Steiner provides a counterbalance to Harlow – very pro-European integration and supportive of the expansion of ECJ prerogatives.

10

Law and European Integration

Mark Schieritz and Jess Clayton

The case law of the European Court of Justice (ECJ) has profoundly influenced the way in which the EU works. The rulings of the ECJ have not only guided the development of EU policy, but have also shaped the political structure of the overall Community. In addition, many of the changes stimulated by the ECJ were not necessarily expected or intended by the original drafters of the Treaty. Several policy areas, in particular the Single Market Programme (SMP), have expanded as a direct result of ECJ rulings. As a result, it has become important to explain how and why the Court could assume such a prominent, and arguably political, role in the European integration process.

The facts

A   How the ECJ affects EU integration

The Court has used its mandate as interpreter of the Treaty to shape the basic principles of the Treaty, and therefore the political structure of the EU. In so doing, the Court has substantially furthered European integration. This became particularly evident in the 1960s and 1970s: while the EC legislative process was stalled, due to *de facto* unanimity in the Council of Ministers (resulting from the Luxembourg Compromise of 1966), the judicial rulings of the Court allowed European integration to continue. However, the activities, and therefore the activism, of the Court are limited by several factors.

- The ECJ can affect integration only through its case law. In other words, it must wait for either the EU institutions or the national courts to present cases for review, before its rulings can have an effect on the integration process.

- As the ECJ has no police force, it must depend on the member states to enforce its rulings.
- The Court has not been given the right of judicial review in all areas of the Treaty.

B Cases that have changed the EU

Judgments made by the Court have affected almost all areas of EU policy. They have been used by different actors to change the shape of the EU and to broaden the scope of EU competences. Below are three examples of cases that have advanced and strengthened EU policies.

1   Facilitating the common market

The most prominent example of ECJ case law furthering European integration is the *Cassis de Dijon* case (Case 120/78, *Rewe Zentral AG* vs *Bundesmonopolverwaltung für Branntwein (a.k.a. Germany)* (1979)). In *Cassis*, the ECJ ruled that a German liquor regulation that forbade the importation of certain liquors constituted an illegal trade barrier to the free movement of goods within the Community. In addition, the Court recognized that what was legally for sale in one member state should be legally for sale in all. This became known as the principle of mutual recognition.

Although based on the precedent set by the *Dassonville* case (Case 8/74, *Procureur du Roi* vs *Dassonville* (1974)), the *Cassis* case became important because it inspired a new Commission initiative: namely, the SMP. Since the 1960s, European market integration had decelerated as a result of the slow progress of product harmonization. The principle of mutual recognition enabled the Commission to bypass the need to harmonize all product standards, and was therefore one of the key concepts behind the SMP, which also led to the Single European Act (1987) (see *The Single Market*).

2   Sex discrimination

The ECJ influenced both the development of Social Policy and the legal structure of the EU through Case 43/75, *Defrenne* vs *Sabena* (1976). In *Defrenne*, the ECJ ruled that Ms Defrenne could not be forced to retire early from her position as a flight attendant just because she was a woman. The significance of this case is twofold.

- *Defrenne* allowed Treaty Article 141 (ex-Article 119), establishing equal work for equal pay, to be invoked by private parties against other private parties, thereby developing the principle of direct effect (see *Judicial Processes*).
- *Defrenne* clarified that EU law on sex discrimination could be used by EU citizens, even if there was no national law in this area. This resulted in a strong EU policy against sex discrimination, which was more advanced than the policy of any member state at the time.

Both developments helped to tie the member states into the Community's legal system. Following the *Defrenne* case, many other cases extending the parameters of Article 141 were brought before the ECJ. These cases, including several dealing with pregnancy and employment, provided legal support for Commission directives in the area of EU Social Policy, notably the somewhat controversial Parental Leave Directive of 1996.

3   Environmental Policy

More recently, ECJ case law has been expanding environmental legislation beyond that originally envisaged by EU legislators. In Case 302/86, *Commission* vs *Denmark* (1989) (known as the *Danish Bottle* case), the Court decided that Danish rules regarding glass beverage bottles, which acted as a restriction to the free movement of goods within the Community, were permissible – as long as these rules were genuine attempts to protect the environment. In another instance, Joint Cases 206 and 207/88, *Vessosso and Zanetti* (1990), the ECJ enlarged the definition of what types of waste are subject to EU regulations, making it much wider than had been foreseen by EU legislators. These cases demonstrate that the Court is sometimes prepared to protect the environment even at the expense of economic integration. More importantly, the resulting expansion of environmental legislation can also be understood as a form of political integration: through cases such as these, the ECJ expanded EU competences in ways that had not been foreseen by the member states (see *Environmental and Social Policies*).

C   The role of national courts in the EU legal system

The ECJ is not only dependent on member states to enforce its rulings; it is also dependent on the national courts of member states to provide it with cases to rule on. While the Commission and other member states can bring cases before the ECJ, the majority of decisions are 'recommendations' on the interpretation of EU law requested by national courts. This 'preliminary reference procedure' is outlined in Treaty Article 234 (ex-Article 177), and allows national courts to request an opinion or recommendation from the ECJ on matters of EU law. It has been estimated that the national courts accept 90 per cent of ECJ rulings through Article 234.

D   The actors in legal integration

Many actors besides the ECJ and national courts have been important in promoting EU integration through the use of EU law.

I   Private actors

Private actors such as firms often find it advantageous to have regulations set at the European level rather than at national levels, as it is easier for them to sell their products throughout the Union if they only have to comply with one regulation rather than fifteen different national regulations. Consequently, it is argued that firms have often taken member states to court in order to satisfy their commercial interests. Case 46/93, *Brasserie du Pêcheur* (1996), is an excellent example of this. The case was brought by a private firm, which wasn't allowed to export its beer into Germany because of sixteenth-century German Beer Purity law. Non-tariff barriers to trade such as this regulation were one of the reasons why economic integration had progressed so slowly in the EU before the principle of mutual recognition was introduced.

2   EU citizens

EU citizens have also been vital in promoting integration through EC case law. Many important legal concepts, such as direct effect and state liability, have been developed as a result of individuals insisting on their EU-level rights in national courts. A good example of this is Case 6/64, *Costa* vs *ENEL* (1964), a case brought by an EU citizen. *Costa* allowed the ECJ to establish the doctrine of the supremacy of EU law, upon which the entire structure of EU law is based (see *Constitutionalism* for more details).

3   The Commission

The Commission has also utilized the EU legal system to promote its agenda. For instance, the Commission recognized the potential of the *Cassis de Dijon* ruling, and made it the basis of its new programme to complete the Single Market. However, as Stein and others point out, the interaction between the Commission and the ECJ is two-way: in major constitutional cases, the Court has almost always agreed with the Commission's position on the issue being decided. Neo-functionalists argue that the ECJ uses the Commission as a political 'bellwether' to determine the degree of integration that is acceptable to member states at the time of a ruling. The relationship between the two institutions is not surprising, since both EU institutions are mandated by the Treaty to promote European integration.

The problems/issues

A Why member states created the ECJ

Some legal scholars maintain that the ECJ has developed into a political actor with a pro-integration agenda. In its legal capacity, the ECJ has the ability to rule on case law, which then becomes the basis of the Community legal framework. This allows the ECJ to influence the development of the EU in ways not predicted or even supported by the member states. Why, then, did the member states create the ECJ? Academics offer several explanations.

- The establishment of the rule of law helps to solve the 'incomplete contract' problem. Given the complexity of political interaction and the unpredictability of future situations, it is impossible for a treaty to provide instructions for all possible future circumstances. So, rather than attempt to write a complete contract, member states agreed on a framework for interaction between members, reinforced by the establishment of a legal system. For example, EU Environmental Policy, which developed as a result of the growth of the Single Market, was not part of the Treaties of Rome. However, Article 95 (ex-Article 100a) provides for the establishment of other EU policy areas as necessary to address problems created by the Single Market. The incomplete contract allows the Community to adapt and develop without the need for constant Treaty revisions. It is therefore necessary to have a body such as the ECJ to monitor the contract, in order to ensure that new legislation falls within the parameters of the Treaty.
- The Court was also established in order to resolve 'collective action' problems. Since member states often have strong economic and/or political incentives to ignore international obligations, the establishment of an independent court, to monitor compliance and identify transgressors, encourages individual member states to fulfil their Treaty obligations. In 2002, the Commission took action against member states for failure to fulfil Treaty obligations in over 100 cases brought before the ECJ. Without this external discipline, inconsistent compliance with EU law and legislation would greatly decrease the effectiveness – and therefore the benefits – of the Single Market (see the principal-agent framework in *Theories of European Integration*).
- A central task of the Court is to keep the Community powers in check by ensuring that EU institutions do not exceed their authority. This has taken place on several occasions, especially with regard to the balance of power between the European Parliament (EP) and other EU institutions. Maintaining the balance of power between EU actors allows each institution to work more effectively.

B Why member states support ECJ rulings

Although member states have agreed to uphold ECJ rulings, the ECJ is still dependent on the member states to enforce EU law. This is because the ECJ cannot implement rulings itself – unlike national courts, the ECJ has no police force to ensure that citizens and member states follow its judgments. If a member state should decide not to uphold a ruling by the ECJ, it would also challenge the authority of the ECJ. If other states were to follow suit, the repercussions could, in theory, undermine the legitimacy of the entire EU legal system.

However, member states have decided to accept the vast majority of ECJ rulings, allowing the ECJ to expand EU powers and responsibilities, often at the expense of the nation-state's sovereignty. There are several explanations for this, including those related to the incomplete contract (see above). In addition, member states may be playing a 'two-level' game. In other words, while it may appear that a ruling works against the interests of a particular economic sector in a member state, the ruling may be beneficial to the economy of that state as a whole. Consequently, national governments may accept ECJ judgments, and claim credit for any beneficial effects of these judgments, while simultaneously using the ECJ as a political scapegoat for the necessary political reforms that hurt particular economic sectors. This, academics such as Garrett argue, is what happened in the *Cassis de Dijon* case: while Germany blamed the ECJ for hurting its liquor industry, it was actually in favour of the principle of mutual recognition, as this would stimulate increased trade of its industrial goods. Therefore, Germany offered only token resistance to a ruling that it secretly supported.

C The relationship between the ECJ and national courts

The use of the preliminary reference procedure by the national courts (through Article 234) has been crucial to the ECJ's ability to create EU case law, and thereby to affect EU integration. The national courts of the member states also have an obligation to take EU legislation into account in their decisions (this interpretative obligation is known as indirect effect – see *Judicial Processes*). However, national courts may also choose to utilize Article 234 because they have been empowered by it: through direct interaction with the ECJ, national courts increase their power and prestige in domestic political and judicial systems, especially *vis-à-vis* the executive and legislative branches of government. Lower national courts may view Article 234 as a way of circumventing their higher (constitutional) courts. Through this system, judges in lower courts have, in theory, a rare opportunity to affect national and EU law.

Who wins/who loses

The ECJ has gained power and status as a consequence of the increasing competences of the Union. This power has come at a price, however: several member states
have become suspicious of what they view as the Court's activism, and hence have
proposed that the ECJ's role in the Community be circumscribed. In the Treaty on
European Union (TEU, 1992), judicial review was highly restricted in policies
created in the third Pillar of the Treaty, known as Justice and Home Affairs
(JHA). While this restriction was modified in the Treaty of Amsterdam (1997),
areas of the Treaty such as issues concerning EUROPOL (the EU-level policing
organization) remain outside the jurisdiction of the ECJ.

Higher national courts (also known as constitutional courts) have lost some of
their status because of increased integration. The ECJ now has the right to rule in
areas which were previously the sole competence of higher national courts. However, some constitutional courts, especially those in Germany and Italy, have
indicated that they reserve final jurisdiction over any laws affecting their citizens.
Such statements, made in Case 11/70, *Internationale Handelsgesellschaft* (1972)
(related to the *Solange* ruling) and *Brunner* vs *European Union* (1994), have
threatened to undermine the legitimacy of the ECJ (see *Constitutionalism* and
Fundamental Rights). **Lower national courts**, by comparison, may have gained
both status and competences as a result of the development of EU jurisprudence.
Through the use of Article 234, they can now circumvent their higher courts by
referring cases with EU ramifications directly to the ECJ.

Member states can be considered either winners or losers from the development of
EU case law. Member states are constrained by the laws that the ECJ imposes on
them, and they must modify their legislation accordingly. Yet, as the two-level game
theory demonstrates, member states can use the ECJ as a scapegoat for unpopular
but necessary reforms.

Private firms and **the Commission** have both gained from the integration related to
EU case law. Firms have the ability to petition the ECJ for the removal of unwel-
come barriers to trade. However, in several important cases (such as *Cassis de Dijon*
and *Brasserie du Pêcheur*) the Court has furthered integration while denying the
complaints of the actual litigants. The Commission, as Stein points out, has gained a
strong partner in the creation of new areas of EU competence. However, this
partnership is not always consistent, as the ECJ has ruled against the interests of
the Commission on several occasions.

EU citizens may have gained rights through the extension of EU law, but these
new rights have come at a cost. By furthering integration through the courts rather
than through the legislative process, the ECJ has increased the democratic deficit in
the EU, since citizens have not elected the ECJ judges, but rather the members of the
EP, to provide them with laws.

Food for thought

Is the ECJ a dynamic political actor with a pro-integrationist bias or an instrument of the member states? There are many reasons to assume that the ECJ is a pro-integrationist actor with its own agenda. However, academics such as Garrett argue that the ECJ cannot afford to make decisions that diverge too far from member states' interests. If member states were to rebel against its rulings, the legitimacy of the Court and therefore the entire EU legal system would be under-mined. However, as the legal system of the EU provides several benefits for the member states, non-compliance with EU law could also work against the interests of the member states.

Are treaty revisions an effective way to control the integrationist tendencies of the ECJ? Some academics have argued that the exclusion of the ECJ from the second and third Pillars of the Maastricht Treaty was an attempt by member states to limit the ECJ's ability to promote integration. This is because the policy areas of defence and home affairs are of particular political sensitivity for several national govern-ments. Does exclusion from these Pillars indicate that the member states are unhappy with the pace or type of integration encouraged by EU case law? It has been argued that the Maastricht Treaty was an attempt by member states to regain control over the integration process; if this is true, why did the member states expand the judicial review of the Court in the Amsterdam Treaty?

Is Cassis de Dijon *the only example of the ECJ–Commission alliance having a profound effect on EU integration?* Many scholars agree that the *Cassis de Dijon* case has had such a profound effect on the EU. However, one might expand Stein's thesis to argue that the EU institutions often work together to promote their own interests. Does the rapid development of policy in the area of environmental policy and sex discrimination indicate that the ECJ and the Commission are working in tandem to further EU integration?

Student-to-student tip

Do not ignore the legal references that occur in your academic reading; instead, use the legal cases to support your arguments. The key to any legal case is to focus on the ramifications of a ruling, rather than the means by which it was decided or the actual results of the case. Therefore, the brief summaries of cases on the ECJ websites can often be more helpful than a textbook. Visit *www.curia.eu.int* for details.

Summary

- As the interpreter of the EU Treaty, the ECJ is in a position to affect the legal and political structure of the EU. The willingness of the ECJ to rule in favour of integration has been demonstrated in several cases and in several policy areas. Examples include:

- Case 120/78, *Rewe Zentral AG* vs *Germany* (1979), establishing the principle of mutual recognition and facilitating the Single Market Programme;
- Case 43/75, *Defrenne* vs *Sabena* (1976), developing the concept of equality in the workplace, and the direct effect of EU law;
- Case 302/86, *Commission* vs *Denmark* (1989), strengthening the importance of Environmental policy within the EU.

- There are several actors who use EU case law in order to further EU integration. They include private firms and individuals, who bring cases to national courts based on their rights under EU law, and the Commission, which has used EU case law as the basis for integrationist policy, such as the SMP.
- National courts play a crucial role in the development of EU case law. Through Article 234, national courts can refer cases with EU implications to the ECJ for recommendations.
- Although the extension of EU case law often results in further integration with negative ramifications for national sovereignty, member states have many reasons to accept ECJ rulings, including the resolution of the collective action problem and the positive benefits of the two-level game.

Selected bibliography

Analysis of the ECJ

Stein, E. (1981) 'Lawyers, Judges and the Making of a Transnational Constitution', *American Journal of International Law*, vol. 75: 1–27.
  One of the seminal works on the subject of EU law, this article explores the relationship between the ECJ and the Commission in detail.
Garrett, G. (1995) 'The Politics of Legal Integration', *International Organization*, vol. 49: 171–82.
  An important work outlining Garrett's neo-realist perspective on the ECJ, it uses game theory to describe the creation of EU law.
Burley, A.-M. and W. Mattli (1993) 'Europe before the Court: A Political Theory of Legal Integration', *International Organization*, vol. 47, no. 1: 41–76.
  In this classic neo-functional analysis, the authors focus on the role of national courts and the particularities of the law.
Rasmussen, H. (2000) 'Remedying the Crumbling EU Judicial System', *Common Market Law Review,* vol. 37, no. 5: 1071–1112.
  This article discusses the need to reform the EU judicial system and the role of the ECJ judges in the reform process.
Alter, K. (2000) 'The European Union's Legal System and Domestic Policy: Spillover or Backlash', *International Organization*, vol. 54: 489–518.
  Alter investigates the conditions that domestic actors must satisfy in order to successfully apply EU legal tools to change national policies.

The *Cassis de Dijon* case

Alter, K. J. and S. Meunier-Atsahalia (1994) 'Judicial Politics in the European Community: European Integration and the Pathbreaking *Cassis de Dijon* Decision', *Comparative Political Studies*, vol. 26: 535–61.

One of the few articles focusing on *Cassis*, it links the legal with the political, and EU case law with Commission initiatives.

Environmental law

Sands, P. (1990) 'European Community Environmental Law: Legislation, the European Court of Justice and Common-Interest Groups', *Modern Law Review*, vol. 53: 685–98.
Although an older reference, Sands does a great job outlining the ECJ's role in environmental policy, particularly in the *Danish Bottle* case.

Sex discrimination

Craig, P. and G. de Búrca (1998) 'Equal Treatment of Women and Men', in *EU Law: Text, Cases and Materials*, 2nd edn, New York: Oxford University Press, chapter 19: 841–65.
This chapter provides a comprehensive introduction to the legal aspects and development of the sexual discrimination policy of the EU, offering information on both case law and directives.

Part IV

Economic and Monetary Integration

11

Economic Theories of Regional Integration

Alexis Iche

The Treaties of Rome (1957) were signed on the premise that regional economic integration could be the engine for a political aim: namely, an 'ever closer union' between the peoples of Europe. In theory, the economic benefits from regional economic integration would convince the citizens of Europe that deeper political links between member countries would have similar benefits. In order to analyse the economic rationale behind EU programmes such as the Single Market Programme (SMP) or Economic and Monetary Union (EMU), it is necessary to understand the fundamental economic concepts and theories used to justify regional economic integration, as well as the problems associated with these theories.

The facts

A   Types of integration – negative vs positive integration

In 1954, the Dutch economist Jan Tinbergen outlined a distinction between two different types of integration:

- *Negative integration* – the elimination of obstacles to the free movement of goods and factors of production. An example is the removal of tariff barriers, such as quotas, as well as non-tariff barriers, such as differing technical standards between member states.
- *Positive integration* – the replacement of various national rules with one set of EU rules and the adoption of common policies. An example is the EU's Common Commercial Policy (CCP).

B Stages of regional economic integration

Regional economic integration is a gradual process that can exist in several different forms. In the 1950s the economist Bela Balassa defined the process of complete economic integration as one that progresses through various stages as it moves towards more integration. The best example of economic integration is the EU, which has developed from a free trade area (FTA) towards a full economic and monetary union. Integration is an ongoing process with its own in-built momentum, because each further step creates problems that can be solved only by deeper regional integration (a phenomenon known as spillover; see *Theories of European Integration*).

Stage 1 – free trade area (FTA)

- Exclusively focused on trade in goods (services, labour and capital remain restricted).
- Tariffs (i.e. import taxes imposed on foreign goods) are abolished within the group.
- Each member keeps its own external tariffs policy toward the rest of the world.
- Example: NAFTA (North American Free Trade Area)
- *Problem*: in an FTA, each country keeps its own external tariff on goods from outside the FTA. Once these goods are inside the FTA, however, they can move freely without additional tariffs. This means that in an FTA between Sweden and Finland, if Sweden has a lower tariff than Finland on coffee, companies in Finland will import coffee through Sweden in order to pay lower tariffs.
- *Solution*: to avoid this, the FTA needs to become a customs union, with a common external tariff (CET).

Stage 2 – customs union (CU)

- Exclusively focused on trade in goods (services, capital and people remain restricted).
- Tariffs are abolished within the group.
- A CET is established for the group.
- Example: European Economic Community (EEC), 1957–87.
- *Problem*: the CU eliminates the tariffs and quota restrictions (tariff barriers), but still allows non-tariff barriers (NTBs) (such as technical standards and health/safety requirements), which hinder free trade.
- *Solution*: to avoid this, NTBs should be eliminated through mutual recognition or product harmonization.

Stage 3 – Common Market (CM)

- Has all the properties of a customs union.
- Free movement of the factors of production (goods, services, labour, capital) between all members of the group is established.
- Example: European Community (EC)/European Union (EU), 1987–99.
- *Problem*: to achieve complete free movement, the last NTB must be eliminated: namely, the different currencies in the member states. This is because the exchange rate (ER) does not reflect the 'true' price of goods and acts as an NTB, distorting prices (and hence information) between member states
- *Solution*: to avoid this, a common currency should be adopted, eliminating the problems associated with the ER.

Stage 4 – monetary union

- Has all the properties of a common market.
- A common currency is adopted within the group.
- Example: European Union (EU), 1999–present.
- *Problem*: in the past, strains between the different economies, caused by different growth rates between member states, were partly eased by having different exchange rates. These floating exchange rates allowed national central banks to set individual interest rates, suited to the needs of their economies. In a monetary union, exchange rates are (irreversibly) fixed, and the other adjustment mechanisms (such as the movement of capital and labour) may be insufficient to counterbalance tensions in the system caused by different growth rates between countries.
- *Solution*: the only option is to adopt one common economic policy, including some form of common or co-ordinated fiscal policy. This would permit fiscal transfers from regions experiencing positive growth to regions suffering from negative growth, in order to maintain the stability of the system.

Stage 5 – economic union

- Has all the properties of a monetary union.
- Common economic policies, co-ordination and harmonization on fiscal issues (single policy for the entire zone) are established.
- Example: there is no good example available between equally sovereign nation-states. The relationship between individual US states may be the nearest example.
- *Problem*: the loss of control over economic and monetary policy is a serious loss of sovereignty for member states.

- *Solution*: there is a need to find a new balance between nation-states' sovereignty and their economic powers, or to integrate further into a full political union modelled on already existing federal states (such as Germany).

The further regional integration progresses, the more its economic developments clash with the individual political prerogatives of the member countries. This is especially true with regard to issues such as monetary policy, taxation and all forms of redistributive policy – that is, issues connected with a state's *raison d'être*. As a result, while further economic integration leads to a need for more political change, member states are reluctant to yield the sovereignty necessary to move to the next level of integration.

C   Theories of regional integration

In order to determine whether economic integration increases the welfare of participants, it is necessary to analyse the costs and benefits expected from integration. Two main approaches provide the foundation for the economic rationale behind regional economic integration.

I   The Viner approach

Presented in the 1950s, Viner's CU theory is directly derived from the Ricardian approach to international trade, according to which countries trade with one another because they are different and have advantages, compared to other countries, in the production of certain goods ('comparative advantages'). This means that each country will specialize in the production of goods in which they have the strongest comparative advantage; for example, Spain, rather than Denmark, will specialize in the production of oranges, and vice versa for cheese. Viner's study also exposed trade diversion and trade creation effects. The creation of a customs union can be either trade-diverting or trade-creating, depending on the levels of external tariffs (those with the rest of the world) and internal tariffs (those between members of the regional group).

- *Trade creation* increases the overall welfare of members of the group. Because customs duties between members are abolished, countries are encouraged to import goods that are produced more cheaply in a partner country than can be produced domestically (thus moving away from high domestic costs towards lower partner costs). This results in a shift to a more efficient producer.
- *Trade diversion* decreases the overall welfare of the members of a CU, by encouraging inefficient production. This occurs if the external tariff with the rest of the world is set high enough to prevent less expensive goods produced outside the customs union from competing with more expensive goods produced

inside the CU. For example, even if Greek olives are more expensive to produce than Moroccan olives, the members of the group would buy olives from Greece if the external tariffs on Moroccan olives are higher than the additional price of producing Greek olives. This situation can damage the overall welfare of the region, because members of the group end up paying more than is necessary for products, representing a shift to a less efficient producer as a result of the establishment of a CU.

In sum, the balance between trade creation and trade diversion determines whether regional economic integration is beneficial for the partners. Note that even if, in overall terms, a CU is beneficial, this still does not mean that all countries in a CU will benefit, or benefit to the same extent.

2 The new theory of market integration

The Vinerian theory describes only the static, one-off benefits to be gained from forming a customs union. The 'dynamic approach', supported by economists like Krugman, takes into account economic elements overlooked in the Vinerian approach, arguing that there are also dynamic gains to be achieved in a CU. These gains occur because the formation of a CU forces economic actors to restructure their activities. Two effects are of particular importance here:

● Firms faced with *increased competition* must lower their costs in order to remain competitive.
● The increase in market size allows firms greater scope for *economies of scale*.

Thus dynamic effects lead to long-term gains, as production is forced to become more efficient in order to remain competitive. It is estimated that such gains are much larger than the one-off static effects. This approach illustrates that the benefits from regional economic integration may be more significant and long-lasting than simply the benefits from comparative advantage, hence allowing for a larger opportunity for economic integration to be beneficial overall.

The problems/issues

A   Assessing economic integration in Europe

Following the completion of the SMP creating a Single Internal Market (SIM) within the EU, academics continue to debate several issues related to regional integration. These include whether or not regional integration in Europe has created welfare gains (i.e. really contributed to greater economic wealth in Europe) and to what extent increased economic growth can be attributed to the process of European integration.

There is no conclusive answer to these questions, as it is very difficult to empirically isolate the impact of European economic integration on economic growth from other factors such as globalization, liberalization, technological innovation, etc. Nevertheless, the debate has resulted in some serious reports and analysis of the subject. Most reports agree that the SMP has had an overall beneficial impact on the European economy, producing welfare gains for the population that can be measured in terms of GDP. However, they disagree as to what precise economic factors have generated these gains.

B   Trade effects

Academics generally agree that the SIM has been trade-creating, based on the explosive rise of intra-European trade between member states of the EU. Further, according to calculations by Sapir, the growth of intra-EU trade has not been detrimental to the rest of the world and has not reduced trade flows with non-EU countries, as was originally expected. Balassa supports this conclusion, asserting that trade creation has been exceeding trade diversion (except for agricultural goods, where the CAP has closed the EU market to non-members). However, most assessments of the SIM by scholars (such as those by Helm or Sapir) tend to agree that trade effects should not be over-emphasized, as these are outweighed by the dynamic effects of increased competition and economies of scale.

C   Growth estimates

Although a consensus on the positive economic results of European regional integration exists, *ex ante* estimates of integration impact vary significantly from *ex post* calculations. In 1988, the Commission conducted a study known as the Cecchini Report (formally known as *The Cost of Non-Europe*), in order to assess the impact of the SMP. It estimated that GDP gains from integration were expected to be in the 6 per cent range. In comparison, an *ex post* 1996 estimate by the Commission indicated that GDP gains for the EU have been between 1 and 1.25 per cent.

Who wins/who loses

Consumers/taxpayers win from integration, as a result of increased efficiency in the allocation of resources through increased competition. This reduces prices and extends product choice. Furthermore, if regional economic integration accelerates economic growth, this should result in less unemployment. However, market integration can also lead to industry concentration, creating oligopolistic situations that could, in the long run, prove detrimental for the EU consumer (see *Competition Policy*).

EU businesses are the primary winners of the process of economic integration, as they are directly concerned with the opening of market frontiers, the growth of market size, and the harmonization of market conditions. Although businesses will face increased competition from firms across Europe, the new distribution opportunities for competitive products should counterbalance any negative effects created by competition. Furthermore, companies benefit from having only one tariff per product rather than fifteen. Large businesses, especially multi-national corporations, have enthusiastically supported further economic integration. However, increased competition also means that inefficient businesses will suffer, resulting in potentially large-scale restructuring, when protective barriers are eliminated. This could lead to unemployment in vulnerable sectors of some economies.

Member states lose power as political entities, as they gradually transfer their economic sovereignty to the EU level. Integration means the ability to levy customs duties, control competition, nationalize industries and enact economic policies that protect 'national champion' industries is shifted from member states to the EU or eliminated through the integration process. Yet, in economic terms, the extent to which member states win or lose also depends on the openness of their economies. In terms of trade, the more open an economy is, the bigger the benefits that it will gain from regional economic integration. Therefore, very open countries, such as the Netherlands, will benefit the most from integration.

The impact of a regional grouping on the **rest of the world** depends on the CET levied by the group. In general, the less protectionist the integrating region is, the better a common market is for the world economy as a whole. The impact of the CM is usually concentrated on sectors, rather than countries. For example, countries with strong agricultural sectors suffer more, since CAP levies increase tariffs on products that constitute a core part of their economy.

Food for thought

To what extent can economic integration proceed without complementary political developments? Most proponents of the EMU, such as Mundell, argue that successful monetary integration must be paired with political co-ordination and harmonization, especially with respect to fiscal systems and labour market regulations. Without these components, the EMU is more likely to cause economic hardship than to enhance economic welfare. Are national governments ready to implement the strategy outlined in the Treaties of Rome – namely, to co-ordinate sensitive political issues in order to politically consolidate economic market integration? Or are concerns about sovereignty likely to hinder this type of political integration?

Student-to-student tip

When studying economic theories, you always run into a lot of graphs. Economists love graphs, as an alternative way to communicate ideas. However, you should not be intimidated by them; if you read the text of most books on integration, you will be able to develop a strong understanding of the theories. Remember that everything in a graph has already been explained in the text. Therefore, if the graphs confuse you, you can safely ignore them.

Summary

- Regional economic integration is the process of deepening economic co-operation between a group of countries.
- Regional economic integration is a gradual process, which can take various forms according to the degree of co-operation between member countries, ranging from arrangements exclusively focused on trade in goods to full monetary and economic union.
- There are two potential benefits of economic grouping:
  - *Static effects*, as outlined in the Vinerian principles of trade creation/diversion, based on the principle of comparative advantage. The balance between these two factors determines the overall welfare benefits from regional integration.
  - *Dynamic effects*, as proposed by the new theories of market integration based on the principle of increased efficiency through economies of scale. The dynamic gains from market integration are thought to be much larger than the static ones.
- Traditional theories of customs unions concentrate only on the static economic effects; therefore, they fail to predict the net gains/losses from economic integration. The concept of economies of scale allows the dynamic effects to be taken into consideration and to add a new source of benefit from integration, over and above the benefits from comparative advantage.
- So far, economic integration in Europe seems to have had an overall positive impact on the economies of member states. However, gains from market integration are not equally distributed between all member states. This leads to political problems, as no countries want to be part of an economic union that leaves them worse off. Economic integration has therefore been accompanied by measures to strengthen weaker economic areas.
- One of the primary political arguments regarding integration is that deeper economic integration needs to be complemented by increased political policies and structures, in order to ensure the long-term viability of the SMP. This is controversial, because political integration means an increased loss of sovereignty for the member states.

Selected bibliography

Overview of SIM

Hansen, J. D. and J. U. Nielsen (1997) *An Economic Analysis of the EU*, 2nd edn, London and New York: McGraw-Hill, chapters 1–5: 3–96. Assessing EU co-operation from an economic viewpoint, the microeconomic section of this book covers the classical theory of customs unions, as well as the 'new' trade theory, dealing with imperfect competition and economies of scale.

Economists on SIM

Krugman, P. (1989) 'Economic Integration in Europe: Some Conceptual Issues', in
  A. Jaquemin and A. Sapir (eds), *The European Internal Market: Trade and Competition*,
  Oxford: Oxford University Press.
  Krugman, a leading economist in the field of integration economics, provides excellent material on
  the effects of regional integration.
Robson, P. (1998) *The Economics of International Integration*, 4th edn, London: Routledge,
  Introduction and chapters 1, 2, 3, 6, 7 and 11.
  In this excellent volume on the economics of market integration and economic union, Robson is not
  too technical and describes the new theories, the dynamic effects of integration, and further political
  needs of the Union very thoroughly.

Commission evaluation of SIM

European Commission (1988) 'The Economics of 1992: An Assessment of the Potential
  Economic Effects of Completing the Internal Market of the European Community',
  European Economy, no. 35.
  This is the famous Cecchini Report, an *ex ante* analysis of the SMP.
European Commission (1996) 'The Economic Evaluation of the Internal Market', *European
  Economy*, no. 4.
  This is the *ex post* analysis by the Commission. It is especially interesting to compare the two reports.

Economic evaluations of the SIM

Sapir, A. (1992) 'Regional Integration in Europe', *Economic Journal*, November: 1491–1505.
Helm, D. (1993) 'The Assessment. The European Internal Market: The Next Steps', *Oxford
  Review of Economic Policy*, vol. 9, no. 1: 1–14.
  Both of these references offer estimates and evaluations of the impact of market integration in
  Europe, and can be very useful for understanding the practical implications of these theories.

12

The Single Market: achieving the free movement of goods, services, capital and people

Marc Gafarot

Although the free movement of goods, services, capital and people was one of the primary goals of the Treaties of Rome (1957), many barriers to free movement between member states were not addressed by the Community until the early 1980s. The presentation of the Commission's initiative on the completion of the Single Market in 1985 marked a turning point in European integration. The Single Market Programme (SMP) proposed to increase competition and the free movement of goods, services, capital and people – without requiring the member states to co-ordinate all their national standards through the creation of new legislation. However, this process could be accomplished only through changes to the legislative framework of the Community, and therefore led to the creation of the Single European Act (SEA, 1986). As a result, the SMP launched a renewed period of dynamic growth in the competences of the European Union, and created the momentum for further integration in ways that are only currently being realized.

The facts

A   Barriers to development

The central element of the Treaties of Rome was the creation of a common market, defined as 'an area without internal frontiers in which the free movement of goods, services, capital and people is ensured'. While the successful completion of the Community customs union was announced in July 1968, this referred only to official barriers to trade, and did not take into account policies favouring domestic producers, such as discriminatory product specifications, different VATs, nationalistic public purchasing policy, and unreasonable bureaucratic barriers. In addition, two institutional barriers were impeding the development of the common market: product harmonization and unanimity in the Council.

I Product harmonization

The lack of common standards across all EU countries meant that free movement of goods between countries could be blocked if products from one country did not comply with the regulations in another. Therefore, national standards and regulations on products formed extensive non-tariff barriers (NTBs) to intra-EU trade. The Community attempted to eliminate these NTBs through product harmonization, which is the process of co-ordinating national standards through detailed legislation agreed at the Community level. Since all member states had to approve these common technical standards in order to harmonize legislation, harmonization proved to be a slow and inefficient method of eliminating NTBs. It required that each member state agree to the minutiae of regulations on products, ranging from the proportion of ingredients in pasta to the decibel levels of lawn-mower engines. Not only was this process time-consuming, it was also very difficult politically in periods of economic stagnation, when each country was concerned primarily with protecting the interests of its own national industries.

2 Unanimity in the Council

Although the Treaties of Rome made provisions for the use of majority voting within the EU, the Luxembourg Compromise of 1966 gave each member state the *de facto* right to veto proposals on the basis of national interest (see *A History of European Integration*). Since member states could always claim that an aspect of a new directive acted against its national interest, the Commission was forced to accept the position of the most reluctant member if it wished to get a directive approved. Thus, unanimity led to lowest-common-denominator decisions, and slowed the legislative process, as member states argued about each aspect of any harmonization proposal that might have a negative effect on their national industries.

B The 1970s and Euro-scepticism

The Golden Age of European integration came to an abrupt end following the OPEC oil crises and the collapse of the Bretton Woods monetary system in the early 1970s. The oil crises increased the cost of production of goods around the world, and initiated a contraction in global markets. As a result, Europe experienced a decade of high unemployment, low economic growth, and a sharp rise in inflation.

This situation was called 'stagflation' (stagnation of the economy concurrent with inflation of prices), and led many member states to retreat from their EC commitments and concentrate on their economic difficulties at home.

In August 1971, the collapse of the Bretton Woods system increased the instability of world markets by allowing currencies to float freely against each other for the first time since World War II. This new situation led to balance-of-payments problems, to which the EC proposed several solutions. However, the Community's first attempt to address this problem in the system of payments, known as the 'Snake in the Tunnel', failed just three years after its launch in 1973 (see *Economic and Monetary Union*).

The increasing withdrawal of member states from the creation of new Community policies and the inability of the EC to counteract the effects of the recession led to a period of Euro-scepticism. This situation was exacerbated by the lack of consensus among member states about future integration. As a result, very few policy measures were adopted during the 1970s, and most scholars, politicians and newspapers predicted the end of the European project.

C   The advent of a new economic orthodoxy

In response to the decade-long recession and high levels of inflation, the economic policy preferences of European governments began to shift. *Keynesian* policies, which focused on maintaining high levels of demand and employment, had been practised by most national governments since World War II. However, as Keynesianism was unable to combat stagflation, governments started to embrace a neo-liberal economic philosophy known as Monetarism. Based on supply-side economics, economic liberalization, privatization and market deregulation, *Monetarism* (also referred to as the 'new economic orthodoxy') encouraged less state involvement in the economy, and focused on interest rates and inflation control, in order to stimulate the economy. This shift toward monetarism meant that any programme proposed by the Commission to reinvigorate the European project had to be compatible with deregulation and liberalization.

D   Mutual recognition

The principle of mutual recognition enabled the EU to overcome the barriers presented by product harmonization and unanimity, and helped reinvigorate the European project. First identified in the *Cassis de Dijon* case of 1979, mutual recognition developed as a direct result of ECJ rulings (see *Law and European Integration*). This principle states that any product legally manufactured in one member state, in accordance with the regulations of that member state, must be allowed into the market of any other member state in the Community.

The key to the success of this proposal was the fact that mutual recognition was both compatible with the new economic orthodoxy (which focused on deregulation and liberalization) and avoided the problems associated with harmonization (namely, time-consuming, lowest-common-denominator decisions). It limited legislative harmonization to the minimum needed to provide for health and safety standards, and allowed for flexibility, so that legislation could be adapted to the individual needs of each member state. It also allowed the Delors Commission to delegate most of the responsibility for detailed technical standard setting to the CEN (European Standards Committee), CENELEC (European Electrotechnical Standardization Committee) and ETIS (European Telecom Standards Institute), the private European standard-setting bodies composed of industrial representatives. The Commission provided these bodies with mandates on deadlines and financial provisions for setting voluntary EU-wide standards.

E White Paper and Commission initiative

The Cockfield Report (also referred to as the '1985 White Paper on Completing the Internal Market') identified over 280 remaining barriers to the completion of the Single Internal Market (SIM), including the partial implementation of Treaty provisions. The report established three categories of barriers preventing the completion of the SIM:

- *Physical barriers*, which included frontier controls such as quantitative restrictions (QR) on goods within the EC. The report also referred to the lack of a common transport policy and the elimination of interior border controls.
- *Technical barriers*, including NTBs caused by national regulations on technical standards on products within the EC.
- *Fiscal barriers*, focusing primarily on the different rates of indirect taxation, and especially taxation on the consumption of goods and services (VAT).

The Commission proposed to reinvigorate the European project through the completion of the SIM. The SMP (also known as the '1992 Programme') proposed to:

- *circumvent* the problems caused by product harmonization through mutual recognition; member states could make exceptions to mutual recognition for health and safety reasons, but only with the approval of the Commission;
- *legislate* only on essential issues (such as safety) in the form of directives, which allowed for some legislative flexibility at the national level (see *Judicial Processes*);
- *develop* European-wide standards for products through the voluntary co-ordination of industry in the form of European norms (EN) under the control of the European Standards agencies;
- *reform* the VAT system, in order to remove the need for border controls;

- *liberalize* public procurement of goods so that national governments could not favour their national industries, which was restricting trade.

The 1985 White Paper appealed to the member states for several reasons: it had an economic, rather than a political, goal that would assist in the recovery of the depressed European economies, and it suited the new monetarist economic philosophy, which focused on the liberalization of markets in order to achieve economic growth. Since the creation of regulations places the onus of change on the national governments of the member states, mutual recognition did not require an increase in the EU budget. The SMP was also preferable to other suggested EC projects, such as monetary union, because it was not seen as a threat to national sovereignty. Therefore, the SMP appealed both to pro-integrationist member states such as France and Germany, as well as member states such as the UK which were reluctant to increase Community powers and responsibilities.

F   The Single European Act

In order to accomplish the SMP, the Commission indicated that an institutional reform of the Community was needed. In particular, the Commission requested a new legislative tool: qualified majority voting. QMV is a weighted form of voting, whereby each member state has a different number of votes, based on population. Currently, of a total of eighty-seven votes, a 'qualified majority' of sixty-two votes is required to approve proposals. The member states, still reluctant to give up their national veto, decided to limit the use of QMV to issues that fell within the scope of the SIM. This package of institutional reforms became the Single European Act (SEA, 1986) and was accomplished in co-ordination with the accession of Portugal and Spain to the EC. The SEA included:

- acceptance of the goals of the White Paper and the definition of the internal market;
- use of QMV in the Council of Ministers for defined policy areas dealing with the SIM, such as Environmental Policy;
- greater transparency and the reduction of the democratic deficit through the introduction of the co-operation procedure in defined policy issues dealing with the SIM;
- integration of the European Political Community (EPC) into the Treaty structure;
- creation of the Structural Funds through the expansion of Regional Policy in both scope and funding;
- integration of some aspects of Social Policy, such as the European Social Fund (ESF), into regional policy.

Two of the most significant aspects of the SEA are the introduction of Article 95 (ex-Article 100a), and the co-operation procedure for the EP. Article 95 authorizes the Council to adopt new measures concerning the internal market through QMV. Its wide scope also allows the Commission to propose legislation in fields related to the Single Market but not originally addressed in the Treaty. It can be argued that the Commission has used Article 95 to slowly expand supranational competences into new policy areas, thereby fostering positive integration. The SEA also created the co-operation procedure, which gave the EP a greater role in the legislative process. While the use of the co-operation procedure was circumscribed, it led to the development of the stronger co-decision procedure, introduced in the Maastricht Treaty (1992).

The problems/issues

A   Achieving the free movement of goods, services, capital and people

The SMP has been largely successful in removing the non-tariff barriers to trade within the SIM. While successful liberalization in one area has often facilitated liberalization in others, these successes have not been equally distributed between the four fundamental freedoms; in particular, the free movement of services and people has remained less developed than the free movement of goods and capital. In addition, negative integration in certain sectors has created pressures for positive integration in others.

I   Goods

Trade of goods within the Community faced many problems in the early 1950s: customs formalities, paperwork and inspections at borders, different tax systems and different regulations, all of which hindered the trade of goods. Since trade between EC countries was based on goods at the time, the Treaties of Rome were primarily devoted to the elimination of tariffs and quantitative restrictions (QRs) on these goods. Therefore, the removal of barriers to free movement through the elimination of NTBs (the aim of the SMP) has seen the most success in this area – of the eighty-one measures identified in the 1985 White Paper in this area, the Community had implemented all but three by 1992. In particular, the removal of physical barriers through the abolition of border controls and the creation of the Common Customs Code (1992) has increased competition throughout the Community. European norms (EN) and standards created by the CEN and other standard-setters have also drastically reduced technical barriers within the Community. However, the elimination of fiscal barriers, which required the reform of the VAT system, proved to be much more difficult, and has resulted in a bureaucratic burden for EU importers and exporters. These problems have generated pressure for further tax harmonization, which is resisted in member states with liberal tax regimes, such as the UK and Luxembourg.

2 Services

Article 49 (ex-Article 59) establishes free movement of services between the member states. However, increasing the free movement of services has proved much more difficult than liberalizing trade in goods, due to a long history of government intervention in the service sector. The SMP focuses on four areas of service, and has established a timetable for the liberalization of each.

- *Financial services.* The SMP has led to a restructuring of the banking sector. The Single European Banking Licence (Directive 89/646 EEC), with its corresponding minimum solvency rates and capital requirements, allows a bank in one member state to easily establish a branch in another member state. EU directives pertaining to the free establishment of insurance services have created a more liberal insurance regime in the EU than currently exists between individual US states. In addition, the Investment Services Directive (ISD) allows for banks to have access to stock exchanges in all member states. The Second Banking Directive also provided a list of financial activities recognized by the Community members, and acts as a passport for firms to engage in investment activities throughout the Community. As a result of this legislation, the EU financial services sector has been largely liberalized.
- *Telecoms and postal services.* While both telecoms and postal services have traditionally been dominated by state monopolies, telecoms have been privatized much more quickly than postal services, which are still partially state-owned. In an effort to reduce state ownership and aids, open competition in telecoms equipment began in 1998, and the open networks provision for both mobile and fixed telephone services was initiated in 1998. However, liberalization in some aspects of this area remains slow.
- *Transport services.* These are divided into air, road and maritime sectors. While air transport has a long history of state ownership, the SMP encouraged privatization and competition. Newly privatized European airlines can now operate in various member countries, and national governments can no longer subsidize these companies. (However, after the events of 11 September 2001, some subsidies have been allowed to counteract the effects on the airline industry.) The Prodi Commission has also pushed for the creation of a 'European Sky', which should also help to increase competition in this area. In road and maritime transport, national licences and quotas for intra-EC transport of goods created barriers to free movement, thereby increasing transport costs. These problems were significantly reduced by the introduction of full cabotage rights (the right to carry goods within another member state) in 1993, and signalled the first step toward a single transport market.
- *Professional services.* The SMP has facilitated a growth in the mutual recognition of professional qualifications and diplomas throughout the EU, especially through the extension of rights of establishment. In order to facilitate free movement of people, the Commission has also established equivalences among

various professions. However, this is much more developed in some areas, such as medicine and legal services, than others, such as vocational training fields. There is still some room for improvement in this area, since EU citizens have yet to take full advantage of their rights in this regard. Increased recognition of professions would therefore facilitate movement.

3 Capital

National governments have traditionally controlled capital to avoid adverse effects on macroeconomic policy objectives. However, the development of the SMP required the liberalization of capital, principally in order to avoid capital flight between member states. The full liberalization of capital movements, which ended all capital controls, took place on 1 January 1994, when Greece liberalized its capital movements (the first eight member states liberalized on 1 July 1990, as part of the launch of Stage I of the EMU). Liberalized capital movement was a crucial step toward the elimination of the final non-tariff barrier to trade: namely, individual currencies. Although capital movements are fully liberalized in the EU, there is no EU Stock Exchange; nor does the EU have the ability to accrue debt, which has a restricting effect on the EU economies.

4 People

The Treaties of Rome established the free movement of people as a fundamental objective of the European Economic Community, but this provision originally applied only to cross-border economic activities: namely, the activities of workers. The SMP has expanded the rights of residence for non-workers, with various directives extending these rights to students and retirees. In addition, the Schengen Accords have eliminated border controls between certain countries in the Community. This has generated pressure for further harmonization of immigration and asylum policies (see *Justice and Home Affairs*).

B Implementation of SMP regulations

The principle of mutual recognition has been strengthened by Directive 89/34/EEC, which requires member states to inform the Commission of any proposed technical regulations before they become law, in order to ensure compliance with this principle. In addition, while Article 36 (ex-Article 30) allows for exceptions to mutual recognition for reasons of public safety, health and morality, all exceptions must be approved by the Commission. However, the SIM remains incomplete so long as the directives created under the SMP are not implemented in the member states. The Sutherland Report of 1992 indicated that implementation of directives had become a problem in the Community. Whilst 90 per cent of legislative projects listed in the 1985 White Paper had been adopted, member states consistently failed to transpose directives within the assigned time limits; of the directives that were transposed, many were transposed incorrectly or were poorly implemented by national authorities. In order to address these problems, the Commission has used two approaches.

- By utilizing its powers under Article 226 (ex-Article 169), the Commission began prosecuting SIM infringements by member states, such as delayed or faulty transposition of directives and poor implementation of directives by national authorities, by sending these cases to the ECJ.
- The Commission also hoped to increase transposition and implementation through the creation in 1997 of the Internal Market Scoreboard, which publicizes the implementation record of each individual member state. The May 2002 edition of the Scoreboard indicates that the implementation deficit for internal market directives has shrunk from 20 per cent in 1997 to 1.5 per cent in 2001.

In order to maintain pressure on member states, the Scoreboard continues to set higher goals for complete implementation; it indicates the implementation records in various subcategories (such as Environmental Policy), and publicizes alleged infringements to internal market rules. This allows interest groups and the EU public as a whole to assist the Commission in placing pressure on member states for full implementation.

C Integration theories of the SMP

Academics disagree about the source of political stimulus behind the SMP. Neo-functionalists, focusing on the effects of spillover, view the SMP as a Community initiative, instigated by the ECJ in the *Cassis de Dijon* ruling and developed by the Commission through the 1985 White Paper and through the leadership of Jacques Delors. Indicating the involvement of European business and through interest groups in the creation of the White Paper, and the co-ordination between the EP, the ECJ and the Commission in developing the programme, neo-functionalists (such as Sandholtz and Zyman) argue that the SMP provides an excellent example of the spillover effects of negative economic integration on positive political integration.

By contrast, intergovernmentalists contend that the SMP, and in particular the SEA, result from a convergence in the political goals of the three largest member states – namely the UK, France and Germany. As Moravcsik argues, the top political forces in each government believed that the SMP and the SEA could work to their best advantage. France viewed the SMP as a way to regain political prestige and a position of international leadership after the failure of the socialist experiment in the early 1980s. Germany perceived the SMP as a way to increase the market for its export goods. And the UK believed that the SMP was an ideal vehicle to export neo-liberal economic ideals regarding deregulation to Europe, without further positive integration. In addition, intergovernmentalists contend that the development of further legislation to support the SMP, such as Regional Policy and EMU, is the result of side-payments between those member states who gain through further integration and those who are more vulnerable to increased competition (such as the Cohesion countries – see *Theories of European Integration*).

Who wins/who loses

The **Union** as an entity is the largest winner from the SMP. The EU institutions have gained new powers to implement and enforce EU legislation instituted in the SEA. In particular, the Commission and the EP received both increased power and enhanced status through the institutional restructuring achieved by the SEA. The SMP also created pressures for further European integration in a variety of policy areas, such as EMU, tax harmonization and fiscal co-ordination. These pressures have resulted in the need for several Treaty revisions over the last ten years (i.e. Maastricht, Amsterdam and Nice), each of which has enhanced the competences of the EU.

Member states have gained as a result of the SMP, especially as regards overall long-term economic benefits. However, the programme has also facilitated the shift of many policy competences from the national to the EU level, particularly in relation to control over the economy. This loss of sovereignty by member states has caused tensions between the national governments, EU citizens and EU institutions.

EU-level business has profited in many ways from the SMP. Through the voluntary standardization process in the area of technical standards, European firms not only can produce goods that are easily distributed and sold throughout the EU, but they also play a crucial role in shaping the standards themselves. In addition, the liberalization of capital movements has facilitated investment. The gradual increase in business representation in Brussels testifies to the fact that business is one of the main beneficiaries of the SMP (see *Interest Groups*). However, national champions have lost the protection of state subsidies, and face increased competition. If this leads to an oligopoly of large EU firms, it could result in a decrease in the variety of goods available for the consumer (see *Competition Policy*).

EU citizens are often considered to be both winners and losers from the SMP. Consumers should see lower prices, as a result of the increased competition and price transparency brought about by the SMP. In addition, the SMP has led to EU legislation in areas such as the free movement of people, which provides benefits for all EU citizens. However, as employees, EU citizens may have lost some of the social protections they enjoyed from the national government, such as the job security provided by labour unions and state aids to national businesses. At the same time, the dynamic effects of the SMP may increase EU employment levels in the long term. Therefore, the overall effect on EU citizens remains unclear. It will likely affect some citizens positively (such as high-skilled workers) and others negatively (such as low-skilled workers and the unemployed).

Food for thought

Has mutual recognition led to an erosion of standards? Through deregulation by mutual recognition (rather than harmonizing standards through new regulations), the SMP received the support of both pro- and anti-integrationist member states. However, some politicians and consumer groups predicted that large-scale deregulation could lead to an erosion of standards across Europe, by creating a 'race to the bottom' – in other words, all member states might be forced to lower their standards to the lowest possible level permitted by EU regulations, in order to remain competitive with other member states (a.k.a. the Delaware Effect – see *Environmental and Social Policies*). However, as Hix points out, this phenomenon has not yet occurred in the EU. Have the Commission and the EP been successful in counteracting the effects of deregulation, through re-regulation in the fields of Environmental and Social Policy? Or will the predicted erosion of standards, like the economic benefits, be a longer-term effect of the SMP?

Was the early success of the SMP the result of economic liberalization, or the by-product of the economic boom of the 1980s? Scholars such as Tsoukalis explain the success of the SMP as the result of a 'virtuous circle' of economic and political events. In other words, the elimination of NTBs led to more competition, which in turn reduced costs and increased profits for producers, thereby lowering prices for consumers. Tsoukalis also argues that the liberalization of the banking sector resulting from the SMP increased investment by and into firms across Europe, creating more aggregate demand, and thereby strengthening the economy. However, can the economic expansion of the 1980s be attributed to the beneficial effects of the SMP? Or was the economic situation in Europe the result of global economic factors, and the success of the SMP a by-product of the economic prosperity of the period?

Student-to-student tip

As the study of the SMP is based on cause and effect, it is crucial to be clear on the chronology of events. The Commission website provides a fairly comprehensive and up-to-date timeline at *http://europa.eu.int/abc/history*. In addition, the Internal Market DG keeps a running implementation scoreboard, and produces several press releases per month about infringement proceedings against member states. As such, it provides up-to-the-minute information about how the internal market is developing. Visit the website to sign up to receive these press releases by email every time they are published, or use their free, searchable database of recent press releases.

Summary

• The SMP was a Commission initiative, based on a ruling by the ECJ that established the principle of mutual recognition. Mutual recognition solved several of the problems that had stalled the integration process in the 1970s, such as the need for harmonization of all technical standards. The deregulatory nature of both mutual recognition and the SMP made it acceptable to both pro- and anti-integrationist member states.

• In order to implement the SMP, the Commission required several new institutional tools, including QMV, the co-operation process and Article 95; these tools were incorporated in the Treaty through the SEA in 1986.

• The SMP has successfully removed the majority of the barriers to trade outlined in the 1985 White Paper; this success has generated pressure for further integration, into fields such as EMU and Social Policy. In effect, the negative integration that characterized the SMP has created a need for positive integration, in order to complete the internal market. However, positive integration requires the member states to delegate more competences and therefore relinquish more sovereignty to the EU level, which has been resisted by several national governments.

Selected bibliography

History and analysis

Tsoukalis, L. (1997) *The New European Economy Revisited*, 3rd edn, Oxford: Oxford University Press, chapters 3–5: 33–108.
  Providing both political and economic analysis, Tsoukalis offers an excellent narrative on the evolution of the SMP.
Dinan, D. (1999) *Ever Closer Union*, 2nd edn, London: Macmillan, chapters 4–7: 103–204.
  Dinan concentrates on providing a detailed historical analysis of the SMP.
Wallace, H. and A. Young (2000) 'The Single Market: A New Approach to Policy', in H. Wallace and W. Wallace (eds), *Policy-Making in the European Union*, 4th edn, Oxford: Oxford University Press, chapter 4: 85–114.
  This chapter offers a succinct and broad introduction to the SMP, from a political economy point of view.
Smith, M. (2001) 'In Pursuit of Selective Liberalisation: Single Market Competition and its Limits', *Journal of European Public Policy*, vol. 8, no. 4: 519–40.
  Smith emphasizes the role of private companies in the way governments form preferences in relation to liberalization of different markets. The article thereby explains why some sectors of the economy have been more liberalized than others, and plays down the role of the Commission and the ECJ in the development of the SMP.

Political theory

Moravcsik, A. (1999) *The Choice for Europe: Social Purpose and State Power from Messina to Maastricht*, London: University College, London, chapter 5: 314–78.
  In this volume, Moravcsik outlines a very convincing intergovernmentalist explanation for the creation of the SMP and the signing of the SEA.
Fligstein, N. and I. Mara-Drita (1996) 'How to Make a Market: Reflections on the Attempts to Create a Single Market in the EU', *American Journal of Sociology*, no. 1: 1–33.
  This article is unusual, as it provides a step-by-step account of the political developments that led to the SMP, using a sociological approach. The authors present an explanation of the process that combines elements of both neo-functionalism and intergovernmentalism.

Supportive websites

http://www.europa.eu.int/pol/singl/index_en.htm   Internal Market DG website (for current developments) in the SMP, as well as the Internal Market Dialogue with Citizens. The Commission offers an overview of the EU's internal market, including the SMP Scoreboard.

http://www.europarl.eu.int/factsheets/default_en.htm   *EP Fact Sheets* provide a critical assessment of Commission progress on implementing the SMP.

www.bis.org   The Basle Committee provides the annual report on the SMP.

http://www.europa.eu.int/business/en/index.html   Dialogue with Business provides data, information and advice for business from many sources.

13

Economic and Monetary Union

Jorge Juan Fernández García

Full monetary union will directly affect the daily activities of EU consumers, as well as the traditional functions of the nation-states. While citizens must learn to use euros instead of pesetas or Deutschmarks, central governments must learn to continue to manage their economies while losing some of their traditional powers (such as the establishment of the exchange rate and management of monetary policy). As a result of its wide-ranging economic and social implications, economic and monetary union (EMU) creates pressures for further integration.

The facts

A International monetary arrangements

Consumers and investors buy other countries' currencies in order to purchase the goods and services of these countries. This simple fact has significant implications in the international arena. In the interdependent EU economies, large fluctuations in the exchange rate (ER, the domestic price of a unit of foreign currency) create instability for the countries involved. That is why countries attempt to resolve this problem collectively, rather than individually, by organizing multilateral monetary arrangements. There are two theoretical types of monetary arrangements, although in practice most arrangements lie between these two extremes.

I   Fixed exchange rates

Under such arrangements, national governments intervene in foreign exchange markets to maintain the convertibility of their currency at a constant ER. Maintaining a fixed ER is not easy, as supply and demand of currencies in foreign exchange markets fluctuate due to changing market demand and supply for that currency. Governments counteract these fluctuations by holding reserves of foreign currencies, which they then use to buy or sell their own currency on the market in order to defend the fixed parity. However, due to the large volume of money available to speculators in the foreign exchange market, it is not always possible for governments to keep ERs at their preferred level.

2   Floating exchange rates

Under such arrangements, national governments do not intervene in foreign exchange markets, and the ER is allowed to reach its market equilibrium level freely. The advantages of this monetary arrangement include the following:

- It allows for a greater degree of freedom in the use of economic policies, as a floating ER arrangement resolves any balance-of-payments problems (difficulties caused by the difference between the value of exports and imports in any one economy). In other words, a country with a floating ER does not need to use monetary or fiscal policies to fight against external disequilibria in the balance of payments, but instead can use those instruments to correct internal equilibrium problems, such as inflation or unemployment.
- It does not require a country to keep international reserves for market intervention.

However, it also presents some disadvantages:

- There is no anchor currency, so it does not ensure ER stability.
- There is a risk of *competitive devaluations* or *beggar-thy-neighbour policies* (ER devaluations by one country in order to gain competitiveness, which leaves its trading partners worse off).

B   The history of European monetary arrangements

I   The Bretton Woods System

The Bretton Woods Conference (July 1944) created the post-war international economic order, by establishing the Bretton Woods System (BWS). The purpose of the BWS was to construct an international monetary system, based on international financial institutions, in order to overcome the economic difficulties following World War II. The BWS had two main characteristics:

- a fixed exchange rate, with all currencies anchored to the US dollar;
- US dollar parity with gold (1 ounce of gold = $US 35.00), with unrestricted convertibility – US dollars could be converted into gold at any time, and vice versa.

In order to maintain parity with the dollar, central banks across the world kept reserves of US dollars, which they used to intervene in foreign exchange markets. The BWS allowed currencies to fluctuate around the dollar only in bands of ± 1 per cent. In addition, parity with the dollar could be changed only to correct 'fundamental disequilibria' in the balance of payments between countries (this was the case when the UK devalued the pound in 1949 and 1967).

While the BWS initially worked fairly well, strong economic growth in the 1960s and the US increase in defence spending due to the Vietnam War created the need for more money in the system. The USA satisfied this demand by printing more US dollars. However, this created a problem: whilst the amount of dollars in circulation increased, the quantity of gold held by the US government did not. As a consequence, other governments began to lose confidence in the convertibility of US dollars into gold. This forced US President Nixon to declare in August 1971 that the dollar was no longer convertible into gold. This announcement resulted in the *de facto* end of the BWS.

2   The Snake

Following the collapse of Bretton Woods, the EEC countries and the UK, Ireland, Denmark and Norway agreed in March 1972 to maintain stable ERs with each other, by preventing ER fluctuations of more than ± 2.25 per cent with respect to the value of the US dollar. This arrangement was called the 'European Snake in the Tunnel'. As the US government did not fix the value of the dollar, this meant that the Community currencies floated as a group within the 2.25 per cent limit, as the dollar itself rose and fell. (Tracked on a graph, this movement was thought to resemble a 'snake in a tunnel', from which the system derived its nickname.)

The Snake was conceived as a temporary arrangement, to be converted into a system of economic and monetary union (EMU) that would incorporate all EC currencies once economic conditions were more favourable. By the end of 1973, continued instability (due in part to the international oil crisis) resulted in the British pound, Irish punt, Danish krøne and Italian lira leaving the system. After this, the remaining currencies stopped pegging their currencies to the US dollar. By 1976, the Snake consisted of only Germany, Denmark and the Benelux countries. As Germany was the participant country with the largest economy, it essentially set the monetary policy for the Snake's participants, turning the Snake into a Deutschmark zone, asymmetrically favouring the German economy.

3   The European Monetary System

The large fluctuations in currency values in the 1970s, compounded by the US policy of 'benign neglect' of the dollar's value (not changing the fixed parity of the dollar with gold) and the reluctance of the USA to construct a new international system, emphasized the need for a new monetary arrangement. A Franco-German initiative led to the launch of the European Monetary System (EMS) in March 1979. The EMS had three main features:

- The *European Currency Unit (ECU)*, as the unit of account for transactions between EC governments. The ECU was a 'basket' of national currencies, each currency's weight within the basket fixed as a percentage determined by the country's gross national product (GNP) and share of inter-EC trade.
- The *European Monetary Co-operation Fund (EMCF)*, comprised of 20 per cent of each member state's foreign exchange reserves, available for short-term concerted central bank interventions in foreign exchange markets.
- The *exchange rate mechanism (ERM)*, devised as a means of minimizing currency fluctuations. Each participating currency had a central ER against the ECU; this allowed for a system of bilateral central rates between EC currencies to be calculated. Each currency was initially allowed to fluctuate by an agreed margin ($\pm$ 2.25 per cent) around these bilateral central rates. If a currency approached its top or bottom limit against another currency, a 'divergence indicator' was triggered, and the national central banks of both countries were then obliged to intervene on exchange markets to defend the fixed parity. Realignments (changes in the fixed ER against the ECU) were allowed, but only if agreed unanimously by all participating member states.

De Grauwe divides the operation of the EMS into four distinct economic periods:

- The first period lasted from March 1979 to March 1983, and was characterized by frequent realignments (twelve in total) of the member currencies. These were caused largely by diverging economic policies in the different member states (e.g. Keynesian expansion in France, monetarist consolidation in West Germany).
- The second period, lasting from 1983 to 1987, was one of consolidation. After France abandoned its Keynesian policy in 1983, the fiscal and monetary policies within the EC converged, resulting in convergent inflation rates. Consequently, there were few ER realignments during this period.
- The third period, lasting from 1987 to 1992, entailed no realignments, and extended ERM membership to other countries. The lack of realignments may have indicated that the EMS had become too rigid. Two important events occurred in this period, which had an impact on the next period: the liberalization of capital movements (1 July 1990) and the reunification of Germany (3 October 1990).
- The fourth period ended with the currency crisis and collapse of the EMS. Market actors began questioning the sustainability of a restrictive German monetary policy during a recession in the other EMS member states. The result was currency speculation against the existing bilateral rates in September 1992. The EMS members were forced to make a series of realignments; the pound sterling and the lira withdrew from the ERM, and in September 1993, the $\pm$ 2.25 per cent bands of fluctuation were widened to $\pm$ 15 per cent.

In general, the EMS was fairly successful in minimizing currency fluctuations, partly due to a new agreement on monetary policy: inflation control. The existence of foreign exchange controls also prevented massive currency speculation by blocking large capital flows (until July 1990). Importantly, the international economic outlook was relatively strong in this period, leading to a firm political commitment to the EMS. In addition, the EMS system itself was flexible, and able to adapt to various economic situations.

However, in the period preceding 1992, all these factors changed. The liberalization of capital movements in July 1990 allowed for large-scale speculative capital movements. In addition, the EMS had developed the N−1 problem: although it had been designed to be symmetrical, only the country with the largest economy (Germany) could set its monetary policy independently. All other participants were forced to adjust their policies to German monetary policy. In a recession, this meant that countries had to either devalue their currency or leave the system.

The asymmetry in the system strained the balance between conflicting monetary policy aims in Europe. With reunification, Germany began a massive public expenditure programme in the impoverished East; since the government chose not to raise taxes, the fear of inflation led the Bundesbank (a highly risk-averse body) to raise interest rates. However, an interest rate hike was the exact opposite of what the other European economies needed at the time, as they were experiencing a recession and needed low interest rates to stimulate demand and investment in their economies. The combination of these factors led to the crisis and collapse of the EMS in 1992–3.

C   Economic and monetary union

I   The history of EMU

Article 2 of the Treaties of Rome (1957) recognized the importance of macroeconomic (and especially monetary) policies as a way of 'ensur[ing] the proper functioning of the common market'. However, the Community initially did not develop competence in this field, partly because EC governments were involved in interventionist domestic politics. As Keynesians, they were committed to retaining monetary and fiscal independence for domestic stabilization purposes. However, the main reason for the lack of progress toward EMU at this time was that the EC members were already participating in the Bretton Woods System.

Increased monetary instability in the 1970s led to talks regarding regional cooperation. The six members of the EEC realized that they were unable to insulate themselves from ER fluctuations. Consequently, at the Hague Summit in December 1969, they decided to pursue further integration by committing themselves to EMU. This was followed by the Werner Report in October 1970, which proposed that monetary union should be accomplished in three stages over ten years. However, the economic downturn of the 1970s, caused by the oil crisis, resulted in very little being achieved. The idea of European monetary co-operation was only re-launched in 1979, with the establishment of the EMS.

EMU was also mentioned in the Preamble to the Single European Act (SEA) in 1986, but the SEA did not outline how this could be achieved. However, the Hanover European Council in June 1988 agreed to set up a 'Committee for the Study of Economic and Monetary Union', composed of central bank governors from the twelve member states and four independent prestigious economists, under the chairmanship of the then Commission President Jacques Delors, in order to prepare another report on EMU.

The Delors Report was submitted on 12 April 1989 and (like the Werner Report) proposed a three-stage blueprint for EMU. Acting on Delors' proposals, the June 1990 Dublin European Council decided to convene an intergovernmental conference (IGC) to discuss the necessary Treaty reforms. This resulted in the 1992 Treaty on European Union (TEU, also known as Maastricht), whose centrepiece was the adoption of a common currency, a fixed ER, and the establishment of the European Central Bank (ECB).

2   The rationale behind EMU

EMU is a qualitatively different type of monetary arrangement in comparison with previous attempts. Until EMU, the Community suffered from the problems associated with Padoa-Schioppa's 'inconsistent quartet'. Padoa-Schioppa argues that in a world of free trade and increasingly mobile capital, governments must make a choice between a fixed ER and an autonomous monetary policy. European countries have generally chosen an autonomous monetary policy, in an attempt both to safeguard their external trade and to allow for competitive devaluations in case of balance-of-payments problems. By contrast, EMU attempts to rectify the 'inconsistent quartet' by eliminating the problems associated with ERs – in other words, by pooling monetary policy. It also institutionalizes a set of macroeconomic policy goals: namely, the anti-inflationary objectives in the common monetary policy implemented by the ECB. Therefore, EMU represents a more advanced form of economic integration.

However, agreement on EMU would have been impossible without a supportive political environment. Several factors contributed to the Community's decision to proceed with EMU.

- An economic neo-liberal (monetarist) policy consensus between the EU governments agreed that monetary policy should be used only to keep inflation rates low, not to control unemployment. This neo-liberal consensus marked a clear break with Keynesianism, as well as with the divergent economic policy paths and diverse priorities of the European states during the Bretton Woods and Snake eras.
- The relative success of the EMS (at a time when negotiations for the TEU were under way) encouraged participant governments to develop the monetary system.

- The dominance of the dollar in the Bretton Woods System and the Deutschmark in the EMS made all other currencies in the system vulnerable to fluctuations in the value of the anchor currency. During EMS, for example, the central banks of most states spent a great deal of their foreign currency reserves trying to maintain the parity of their currency with the Deutschmark. This dependency worsened with the expansion of intra-EC trade (approximately 60 per cent of total EC trade at that time). Therefore, Community members were interested in ways of making monetary arrangements more symmetrical.

3   Three-stage launch of EMU

- The first stage lasted from 1 July 1990 to 31 December 1993, and was marked by the removal of exchange controls (meaning that all capital movements were liberalized) in eight of the twelve member states on 1 July 1990. The remaining EMU member states liberalized capital movements in stages, ending with Greece's liberalization of capital in 1994.
- The second stage lasted from 1 January 1994 to 31 December 1998. In this period, the European Monetary Institute (EMI) was created, to help prepare the launch of the body responsible for European monetary policy (the ECB), and all national central banks were made independent (if they had not previously been so).
- The third stage could have started in January 1997, according to the provisions in Maastricht, had a majority of states been ready. However, the Madrid European Council (December 1995) decided to delay the third stage until 1 January 1999. This stage was marked by the introduction of the euro (€) as legal tender, by fixing participating currencies' bilateral ER in May 1998, and introducing the physical currency – the euro – in January 2002. The ECB began work in June 1998, but only assumed responsibility for maintaining price stability (defined as controlling an annual rise in the Harmonized Indices of Consumer Prices (HICP) to below 2 per cent) in January 1999.

Participation in the third stage of EMU was decided after evaluating the economic performance of the member states. This was measured using the convergence criteria established by the TEU in the areas of inflation, public finances, interest rates and exchange rates. On the basis of financial figures from 1997, the Council announced in May 1998 that eleven countries had qualified to take part in the third stage of EMU. Three countries (Denmark, Sweden and the UK) did not wish to proceed: the UK and Denmark had negotiated an opt-out clause from EMU in the TEU, while Sweden had deliberately decided not to make its central bank independent, and hence had not complied with the convergence criteria. Greece did not initially qualify to take part in the third stage of EMU, but it did join in January 2001. Currently, the only EU countries not participating in EMU are Sweden, Denmark and the UK. In a national referendum on 28 September 2000, Denmark voted not to join the euro-zone. On 28 February 2002, the euro became the sole currency within the twelve participating member states, as the period of dual circulation came to an end. The smooth transition to the new single currency has been considered a success by most of the parties involved.

4   The EU's economic governance

The governance of EMU is controlled by three main institutions: the ECOFIN, the ECB and the Euro-X. At present, the functions of these institutions appear to overlap, and responsibilities are not clearly divided between them:

- *ECOFIN* is composed of the fifteen Ministers of Finance from the EU's member states. The Maastricht Treaty allows ECOFIN to determine when intervention in foreign exchange markets is necessary and to decide on external ER relations. Although ECOFIN can set broad guidelines for fiscal policy, it has no control over fiscal policy itself. It also has the power to determine whether a country has violated the Growth and Stability Pact (GSP, discussed below).
- The *Euro-X* is a 'club' of Finance Ministers from nations participating in EMU. The 'X' stands for the indeterminate number of countries that are members of EMU at any one time. Euro-X has no official powers, but instead serves as a discussion forum. Some states, such as France, have expressed an interest in seeing Euro-X become the 'economic government of the euro'. Others (notably the UK) have expressed concern that Euro-X may undermine ECO-FIN's fiscal co-ordination functions. (The UK is a member of ECOFIN, but not the Euro-12.)
- The *ECB* is the EU's independent central bank. It decides on the monetary policy of the euro-zone, by determining the interest rates for the euro-area economy.

The problems/issues

A   Europe as an optimal currency area

Mundell's economic theory (a cost–benefit analysis) dealing with monetary unions is usually referred to as optimum currency areas (OCA) theory. A group of countries form an OCA if and when the benefits of having a common currency outweigh the costs of abolishing their ER. The determining factor in this cost–benefit analysis is the ability of the currency area to respond to *asymmetric shocks* (demand or supply shocks that affect only a particular region of the currency area). In an OCA, the benefits of a common currency are mainly microeconomic (i.e. positive for individuals and firms), while the costs are primarily macroeconomic (i.e. negative for governments, who must manage the economy). A description of the benefits and costs involved is given below:

I Benefits

- *Reduction of transaction costs.* The benefit resulting from the elimination of the costs of exchanging one currency into another is estimated to be very small (up to 0.5 per cent of EU GDP, according to the EU Commission). However, gains of this sort can be considerable for individual firms or citizens. For example, by removing the cost of exchanging currencies, firms involved in inter-state trade no longer pay ER commissions or need to insure themselves against currency fluctuations. For individuals, a holiday trip in 1992 (travelling through ten EU countries, and on the basis of existing average commissions) would cost nearly 50 per cent more, due to commissions based on the original sum, than travelling in a single currency area.
- *Increased price transparency.* The segmentation of national markets creates price discrimination. A common currency increases price transparency, as prices can be more easily compared across borders.
- *Reduction of ER variability and uncertainty.* ER fluctuations introduce uncertainty about future revenues. Therefore, participation in a monetary union lowers risk premiums on investment by eliminating ER risk as a non-tariff barrier (NTB) to trade (see *The Single Market*). In addition, firms no longer need to insure themselves against currency fluctuations. ER stability increases the certainty of prices and revenues, which improves the efficiency of production, investment and consumption decisions, and therefore increases collective welfare.
- *Reduction of efficiency losses due to lack of co-ordination in monetary policies.* EMU facilitates the process of monetary policy convergence, since countries can no longer pursue different counterproductive monetary policies.
- *Reduction of inflationary bias.* In inflation-prone countries such as Greece and Spain, EMU helps member states reduce inflation through an affiliation with credible inflation-fighting institutions, such as the German Bundesbank.
- *Greater use of the euro as a major currency reserve.* The main reserve currency in the world is currently the US dollar, equalling approximately 60 per cent of the central banks' reserves across the world. The use of the euro as a reserve currency might increase the prestige and political power of the EU, especially in terms of a common monetary policy *vis-à-vis* the rest of the world.

2 Costs

- *The loss of IR and ER as a mechanism to absorb asymmetric shocks.* Without an independent monetary policy (now in the hands of the ECB), each member state becomes more vulnerable to asymmetric shocks to its economy. Membership in the EMU means that national governments cannot devalue their currencies to increase competitiveness during recessions nor use interest rates to affect investment.
- *The ECB's 'one-fits-all' monetary policy.* The ECB is able to provide only one interest rate for the entire euro-zone. Therefore, it does not respond to specific national conditions.

B   Dealing with asymmetric shocks

Economic studies demonstrate that the conditions which define an OCA are not met by the EU member states. Therefore, the EU could suffer an asymmetric shock to the economy. Unfortunately, the two tools in a monetary union that could absorb asymmetric shock – namely, labour mobility and wage flexibility – are both very low in the EU.

- *Labour mobility.* Only 1–3 per cent of the EU working population of each member state is comprised of foreign residents. In the USA, approximately 17 per cent of the population moves every year.
- *Wage flexibility.* Labour markets in the euro-zone are highly regulated, which reduces wage flexibility.

Other solutions to the problem of asymmetric shock include the following:

- *Increasing the size of the EU budget* might help deal with asymmetric shocks, as the budget could provide a stabilization function (see *The EU Budget*). The Commission's MacDougall Report (1977) argued that a budget of 7.5 per cent of the EC-9's GDP was required in order for the budget to be able to perform a stabilization role in the economy. However, the current EU budget equals only 1.27 per cent of the EU-15's GDP.
- *National governments' transferral of tax payments* could help depressed or declining regions. However, this would require an increase in taxes (which is not popular), a change in budgetary programmes (which is not legal), or a budgetary deficit (which is not sustainable in the long run and is limited to 3 per cent of GDP under the Growth and Stability Pact).
- This leaves *unemployment* as the last available mechanism for absorbing economic shocks. If none of the previous shock absorbers work, then asymmetric shocks will translate into different rates of unemployment in the EU.

However, critics argue that concern about asymmetric shocks may be unnecessary, for two reasons. First, although increased risk could raise costs, EMU would still make sense if the benefits outweigh those costs. Secondly, some academics argue that an OCA may not be crucial, as other countries (such as Italy or the USA) that were not OCAs have none the less formed successful monetary unions.

C   Fiscal harmonization and/or co-ordination in EMU

The Single Internal Market (SIM) does not have a united fiscal system. Instead, each country has a different taxation structure, reflecting differences in national institutional structures and national preferences. The existence of different fiscal systems can pose problems, since countries are sometimes tempted to compete with each other by lowering taxes (e.g. Ireland in 1991) or undercutting wages (e.g. the Netherlands against Germany in the 1970s and 1980s), in order to attract investment. Such competition may escalate to a point where it harms the rest of the EU, and undermines the SIM. This problem could be avoided by harmonizing national tax systems.

D Tax harmonization

Arguments in favour of tax harmonization include the following:

- *Increasing allocative efficiency.* Within the internal market, different tax structures act as non-tariff barriers (NTBs) to the free movement of goods, services, capital and labour. It is economically inefficient to have firms and individuals devoting resources to tax arbitrage, tax avoidance and aggressive tax planning. Tax harmonization would therefore allow economic agents (consumers, investors, firms) to allocate their resources more efficiently.
- *Reducing tax competition.* Harmful tax competition between member states may generate a 'race to the bottom' that would erode member states' tax base and tax revenues and result in decreased public expenditure and increased public deficits. This would be particularly problematic for member states that already have large welfare states (Nordic countries) or high public deficits (Italy or Belgium). Harmonizing taxes would therefore limit the scope of intra-EC tax competition.

However, tax harmonization faces several obstacles, including:

- *Concerns about national sovereignty.* Taxation is a fundamental part of states' governing competence, and is closely linked to national sovereignty. Any EU tax harmonization could threaten member states' sovereignty.
- *Taxation's different purposes.* Independent tax policy is necessary if member states wish to maintain their own social and capitalist models. Harmonizing taxes reduces member states' autonomy, and may limit the discretion they have to support the type of society they prefer.
- *Capital flight.* If the EU harmonizes taxes, capital and corporate investments could relocate to non-EU countries, which have more competitive tax structures.
- *Reduction of member states' flexibility.* EMU means that member states have relinquished independent monetary policy. Therefore, they have fewer instruments available for dealing with asymmetric shocks and conducting stabilization policies. If taxes are harmonized as well, the ability of national governments to provide these economic functions will be further restricted.

E   Tax co-ordination

Given that tax harmonization is such a sensitive subject, a less drastic option would be to co-ordinate tax systems between member states. This might be sufficient to prevent tax competition in the EMU. The situation in the USA (where different states have different tax rates) demonstrates that a single currency does not necessarily require uniform tax rates. The fact that decisions on fiscal co-ordination are still taken under unanimity in the Council indicates how politically sensitive even a partial co-ordination of taxation policy remains for the member states. However, fiscal co-ordination may become essential, as some mechanism must be established in order to prevent tax competition.

F   Economic discipline

In order to ensure that EMU is successful, member states have agreed to abide by certain economic rules. These rules are the convergence criteria and the Growth and Stability Pact (GSP).

I   *The convergence criteria*

These are requirements established in the TEU, setting out the conditions that member states must fulfil in order to participate in the third stage of EMU. The objective of the convergence criteria was twofold. Economically, they were designed to ensure the convergence of participating economies, the adoption of a single currency therefore being the realization of full economic convergence. Politically, they reflect German preferences for very strict criteria, in order to restrict participation in EMU. The convergence criteria are:

- *Price stability*. Participating countries cannot have an inflation rate that is more than 1.5 per cent higher than the average of the three lowest-inflation countries.
- *Interest rates*. Long-term interest rates (twelve-month government bonds) must not be more than 2 per cent higher than those of the three lowest-inflation countries.
- *Exchange rates*. Participating countries must not have experienced an EMS devaluation in the two years prior to entering monetary union, and fluctuations should be within the normal bands of the ERM.
- *Public finance*. Government budget deficits must not be higher than 3 per cent of that country's GDP, and the accumulated public debt should not be more than 60 per cent of its total GDP.

The convergence criteria have been criticized for two reasons. First, it is generally argued that they do not ensure the real convergence of participating economies, but merely reflect a nominal convergence. Secondly, de Grauwe maintains that the criteria have not been selected on the basis of economic fundamentals, and that at best they provide only a very rough indication of economic stability.

The political situation during the establishment of the convergence criteria largely explains their economic shortcomings. They reflected German preferences, which were intentionally strict. It has been argued that Germany wanted to restrict the initial number of participating countries, in order to ensure the success of EMU, rather than to ensure the economic convergence of participating countries. Yet the convergence criteria acted as a very important reference point for the macroeconomic policy of member states, which worked hard to satisfy the requirements for membership. By 1999, however, only four states actually fulfilled all aspects of the convergence criteria (Luxembourg, Finland, France and the non-participating UK). In order to allow member states to proceed to the third stage of EMU, the convergence criteria were therefore interpreted rather loosely. In addition to some creative accounting methods, flexibility was also allowed on the public debt criterion (which was interpreted as requiring candidates to be 'moving in the direction of', rather than actually achieving, 60 per cent of national GDP).

2   The Growth and Stability Pact (GSP)

Once a member state enters the third stage of EMU, it must abide by the conditions established in the GSP. Adopted by the Amsterdam European Council in July 1997, the GSP aims at ensuring that the member states continue their efforts at budgetary discipline once the single currency has been introduced. The main condition of the GSP is that government budgetary deficits should not exceed 3 per cent per year.

Exceptions to this rule are allowed only during recessions or other significant events. If governments exceed this limit, then they can be fined, with ECOFIN deciding whether fines should be imposed. Therefore, the GSP is an attempt to ensure sound economic governance by the member states participating in EMU. This means that member states with a history of weak fiscal control will be prevented from returning to a more expansive fiscal policy once inside EMU, as this would generate problems for the rest of the participants. However, member states are likely to pursue a more expansive fiscal policy only during a recession. In such a scenario, the fines imposed by ECOFIN would worsen the situation for the member state, and create greater problems for the euro-zone as a whole. In early 2002, the Commission threatened sanctions against Portugal if it remained in breach of the GSP. Germany and France received formal warnings as well, since their deficits were exceeding the 3 per cent of GDP threshold outlined in the GSP.

G   The politics of EMU

It remains unclear whether EMU makes sense for the EU from an economic point of view (i.e. if the benefits outweigh the costs). Politically, however, EMU was able to achieve many of the priorities of the main actors involved in the process at that time. Outlined below are the positions of these actors, and the rationale behind their decision to proceed with EMU.

- *Germany* perceived a need to reaffirm the country's commitment to European integration in the wake of German unification. The German decision to proceed with EMU was therefore primarily political. In fact, joining EMU had a negative effect on Germany in economic terms, since it forced Germany to forego its dominance in the EMS and associate itself more closely with countries with weaker financial credibility. As compensation, Germany was able to secure a number of key concessions, including the location of the ECB in Frankfurt, the institutional design of the ECB (modelled on the Bundesbank), and the choice of the convergence criteria, which were aimed against countries with histories of fiscal laxity.
- *France* was one of the main forces behind EMU, for three reasons. First, it was dissatisfied with the asymmetrical nature of the EMS, and therefore wanted a more equitable monetary arrangement. Secondly, EMU allowed France a formal role in the formulation of European monetary policy. Thirdly, EMU was intended to ensure that a powerful, reunited Germany could still be controlled through its participation in the EU. France also managed to win several concessions in the construction of EMU, including a definite timetable, the creation of the Euro-X Committee, and the imposition of a supervisory board for the ECB, which includes representatives of the member states (i.e. the heads of the national central banks).
- *The United Kingdom* was opposed to EMU, fearing that EMU would lead to further integration. It acquiesced to EMU only after securing an opt-out clause in the TEU.
- *Other EU states* agreed to EMU either for ideological reasons (i.e. they were interested in furthering the European project) or, in the case of the Cohesion countries, because EMU was linked with additional regional aid, in the form of the Cohesion Fund.
- *The Commission* also played an important role in the build-up to EMU, partly because it viewed EMU as a logical continuation of the Single Market Programme (SMP) and as a means of furthering European integration, which would also increase its own powers.

Who wins/who loses

Among the member states, **France** is generally considered a winner, as it has regained some decision-making power over monetary policy. Other smaller member states with open economies, such as Belgium and the Netherlands, have also gained through receiving a voice in monetary policy and by the further integration that EMU represents. By contrast, **Germany** is often considered to be a net loser, as it has given up the monetary dominance it enjoyed in the EMS. However, German participation in EMU won international support for German reunification, and Germany has been given substantial power in determining many of the convergence criteria and the structure of the ECB.

The fact that the **United Kingdom** has not adopted the single currency does not mean that it is immune to the effects of EMU. The effect of the euro-zone on firms located in the UK has been pronounced, and the strength of the UK pound has harmed some UK industries, especially those which trade within the EU, as they assume costs in pounds (which are high) and receive revenues in foreign currencies (which are low). In addition, the UK's lack of participation in the euro-zone has arguably resulted in some loss of influence within the EU.

Mediterranean EU countries have largely profited from EMU. By joining at the same time as states with a good record of fiscal discipline, they have gained some of their monetary credibility (i.e. from the Bundesbank). These member states, along with Ireland, have also gained funds from the Cohesion Fund. However, the loss of the ER as a tool may expose the weaker areas of their economies to increased competition (as there is no possibility for competitive devaluations – see *Regional Policy*).

As regards the **EU institutions**, despite the fact that it has gained few formal powers, the Commission is seen as a winner in EMU, as EMU supports the integration process. The two other supranational institutions may be considered losers, since the EP does not have the power to hold the ECB to account, and new competences assumed by the Union do not fall within the jurisdiction of the ECJ.

As for the **rest of the world**, if the euro is successful in partially replacing the US dollar as the reserve currency held by most central banks, this might strengthen the EU's position, especially on monetary and commercial issues.

As consumers, **EU citizens** are winners, since the fixing of ERs will increase price transparency and competition, and could eventually lead to a reduction in prices. As workers, they may be losers, since the EU appears unable to deal with asymmetric shocks, which could result in higher unemployment. EMU will also affect wage bargaining, since large national trade unions, which often determine wage levels, will become medium-sized EU-level trade unions, and will therefore lose influence.

EU businesses are winners, because EMU equals bigger markets, ER stability, lower transaction costs and larger capital markets. However, increased competition will pose extra difficulties for inefficient businesses.

Food for thought

Can EMU be maintained effectively? EMU faces two main problems: namely, asymmetric shocks and the ECB's 'one-fits-all' monetary policy. Not only do the instruments currently available within EMU not provide any means of minimizing the effects of asymmetric shocks, but monetary policy is normally tailored to the economic needs of a specific economy. Since the ECB must decide on a monetary policy that meets the needs of the entire euro-zone, there is a danger that certain regions or even countries may be forced into an inappropriate monetary policy. This also creates political pressures on the ECB. With neither a large budget nor labour market flexibility to provide a shock absorber for the economy, EMU could create economically depressed regions within the EU.

Is EMU the next step toward a federalized Europe? The incomplete state of the SIM created pressures to proceed with EMU. EMU, in turn, has increased pressures for further economic integration, including possibly tax co-ordination or harmonization and/or a bigger EU budget. The political implications of the adoption of a single currency, and the pressures that this will create for further integration, may indicate that the EU is evolving into a type of federal state. Such a development has implications for the national sovereignty of the member states, but also gives rise to other issues. Countries not participating in EMU fear that member states in the euro-zone may form closer links amongst themselves, and begin excluding those who have opted out of EMU from new policy developments (see *Flexible Integration*).

Student-to-student tip

The literature available on EMU is vast. We recommend that you begin your analysis of the subject with de Grauwe, who provides a strong yet simplified economic explanation of the subject. Econometric studies of EMU should be approached only once the basics of both the economic and the political arguments are understood; otherwise, the subject can appear much more opaque than it actually is. It is also important to remember that there are two sides to the EMU debate: those in favour and those against. Most academics align themselves with one of these positions, which means that their analysis will also be biased in this direction. Therefore, it is crucial to understand the perspective from both sides of the debate (by, for example, visiting anti-euro websites), before performing your own analysis.

Summary

- Since World War II, the Community has experienced four monetary arrangements, all of them fixed ER regimes with varying degrees of flexibility: the Bretton Woods System, the Snake in the Tunnel, the EMS and EMU.
- The Treaties of Rome did not provide for the establishment of a regional currency. After the collapse of Bretton Woods, the Community made two attempts to achieve full monetary union: first with the Snake and secondly with the EMS. EMU was finally realized in the 1992 Maastricht Treaty. The result has been the creation of a new common currency.
- Twelve of the EU countries share a single currency (the euro) and a single central bank (ECB), responsible for maintaining price stability for the whole euro-zone. The number of countries participating may change with enlargement or shifts in the preferences of the non-participating countries.

- OCA theory is the economic theory used to assess whether or not it makes sense for a country to join a monetary union. It argues that the cost of joining the EMU is the loss of an independent ER, a policy tool useful for dealing with asymmetric shocks. However, the loss of an exchange rate could be overcome if the participating countries have high labour mobility and/or wage flexibility. According to the economic analysis, the EU does not currently form an OCA.
- EMU also has important political implications. It creates pressures for further integration in areas such as tax co-ordination and harmonization, and moves the EU closer to a conventional state-like structure.

Selected bibliography

General guide to EMU

Grauwe, P. de (2000) *Economics of Monetary Union*, 4th edn, Oxford: Oxford University Press.
  This book is the ideal starting point for students new to EMU. Those without an economics background should read the first four chapters; others can skip to the last six, especially to chapters 5 and 6: 97–149.

Overviews

Tsoukalis, L. (1997) *The New European Economy Revisited*, 3rd edn, Oxford: Oxford University Press, chapters 7–8: 138–83.
  Tsoukalis outlines both the economic and the historical arguments that have led to EMU, and the interests involved in the process.
Hix, S. (1999) *The Political System of the European Union*, London: Macmillan, chapter 10: 278–306.
  Hix explains why EMU was launched when it was, how it achieved its distinct design, and why certain states joined whilst others did not. He also explores the accountability, legitimacy and reputation problems caused by EMU.
Wildasin, D. E. (2002) 'Fiscal Policy in the Post-EMU Europe', *European Union Politics*, vol. 3, no. 2: 251–60.
  This article discusses the democratic deficit problem as it relates to the EMU. This includes the limitation on the possibility of governments to reflect the policy preferences expressed by the electorate in the area of fiscal policy after the introduction of EMU.

Economic analysis of EMU

McNamara, K. R. (1998) *The Currency of Ideas: Monetary Politics in the European Union*, Ithaca, NY: Cornell University Press.
  McNamara provides a solid explanation of the ideas behind the euro and the previous fixed rate systems.
Eichengreen, B. (1997) *European Monetary Unification: Theory, Practice and Analysis*, Cambridge, MA: MIT Press.
  This is an excellent compilation of essays by Eichengreen (from 1989 to 1997), using the US experience as a guide by which to assess the operation of EMU.

Financial Times ECB Watch.
This is the weekly section of the *FT* on policy making in the euro-zone, published on Tuesdays, and has an estimated reading time of two minutes – it is a great way to stay up-to-date on European monetary policy.

Supportive websites

http://europa.eu.int/euro/html/entry.htm   *EURO* is the Commission Internet site dedicated to the single currency, including documents, legislation and links to other websites. This site was archived in June 2002, so for latest developments on the single currency, visit http://europa.eu.int/comm/economy_finance/euro_en.tm.

http://www.ecb.int   The website of the ECB contains statistical documents and other studies and reports, as well as links to the national central banks. The Bank has established a special euro site, http://www.euro.ecb.int.

http://www.oberlin.edu/~dcleeton/emu.htm   This website consolidates several links and other information on the euro, and provides a reading list of economic research on monetary union.

http://www.x-rates.com/   This website allows you to perform a historical comparison between the euro and most major currencies. Click on 'Historic Lookup' and choose your currencies to access a graph for the selected year.

http://www.dbresearch.com   *EMU Watch* from Deutsche Bank Research also offers extremely helpful analysis.

http://www.obce.org   The *Observatory* of the European Central Bank provides news, research papers and working documents from many different actors.

http://www.no-euro.com   The website of this British anti-euro think tank is useful for its more critical approach.

Part V

COMMON POLICIES

14

Common Agricultural Policy

Ricard Ramon í Sumoy

The Common Agricultural Policy (CAP) is the oldest, most integrated and one of the most controversial Community policies. While the EU agricultural sector represents only 1.7 per cent of EU GDP and employs only 5 per cent of the EU population, the CAP still absorbs almost half of the total EU budgetary expenditure, and more than half of all EU regulations deal with agriculture. Why has the CAP remained the largest EU policy, despite the minuscule size of its constituency? This paradox can be explained by analysing the history of the policy and the symbolic relevance that the CAP acquired as a 'cornerstone' policy of the Union, as well as the difficulties that have been encountered in attempting to reform the CAP.

The facts

A   The beginnings of the CAP

The food shortages after World War II made agricultural policy a top priority for European leaders. The goals of this policy included self-sufficiency in food production, a constant food supply, and price stability for consumers. In addition, agriculture employed a significant percentage of the workforce during this period. A policy was required to keep income levels high in agricultural regions, in order to avoid dramatic labour movement from the countryside to the cities. For these reasons, the CAP became one of the first common policies in the EEC, as it was hoped that a unified approach would result in a more rapid alleviation of the food shortage problem.

Today, with agricultural overproduction and only a small percentage of the workforce employed in agriculture, EU intervention in this sector is justified using two types of arguments:

- *Economic arguments.* Intervention redresses market failures resulting from agricultural production, such as environmental destruction, rural underdevelopment (i.e. negative externalities) and information asymmetries with respect to food quality and safety.
- *Political arguments.* Many politicians believe that bio-diversity, high food safety standards, etc., must be promoted. These new arguments are currently developed around the idea of multi-functionality, which refers not only to the regulation of agricultural markets, but also to the management of the countryside.

Intervention in agriculture is also linked to the creation of social and regional cohesion, thereby reinforcing other EU programmes.

B   How the CAP works

I   The main guidelines

The Treaties of Rome (1957) established the CAP as a central policy of the EEC and the first genuinely supranational policy of the Community. Article 33 (ex-Article 39) set out the objectives of the CAP:

- to increase agricultural productivity by promoting modernization;
- to ensure a fair standard of living for the agricultural community;
- to stabilize markets;
- to ensure the availability of supplies (self-sufficiency in agriculture);
- to ensure that supplies reach consumers at reasonable prices.

2   The three basic principles of CAP

The framework of the CAP was established in the Treaties of Rome, but the basic principles, which form the structure of the policy, were outlined afterwards at the Stresa Conference (July 1958), namely:

- *The Single Market.* The CAP ensures the free movement of agricultural products within the Community and the setting of common prices and aids.
- *Community preference.* The CAP must protect the Community's production from low-priced imports, so that the objectives of the policy can be realized.
- *Financial solidarity.* All member states must pay into the CAP.

C The mechanisms of the CAP

The objectives of the CAP are realized through several economic mechanisms, which can be divided into two categories: price support mechanisms and budgetary control mechanisms.

I Price support mechanisms

The CAP attempts to maintain a high standard of living for EU farmers and internal price stability by controlling the prices of agricultural goods. This means that the EU supports a higher price than the world market price for agricultural goods produced in the EU. The primary price mechanisms are:

- *Intervention price*: the minimum price for a product, guaranteed to farmers, should world prices fall significantly below the target price. The intervention price protects EU farmers from the volatility of the world agricultural market.
- *Direct payments*: during the 1990s, the EU gradually decreased intervention prices, to allow these internal prices to reflect world price levels. As a consequence, the EU has begun to compensate farmers for these reductions by introducing direct income payments to farmers.

Through these mechanisms, the CAP encourages EU farmers to produce enough agricultural products to keep the EU self-sufficient and provide the EU with a stable food supply, while still ensuring EU farmers a decent standard of living.

2 Budgetary control

Because of overproduction, the EU must control the amount of money it spends supporting prices. It has therefore implemented several mechanisms to control agricultural production:

- *Quotas*. These are limits on the quantities produced by farmers. EU quotas include limits on the amount of a product (such as milk or olive oil) produced by a single farmer that is eligible for the target price.
- *Maximum guaranteed quantities*. The EU subsidies apply only to a certain amount of production per farmer, and the EU currently limits subsidies on the production of bananas and cereals.
- *Stabilizers*. The EU penalizes farmers for overproduction of certain products, such as olive oil, through the reduction of payments guaranteed by the intervention price.

- *Export subsidies*. If European farmers produce too much, the EU will subsidize the export of surplus products to countries outside the EU by compensating the farmer for the difference between the world price and the EU price. This is much more cost-effective for the EU than storing or destroying surplus agricultural products (as was done in the past).

D   Common Market Organizations (CMOs)

Each type of food product is regulated by a different CMO, which determines price levels, quotas, subsidies, etc. There are more than twenty CMOs in the EU system, covering more than 90 per cent of final agricultural products produced in the Union, and ranging from cereals to milk and poultry.

E   Funding

CAP funding is channelled through the EAGGF (European Agricultural Guidance and Guarantee Fund). This fund consumes the largest part of the Union budget – around 45 per cent of total EU expenditures. However, the CAP is also a source of revenue for the EU through the common external tariff (CET) (see *The EU Budget*). The EAGGF has two sections:

- *Market policy* (price support) is handled by the Guarantee Section (representing around 88 per cent of the EAGGF budget).
- *Structural interventions* (policies on depopulation and unemployment in rural areas) are dealt with by the Guidance Section (12 per cent of the EAGGF budget).

Structural interventions benefit rural development policy, which consists of aid to public authorities in order to address problems related to depopulation and un-employment in rural areas. Rural development policy currently concentrates on the modernization of agricultural structures, the promotion of environmentalism in agriculture, and the creation of new sources of income for rural communities.

The problems/issues

A   Achieving the objectives of the Treaties of Rome

By the 1990s, the EU had achieved many of the objectives of the CAP:

- *Productivity*. Since the CAP was established, the EU's agriculture productivity has sharply increased, and the sector has experienced extensive modernization.

- *Fair standard of living for farmers.* The income gap between agricultural and non-agricultural personal incomes has generally decreased. However, because the CAP rewards quantity over efficiency, it has a regressive effect on farmers; since smaller farmers cannot produce as much as large farm conglomerates, they are disadvantaged under the CAP subsidy programme, even if they are more efficient than larger farmers. Eighty per cent of the CAP's subsidies currently go to the richest 20 per cent of farmers.
- *Stable markets.* By isolating internal agricultural prices, the CAP mechanisms have avoided the price fluctuations that characterize world markets. At the same time, the CAP's artificially high price supports have disrupted and destabilized world trade in agricultural products, and have hindered the general liberalization of world trade in agriculture. Third World countries, whose major source of revenue is agricultural exports, have suffered most from the distorting effects of the CAP.
- *Self-sufficiency.* The EU is now self-sufficient in most agricultural products, and is, for example, one of the world's largest cereal exporters. However, the system's emphasis on productivity has created large food surpluses. These surpluses (the so-called milk lakes and beef mountains that first occurred in the 1970s) are either stored or disposed of as subsidized exports, at a tremendous budgetary cost to the EU.
- *Fair consumer prices.* Despite this being one of the original goals of the CAP, EU consumers have consistently paid more for food under this policy than they would have at world price levels. In fact, EU citizens pay twice for the CAP: first, through higher food prices, and secondly, through taxes that support the EU budget, half of which is allocated to the CAP. Therefore, the CAP is a regressive policy: it results in food prices that are about 8 per cent higher than in the USA, the burden of which falls most heavily on the poorest consumers, since the poor spend a higher percentage of their income on food than the rich.

B Reforming the CAP

Because of overproduction and disagreements with export partners (such as the USA), in the late 1980s, the EU recognized the need to reform the CAP. However, due to the complex nature of the policy and the political significance of EU support for farmers, policy reform has proved very difficult.

I The MacSharry reforms

After several failed attempts, the first significant set of reforms – known as the MacSharry reforms – were agreed upon in 1992. Unlike the 1988 reform (which contained only a budgetary stabilizer package), the MacSharry reforms significantly changed the CAP, mainly by shifting the focus of the programme from price support of goods to income support for farmers. Direct income support solves two of the CAP's major shortcomings: first, it offers a fair standard of living to small farmers (who were disadvantaged by the CAP's focus on volume rather than efficiency); and secondly, it makes the CAP a less regressive policy by allowing EU food prices to sink to world market level (thereby making food less expensive for EU consumers). Therefore, the main feature of the MacSharry reforms was the transfer of a significant part of the cost of agricultural support from the consumer to the taxpayer. The MacSharry reforms also promoted the following policy changes:

- Lowering intervention prices, to bring them closer to world prices. The EU offered full compensation for loss of income to farms by granting supplementary direct aid payments.
- Attempting to manage overproduction by introducing set-aside measures, and by placing a ceiling on entitlement to premiums for animal production.
- Establishing a set-aside scheme in the arable crop sector, by which farmers were paid to take some of their land out of production.

2 Agenda 2000

The Commission conceived Agenda 2000 as a package of measures preparing the EU for the challenge of future enlargement. However, narrow national interests dominated the negotiations on Agenda 2000, and the final agreement achieved at the Berlin Council in March 1999 resulted in a modest CAP reform, which may not be sufficient to cope with the changes to the EU. Agenda 2000 basically promotes an extension of the 1992 reforms: a drop in intervention prices for arable crops, a relaxation of some supply controls, and the adoption of new provisions to allow the promotion of rural actions. However, the modest nature of the reforms means that, due to several factors (enlargement, World Trade Organization (WTO) negotiations, and a limited EU budget), a more radical reform is still needed in order to maintain the *status quo* (for more on Agenda 2000, see *EU Enlargement*).

It is important to note that the different political environments during the MacSharry and the Agenda 2000 negotiations, especially Germany's position on its budgetary contribution to the EU, affected the outcomes of these two reforms.

C The decision-making structure of the CAP

In order to understand the reasons why CAP reform is so difficult, it is necessary to analyse both the key actors behind the policy and the policy-making dynamics.

1   The key actors

- *The Commission*, in the form of DG Agriculture, formulates guidelines, drafts proposals, executes policy, and oversees the proper implementation of the CAP by member states. Through the administration of the CAP, the Commission tries to keep the policy within the parameters of the WTO agreements. The Commission's management of the CAP is controlled by numerous committees of member state representatives.
- *The Agriculture Council*, composed of national Agriculture Ministers, is the main decision-maker on agriculture in the EU. As most CAP measures are agreed under QMV, all member states have a strong incentive to carry out intensive negotiations to achieve either a blocking minority or a qualified majority, so package deals are common. It is important to note that these Council meetings are prepared by the Special Committee on Agriculture (not by the COREPER), which strengthens the Agriculture Council's position with interest groups (see *Institutional Actors*).
- *The European Parliament (EP)* has very little influence over the CAP, because most CAP issues fall under the consultation procedure, and most agricultural expenditure are considered 'compulsory expenditures', over which the EP has little control (see *The EU Budget*).
- *National administrations* are in charge of the practical management of the policy. Inspections, management of payments, and purchases of agricultural products are in the hands of national bureaucracies. In some countries, the day-to-day management of agricultural policy is in the hands of regional governments, as in Germany, Belgium and Spain.

2   Policy-making dynamics

- *Path dependency*. Once the Council decides to support a certain policy, a qualified majority is usually needed to overturn this decision. As a result, policy decisions are rarely reversed. Moreover, the CAP is redistributive (i.e. it gives money to specific groups), which makes it very difficult politically to take this money away. As a result, the CAP is extremely 'path-dependent', and therefore resistant to change.
- *The 'iron triangle'*. Some academics, such as Hix, argue that the CAP is controlled by the troika of national Agriculture Ministers, agriculture officials in the Commission, and European-level farming organizations, such as COPA. Each of these groups has a vested interest in defending the interests of the rest of the troika. For example, farmers (through their lobby groups) are willing to support Agriculture Ministers with their votes in national elections if these ministers continue to support CAP subsidies. These coinciding interests make a reform of the CAP a difficult task.
- *Concentrated interests/diffuse costs*. Olson's theory of collective action gives a good explanation for the level of interest group involvement in agricultural

policy. Farming interests such as COPA are very well organized and well represented at national and European levels. Since they receive huge subsidies from the CAP, farmers have numerous incentives to mobilize (= concentrated benefits). By contrast, there are few incentives for consumers to mobilize against the CAP, since the cost of the CAP to each individual consumer or taxpayer is smaller than the costs of organizing an anti-CAP campaign (= diffuse costs) (see *Interest Groups* for details).

D   The future of the CAP

There are two broad approaches to agricultural intervention:

- *The liberal approach.* The OECD, WTO, USA and the Cairns Group (agricultural exporters including Australia, New Zealand and Argentina) promote national policies which move away from price support and towards a more market-oriented agriculture. Since the level of price support in the EU is equivalent to an import tariff of 82 per cent (compared to 28 per cent for the USA and 1 per cent for New Zealand), many members of the WTO claim that the CAP significantly distorts world agricultural prices. The CAP costs the world economy at least €75 billion annually, more than a third of which is borne by non-EU countries. While some of these non-EU countries, like the USA and Australia, are able to compete with the EU in other markets, many other countries affected by the CAP depend on agricultural exports for their economic survival (for details on the WTO, see *External Policies*).
- *The multi-functional approach.* Although a consensus exists about the need for further reform, many people argue for the maintenance of a certain degree of regulation in the agricultural sector. According to this approach the state should intervene in order to promote goods and services that the market does not stimulate, such as territorial cohesion, the quality of products, bio-diversity, quality of life in the rural areas, etc. This is the viewpoint currently held by the EU Commission and several EU countries.

Therefore, a new reform of CAP needs to concentrate on issues such as:

- *Further reductions in intervention prices and compensation payments.* Degressivity (the gradual reduction of compensation payments) is one method to relieve the pressure which income support places on the EU budget. It is likely that these funds will be re-allocated to support rural development.
- *Rural development policy.* The new CAP should be focused on multi-functionality in agriculture, such as the promotion of higher food quality, higher environmental standards, and the diversification of rural economies.

- *Re-nationalization* (national delegation of some European measures). Some aspects of the CAP may be re-allocated to national administrations to develop autonomous schemes. This would allow national governments to focus on country-specific problems. In theory, this would increase the incentives for national administrations to be more disciplined and transparent in creating and administering CAP policies, as a percentage of direct payment expenditures would be financed by national governments. It would, however, threaten the principle of financial solidarity within the EU.
- *Changing the European model of agriculture*. Despite outside pressure, Europe continues to have an interventionist agricultural policy. Recent policy liberalization (price cuts, reduction of direct payments, lower tariffs, etc.) has not affected the overall redistributive nature of the CAP. However, the new CAP may be forced to substitute the current market-oriented approach for a new structural approach based on the principles of multi-functional agriculture: rural intervention, the promotion of higher-quality food, higher environmental standards and territorial interventions.

Who wins/who loses

Because of price supports, **EU consumers** have always paid for the CAP. However, the reforms carried out since 1992 have shifted some of the costs to **EU taxpayers**. This is a positive step, since it makes the CAP less regressive (alleviating the burden of higher food prices from poorer EU citizens), while still helping the poorest farmers.

Winners and losers from reform of the CAP among the **member states** illustrate why the CAP is such a problematic policy. Several countries, including Spain, Greece, Ireland and France, all receive a net benefit (in absolute terms) from the CAP; while other countries, like Italy, the UK and especially Germany, are net losers. Denmark, one of Europe's richest countries, is a good example of the inequity of the CAP: on a per capita basis, Danish farmers enjoy the biggest transfers from the CAP of any EU state, yet Denmark is still not a net contributor to the EU budget. One of the reasons behind this inequity is that the most interventionist CAP regimes are applied to Continental products (beef, milk and cereals) rather than Mediterranean products; therefore the regional allocation of resources is clearly biased towards northern Europe.

Food for thought

Why not have fifteen separate agricultural policies? Economically, the creation of a common market in agriculture should increase productivity through competition and specialization. For agricultural goods to move freely within the Community, the intervention regimes that existed at the national level had to be integrated. Therefore, a common policy was necessary, in order to avoid market distortions. In addition, scholars such as Milward argue that the CAP was a political trade-off between German industrial and French farming interests. However, with agricultural overproduction in the Union and the Single Market Programme firmly in place, could the EU now benefit from decentralizing the CAP? Or would decentralization lead to further market distortion?

What reforms are necessary to make the CAP viable after enlargement? Agriculture is a key sector in Central and Eastern Europe, where agriculture represents around 8 per cent of the GDP (compared to 1.7 per cent of GDP in the EU). In addition, agriculture employs 19 per cent of the population in the CEECs (compared to 5 per cent in the EU). Therefore, agriculture is the most difficult issue in the negotiations for enlargement. The main problems in applying the CAP to the CEECs include the inability of citizens of the CEECs to afford the higher food prices that would result from the CAP, the unwillingness of the current EU states to provide direct income support to CEEC farmers upon accession to the EU, and the huge budgetary increase associated with extension of the CAP in its present form. For these reasons, is it possible that eastern enlargement will be the incentive that the EU needs to fundamentally reform the CAP? If the EU is successful in such reforms, will the CEECs lose a major benefit of EU membership? (See Mayhew for statistical information in *EU Enlargement*.)

Is the CAP feasible in this period of globalization? There is growing concern about the ability of the EU to defend its agricultural interests in the new round of WTO talks. The EU may be forced to make concessions in this field if it wants to protect other EU exports. A reform based on the principles of multi-functional agriculture may be the only way to balance the objectives of agricultural liberalization and state protection of rural communities. As such reform will require consensus among many different levels of government (including regional, national, EU and international levels), will the concept of multi-functionality be sufficient to create a reformed, globally competitive CAP? Will an EU concession on CAP reform allow the EU to have more leverage in the globalization of other international markets?

Student-to-student tip

Studying the CAP is not easy, for two reasons. First, it is an interventionist policy – which means that if you want to understand a specific regime in depth, you will need to understand many related regulations and bureaucratic mechanisms. Secondly, the CAP is a sensitive policy, where the analysis is usually very passionate, whether the scholar is for or against the policy. In constructing your arguments on the CAP, it is important to decide whether you support interventionist or free market agriculture. If you choose intervention, you must be able not only to back up your argument, but also to justify why the European model of agriculture is unique (by comparison with the USA, for example), and therefore requires a special agricultural policy.

Summary

- The agricultural sector in Europe makes up 1.7 per cent of the Union's GDP, employing 5 per cent of the EU workforce. However, the CAP consumes almost 50 per cent of the EU budget.
- Arguments for the CAP include income support for farmers, higher food-safety standards, and bio-diversity.
- The objectives of the CAP set out by the Treaties of Rome are:
  - to increase agricultural productivity;
  - to provide for a fair standard of living for the agricultural community;
  - to stabilize markets;
  - to ensure availability of supplies;
  - to achieve reasonable prices for consumers.
- CAP benefits Continental countries and large farmers, at the cost of consumers, taxpayers and small farmers.
- The MacSharry reforms and Agenda 2000 resulted in a lowering of intervention prices, in order to bring them closer to world prices, and direct income support for farmers.
- The future of the CAP is linked to the idea of multi-functionality in agriculture, which regards the CAP as a rural development policy.

Selected bibliography

Economic analysis

Pelkmans, J. (1997) *European Integration: Methods and Economic Analysis*, Harlow: Netherlands Open University and Longman, chapter 11: 164–82.
    This is an excellent source for understanding the basic economic aspects of the CAP for students at all levels.

Political science analysis

Peterson, J. and E. Bomberg (1999) *Decision-making in the European Union*, New York: St Martins Press, chapter 5: 120–45.
    This book explores the role of each institution and the features of the Agricultural Council in relation to the CAP, offering a clear explanation of the decision-making process related to the policy.

The reforms

Ingersent, K. A., A. J. Rayner and R. C. Hine (1998) *The Reform of the Common Agricultural Policy*, London: Macmillan.
    A complete account of CAP reform, it is best to focus on chapters 4 ('Implications of the EU East Enlargement for the CAP', pp. 54–75) and 9 ('The CAP and the WTO after the Uruguay Round Agriculture Agreement', pp. 175–88).

Ackrill, R. (2000) 'CAP Reform 1999: A Crisis in the Making?', *Journal of Common Market Studies*, vol. 38, no. 2: 343–53.
This concise article is highly recommended for those interested in the Agenda 2000 reforms.

Comprehensive general books

Grant, W. (1997) *The Common Agricultural Policy*, London: Macmillan.
Fennell, R. (1997) *The Common Agricultural Policy: Continuity and Change*, Oxford: Clarendon Press.
These are the best two general books on the topic of the CAP.

Supportive websites

http://www.europa.eu.int/comm/agriculture/index_en.htm   This site offers an institutional view of the current policy. The most interesting publication found here is *The Agricultural Situation in the EU: Annual Report*.

http://www.europarl.eu.int/factsheets/default_en.htm   These papers, published by the European Parliament, discuss current issues without requiring an in-depth knowledge of the topic of the reader.

http://www.agra-food-news.com   This site provides updated information about agricultural markets, some interesting reports, and good comments about the most recent news. Its weekly magazine, *Agraa-Europa*, is the reference point for the whole European agrarian community.

http://www.ocde.org   The OECD provides several good reports and analysis of the reform of the agricultural policies from a liberal point of view. Visit the *Agriculture, Food and Fisheries* section for details.

http://www.wto.org/english/   The WTO gives updated information about the ongoing negotiations on agricultural trade. It takes a liberal approach. Visit the *Agriculture* and *Agricultural Negotiations* sections for details.

http://www.copa.be   The COPA–COGECA website represents the position of the largest European agricultural lobby group. The site provides very good fact sheets and position papers on CAP issues.

15

Regional Policy

Jorge Juan Fernández García

According to an EU study conducted in 2000, 22.2 per cent of EU citizens (approximately 100 million people) live in 'Objective 1' regions, where the GDP per capita is less than three-quarters of the EU average. Using similar criteria in the USA, only two states, constituting only 2 per cent of the population (approximately 6 million people), would fall into this category. In addition, the ten poorest regions in the EU-15 are all found on the periphery of the EU: in East Germany, Spain, Greece and Portugal. Moreover, regional disparities cannot be measured by income or GDP alone, as employment statistics are crucial to understanding regional differences in the EU. In 1996, the ten regions with the greatest employment problems suffered from twice the EU average in unemployment.

These studies highlight the regional problem in the EU: namely, that vast discrepancies exist between the rich and poor regions of the Community, and that poverty and unemployment are concentrated in the periphery member states. EU Regional Policy has developed in order to reduce the disparity between different areas in the Community, but politicians argue about how this should be done, and at what cost. There are two main questions here. First, there is the equity question: to what extent should the EU tolerate differences in wealth between regions within the Community? Secondly, there is an efficiency question: is the unequal distribution of wealth, skills and infrastructure likely to impede or aid economic welfare? Given that economic and social cohesion now amounts to 35 per cent of the EU budget, questions such as these have clearly taken on great importance.

The facts

A   Historical development

The Preamble to the Treaties of Rome (1957) refers to the need to 'reduce the differences between the various regions and the backwardness of the less favoured regions'. Despite this, regional policy initially remained the prerogative of the member states, since the founders of the Treaty had intended that any redistribution of resources would be channelled through the Common Agricultural Policy (CAP), or through inexpensive loans to less developed regions sponsored by the European Investment Bank (EIB).

During the 1960s, economic prosperity hid many of the regional problems already inherent in the Community. However, each successive enlargement has added new types of regions, and regional imbalances have widened. The continued integration of the Community has led to the creation of further regional policy instruments, in order to compensate the losers from the integration process.

This process started with the first enlargement in 1973, through the establishment of the European Regional Development Fund (ERDF). The ERDF was created both to compensate the UK for the CAP (it was paying far more into the budget for this policy than it was receiving in return) and to assist Ireland with its industrial decline problem. At the same time, the focus of the European Social Fund (ESF) and the European Agricultural Guidance and Guarantee Fund (EAGGF), which were established in the Treaties of Rome, became much more regionally oriented. In 1985, the Integrated Mediterranean Programmes (IMPs) were implemented, in order to compensate Italy and Greece for increased competition in agricultural products resulting from the Iberian enlargement.

The Single European Act (SEA, 1986) introduced the concept of 'economic and social cohesion' as a counterbalance to the Single Market Programme (SMP). Since the SMP facilitated both deeper economic integration and greater competition through free trade, EU Regional Policy was needed to help weaker economic regions overcome the pressures of increased market liberalization. Yet, until the middle of the 1980s, Regional Policy accounted for an insignificant part of the EU budget (equalling less than 5 per cent in 1975). This changed with the reforms in 1988 (known as Delors Package I), which doubled the resources available to the Structural Funds. These reforms initiated the creation of the first coherent EU-level regional policy, in order to co-ordinate EU intervention at the sub-national level effectively.

With the Treaty on European Union (TEU, 1992), cohesion became one of the fundamental objectives of the Union, and a new Cohesion Fund was set up in order to facilitate economic and monetary union (EMU). The primary motive behind the Cohesion Fund was economic, since weaker, peripheral regions might benefit less than stronger central regions from a single currency. Periphery states argued that disparities would be exacerbated rather than helped by EMU, since the loss of the exchange rate mechanism with the implementation of one currency would prevent national governments from protecting vulnerable sectors of their economies through monetary policy.

The TEU also established the Committee of Regions (designed as a venue for regional participation in the EU) and the principle of subsidiarity (to bring decision making down to the most relevant level of government). In 1992, Delors Package II increased the Structural Funds resources for the period 1993–9. This was followed by the Agenda 2000 reforms (for the period 2000–6), which aimed at improving the efficiency of the Structural Funds and of the Cohesion Fund.

B Policy instruments

There are two regional policy instruments in the EU: the Structural Funds and the Cohesion Fund. These instruments determine how and to whom regional funding is transferred within the various parts of the EU. In 1988, three separate funds were brought together under one framework to form the Structural Funds; a fourth instrument, the FIFG, was incorporated in 1993.

I Structural Funds

The four elements of the Structural Funds are as follows:

- *European Regional Development Fund (ERDF)*. Set up in 1975, the ERDF is the main instrument of EU Regional Policy. It receives 49.5 per cent of the total Structural Funds budget and aims at reducing regional disparities within the Union. It is managed by the Regional Directorate-General (DG).
- *European Social Fund (ESF)*. This fund, set up in 1960, invests in programmes that alleviate long-term and youth unemployment, through training programmes. It receives 29.9 per cent of the total Structural Funds budget, and is managed by the Employment and Social Affairs DG (see *Environmental and Social Policies*).
- *European Agricultural Guidance and Guarantee Fund (EAGGF) – Guidance Section*. Originally set up as part of the Common Agricultural Policy (CAP) in 1962, this fund aims to transform the structure of European agriculture and to develop rural areas for other economic purposes. It receives 17.7 per cent of the total Structural Funds budget, and is managed by the Agriculture DG (see *Common Agricultural Policy*).
- *Financial Instrument for Fisheries Guidance (FIFG)*. Initially, FIFG was financed by the EAGGF. However, following the reform of the Structural Funds in 1992, this fund was made independent of the EAGGF, in order to support diversity in the fishing industry. It receives 2.9 per cent of the total Structural Funds budget, and is managed by the Fisheries DG.

2 Community Initiatives (CIs)

Ninety-four per cent of the Structural Funds budget is allocated to programmes designed and run by member states, whilst approximately 6 per cent is reserved for Community Initiatives (CIs), which are controlled by the Commission. The CIs are separate spending programmes which are co-financed by the Structural Funds. CIs are meant to address specific problems of EU-wide concern. With the Agenda 2000 reforms, the CIs were reduced from thirteen to four initiative areas:

- LEADER helps local action groups address rural development problems.
- EQUAL develops new ways of combating discrimination and inequality that impede access to labour markets.
- INTERREG increases cross-border and trans-national co-operation.
- URBAN assists in the economic and social regeneration of towns, cities and suburban areas in crisis.

C Budget and objectives

Resources under the Structural Funds are allocated on the basis of seven-year programming periods: the present period is 2000–6, and the next period will be 2007–13. Structural Funds assistance is divided up not only between the four regional policy instruments, but also between the different objectives. For the period 1994–9 there were six different objectives (although Objective 5 was divided into 5a and 5b), which were reduced to three Objectives in the Agenda 2000 reforms.

- *Objective 1* By far the most important objective, Objective 1 (replacing old Objectives 1, 5a and 6) promotes the development and structural adjustment of regions which are suffering from slow economic growth and unemployment. This Objective is allocated 69.7 per cent of the Structural Funds budget. Regions are eligible if their average GDP per capita over the last three years is less than 75 per cent of the Union's overall average. The goal of the Community is for 20 per cent of the EU's total population to benefit from Objective 1 policies.
- *Objective 2* contributes to the economic and social convergence of regions that are not eligible under Objective 1. In particular, it targets areas in industrial decline or those suffering from structural difficulties, such as declining rural areas (thus replacing former Objectives 2 and 5b). This Objective is allocated 11.5 per cent of the Structural Funds budget.
- *Objective 3* replaces former Objectives 3 and 4 by concentrating all measures for human resources development. Objective 3 regions receive 12.3 per cent of the Structural Funds budget.

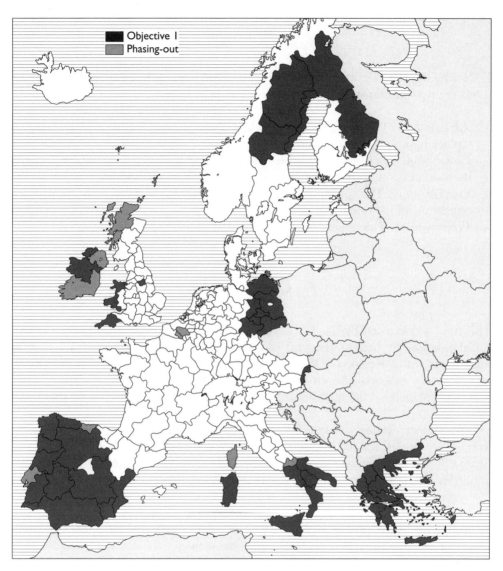

Distribution of EU Regional Policy, 2000-2006
Objective 1 regions.

Germany	14,153	Ireland	0,965	Finland	1,076
Greece	10,476	Italy	19,302	Sweden	0,452
Spain	23,219	Austria	0,275	UK	5,079
France	1,644	Portugal	6,616	EU TOTAL 83,258	

D   Principles

Following the 1992 Delors Package II financial reforms of the Structural Funds, the funds are now administered according to four principles:

- *Additionality*. This principle ensures that Community financing is not used to replace national structural aid.
- *Partnership*. The funds are planned and executed in close co-operation between the Commission, national governments and regional authorities.
- *Concentration*. The spending of funds is concentrated so as to focus on priority objectives and regions.
- *Programming*. This sets the timetable for the allocation of assistance.

E   Cohesion Fund

This fund was created by the TEU, and was intended to strengthen economic and social cohesion by helping the least prosperous states to participate in EMU. It is managed by the Regional DG. Funds are divided equally between transport/infrastructure projects and environmental projects. All the projects are selected and implemented by the member states, but are regularly monitored by the Commission.

Only member states whose GDP per capita is below 90 per cent of the Union average are eligible for the Cohesion Fund (currently Greece, Ireland, Portugal and Spain). Until 1999, access to the Cohesion Fund was conditional on recipient countries pursuing economic policies that enabled them to meet the Maastricht convergence criteria (related to EMU). Currently, Cohesion countries must comply with the Growth and Stability Pact in order to receive funding (see *Economic and Monetary Union*). Although the Commission monitors all projects under this fund, it is the member states that select and implement them.

The problems/issues

A   The economic debate: the Convergence School vs the Divergence School

Economically, regional intervention can be justified based on efficiency grounds; these include market failures (such as imperfect information) and under-utilization of the factors of production (due to lack of infrastructure and unemployment). However, economists disagree as to whether EU integration has increased or decreased the disparities between regions.

- Neo-classical economic theory argues that economic integration will lead to greater prosperity for the entire Union, as increased wealth produced in the core member states eventually spreads to the periphery states. This *Convergence School*, which predicts a gradual reduction in regional imbalances through economic integration, does not support the need for regional policy. The theory is criticized for assuming perfect competition within the EU, full employment and perfect factor mobility, as well as the creation of homogeneous products.
- By contrast, the *Divergence School* expects regional imbalances to grow if regions are not assisted. Unlike the Convergence School, it assumes imperfect competition and emphasizes the importance of agglomeration economies and differentiated products. It argues that firms exploit economies of scale by concentrating production close to markets where they have the most customers (where demand is stronger, and income consequently higher) and suppliers (as this reduces transport costs). As a result, market integration will create incentives for factors of production to move from peripheral to core areas, draining economic resources from the periphery.

Thus, the existence of an EU Regional Policy implies that member states have accepted at least some of the arguments put forward by the Divergence School. Since the EU is responsible for fostering economic integration (through such programmes as the SMP), it should also be responsible for alleviating the negative side-effects resulting from it, such as the increase in regional disparities. In addition, by having an EU-level Regional Policy, distortions of the market through unequal application of national regional policies can be avoided. This eliminates the non-tariff barriers to trade caused by national subsidies, a major concern for the economic integration of the EU.

The costs and benefits from European integration are also unevenly distributed among the participating states, and are sometimes even accentuated by certain EU policies (such as the CAP). This necessitates an EU solution to the regional problem. In sum, economists who favour an EU Regional Policy argue that greater efficiency can be achieved through co-ordination and concentration of resources at the supranational rather than the national level.

B The political science debate: side-payments vs real structural adjustment

Political scientists interpret regional policy in two ways, either as a side-payment or as a policy that is effective in its own right:

- According to academics such as Pollack and Keating, regional policy funds are simply side-payments used to buy support for European integration from the poorer member states. They argue that these funds will not substantially improve the situation of the poorer regions, but are instead little more than subsidies. The IMPs, which many argue were used to convince Italy and Greece to support the 1986 Iberian enlargement, are a perfect example of this argument. The creation of the Cohesion Fund is also often cited as an example of the richer pro-integration member states (such as Germany and France) paying off the poorer periphery states, so that these countries would not block the implementation of EMU. However, even if this were true, regional policy might still have value; according to many academics, side-payments can still be used to facilitate further EU integration.

- Other academics, such as Leonardi, contend that EU regional policy has transformed the supply conditions of the economies concerned. For example, the fact that the four Cohesion countries have experienced higher rates of economic growth than the EU average is often attributed to the application of the Cohesion and Structural Funds. Ireland, a long-term recipient of EU regional funding, is now one of the fastest-growing economies in the Community (see *Basic Statistics*). These academics also point out that a truly viable and well-funded regional policy was created only in 1988 with the Delors Package I reforms. Therefore, more time must pass before a significant reduction in discrepancies between regions will appear.

C Theoretical arguments: multi-level governance vs intergovernmentalism

EU Regional Policy allows political scientists to analyse the emerging EU polity. Two of the several theoretical approaches to regional policy are outlined below.

- Models of *multi-level governance* (see academics such as Marks, Hooghe and Scharpf) emphasize the decreasing role of national governments in the decision-making process and the growing importance of sub- and supranational actors in EU policy making. Regional Policy, they argue, is the result of a complex interaction between political actors across all levels. The role of the Commission as well as of individual regions is viewed as critical in shaping EU Regional Policy. These theorists also maintain that the interaction between all three levels of government is not a step in the progression toward a supranational state (as the neo-functionalists believe), but instead a permanent dynamic within the Union.
- *Intergovernmentalism* (see Allen and Pollack) maintains that the formulation of Regional Policy is still dominated by the national governments of the member states, and that this policy has been used as a side-payment in large intergovernmental bargains in order to buy support for further European integration. According to this view, the Commission and the sub-national authorities have a say only in the management of Regional Policy, not in its formulation.

Who wins/who loses

From a **budgetary point of view**, the winners are the main budget recipients – Spain, Portugal, Greece and Ireland – whilst the losers are the main budget contributors – Germany and the Netherlands (see *The EU Budget*). However, even in economic terms, this argument is incomplete, since much of the funding eventually returns to the contributors (it is estimated that 30–40 per cent of money transferred to Cohesion countries through the Funds leaves again in the form of imports). However, it is important to note that an effective regional policy will always produce budget winners and losers. In other words, if funding is not concentrated on those areas most in need of assistance, the policy would become so diluted as to no longer be effective. Thus, the ultimate goal of Regional Policy will always create these budgetary imbalances.

From a **political point of view**, Regional Policy benefits those states that favour European integration, and therefore the EU as a whole. There is a strong case to be made for the view that Regional Policy also represents side-payments to weaker member states for agreement on further European integration. In addition, as the poorer regions of the Community improve their infrastructure and become wealthier, they offer a better market to the richer core member states. Therefore, EU Regional Policy attempts to foster a virtuous circle of economic prosperity within the Community.

The **regions** themselves are also winners from the increased importance of regional policy. Not only does this policy offer economic planning assistance and funding to regions in need, it has also elevated the political importance of regions within the decision-making structure of the Union. Some multi-level governance scholars, such as Hooghe, argue that increased regional representation in Brussels is a manifestation of new prominence of the regions in EU politics.

Food for thought

Has the process of European integration increased or reduced regional imbalances? According to the Commission, the gap in 1999 between the richest and poorest countries has decreased in terms of GDP per capita (as a result of different economic growth rates among countries, with poorer member states growing faster). However, regional imbalances within individual countries have actually increased. Is this because some regions have applied their regional funds more effectively, or because the European integration process is generating economies of scale and external economies in those regions? In addition, while regional imbalances within regions of different countries have been reduced, inter-personal income differences have tended to grow, especially in countries that have liberalized further (including the UK and the USA). Given these different ways of measuring cohesion, how will the Union be able to determine if regional policy has been effective or not?

Is the current system of regional and structural policy in the EU adequate for dealing with enlargement? The process of enlargement will pose severe challenges to regional policy. In an enlarged Europe, the CEECs will have 29 per cent of the total population, but only 4 per cent of the CEECS. It is probable that Objective 1 funds will be re-allocated to the CEECs at the expense of the current periphery countries.

Student-to-student tip

As it is difficult to obtain reliable data on this subject, we recommend the tri-annual Commission reports, which can be found on the DG's website. However, as this site is run by the DG in charge of Regional Policy, it is in their interest to make this policy look as efficient as possible. In addition, if you want to compare the amount of funds given to each country, you need to have all the funds measured in the same current prices from the same year – the Commission does not provide information in this format. However, that information is available at other websites, such as (surprisingly) the *World Fact Book*, published by the CIA: (*http://www.odci.gov/cia/ publications/*). Remember that these figures are given in US dollars, which need to be converted into euros for the purpose of comparison.

Summary

- EU Regional Policy is constructed from two main instruments, the Structural Funds and the Cohesion Fund, and aims at achieving three Objectives. It is an increasingly important aspect of the EU, as it is the second most heavily funded activity in the Union (equalling 34.2 per cent of the 2001 EU budget).
- Economic theory supports two schools of thought. The *Convergence School* believes that, under certain conditions, market forces will automatically lead to the convergence of economic outputs. The *Divergence School*, by contrast, asserts that, in the presence of the process of European integration, regional imbalances will increase, and market forces will drain the economic viability out of the periphery.
- The political science debate centres on the function that Regional Policy fulfils; some consider Regional Policy to be little more than a side-payment, through which the richer member states can guarantee support for European integration from poorer member states. Others believe that these funds are effective instruments for promoting regional economic convergence.
- EU Regional Policy has resulted in inter-regional convergence (measured in terms of income) between EU countries. At the same time, the regions within a country have suffered from increased income divergence, and income inequality between individuals has grown both at the country and the EU level.

Selected bibliography

Political overviews

Tsoukalis, L. (1997) *The New European Economy Revisited*, 3rd edn, Oxford: Oxford University Press, chapter 9: 187–209.

Tsoukalis provides a very good account of the political economy of redistribution and of Cohesion issues.

Peterson, J. and E. Bomberg (1999) *Decision-making in the European Union*, New York: St Martin's Press, chapter 6: 146–72.
The authors offer a very strong political science account, especially with regard to policy making and possible explanatory theories of EU Regional Policy.

Sutcliffe, J. B. (2000) 'The 1999 Reform of the Structural Fund Regulations: Multi-level Governance or Renationalization', *Journal of European Public Policy*, vol. 7, no. 2: 290–309.
This article discusses the reform of the Structural Funds using a multi-level governance framework. It argues that while national governments are dominant, the Commission and regional actors also play important roles in the development of this policy.

Economic overviews

Vanhove, N. and L. Klaassen (1999) *Regional Policy: a European Approach*, 3rd edn, London: Ashgate.
Vanhove and Klaassen provides a particularly strong explanation of the economics of EU Regional Policy. Chapters 10 ('The Structural Funds') and 11 ('2000 and Beyond'), in particular, are very clear and helpful.

Armstrong, H. and J. Taylor (2000) *Regional Economics and Policy*, 3rd edn, Oxford: Blackwell.
The volume is divided into two independent volumes. Part I on regional economics provides the theoretical framework in regional economics, and Part II on Regional Policy provides a revision of recent changes in Regional Policy and institutions in the EU.

Rodriguez-Pose, A. (1998) *Dynamics of Regional Growth in Europe*, Oxford: Oxford University Press.
This author offers an excellent account of the evolution of regional discrepancies.

To find data, the EU's periodic reports on regional development (*Sixth Periodic Report* (1999), *Fifth* (1994), *Fourth* (1991), as well as the Tri-annual Reports on Economic and Social Cohesion (*Second Tri-annual Report* (2001)), are the best source for official figures and working plans.

Supportive websites

http://europa.eu.int/comm/regional_policy/index_en.htm This site provides detailed and up-to-date information on projects and programmes supported by the ERDF and the Cohesion Fund. In particular, see the *Second Report on Economic and Social Cohesion* adopted by the Commission on 31 January 2001.

http://europa.eu.int/comm/agenda2000/index_en.htm This is the Commission's home-page for the Agenda 2000 programmes.

http://www.europa.eu.int/comm/employment_social/esf2000/index-en.htm The site of the European Social Fund offers detailed information about Objective 3 programmes.

We also recommend visiting the home-pages of regions receiving EU regional funding (such as Catalonia in Spain or South Tyrol in Italy), for information on the application of EU Regional Policy.

16

Environmental and Social Policies

Laurence Baroni and Jess Clayton

Many EU policies focus on market liberalization, specifically the removal of barriers to trade; these policies are often labelled 'deregulatory' policies. By contrast, environmental and social policies are re-regulatory – they create new regulations at the EU level, which control the activities of member states and private actors. The EU has often justified re-regulatory policies by arguing that the increased competition caused by market liberalization could result in 'negative externalities' in the social and environmental fields, such as pollution and social inequities. In addition, re-regulatory policies must be decided at the EU level in order to ensure a level playing field, so that all member states are constrained by the same regulations. While social and environmental policies share this same rationale, each policy has developed at a different pace and to a differing extent at the EU level. Therefore, examining these policies in tandem reveals a great deal about what the member states think is acceptable for the EU to regulate, and what should remain the exclusive competence of the national governments.

The facts

A   Social Policy

I   National vs EU Social Policy

National social policy redistributes resources and makes laws in areas such as social insurance, welfare, housing, health and employment. In so doing, social policy expresses a society's value system. Social policy is also often viewed as a critical part of national sovereignty, due to the historical connection between the creation of the welfare state and the construction of the modern state. Therefore, most traditional areas of social policy (such as housing and social security) remain the competence of the member states. Despite this, EU Social Policy – primarily in the form of social regulation – has developed at the EU level in areas related to economic integration.

2 EU social regulation

Social Policy has been an element of the EU since the Treaties of Rome (now found under Title XI, Chapter 1, Articles 136–45). As this policy is meant to enhance the Common Market, some of the first EU Social Policy directives pertained to the free movement of migrant workers and the establishment of connected social security arrangements, facilitating the free movement of labour. This chapter of the Treaties also created the European Social Fund (ESF), which distributes funds to promote the occupational and geographical mobility of workers. The ESF has become an important tool for economic and social cohesion, and accounts for around 30 per cent of the Structural Funds budget between 2000 and 2006.

3 The Social Action Programme (SAP)

The combination of increased economic imbalances within the EU (resulting from the first enlargement of the EU in 1973) and rising labour unrest in the 1970s led to the implementation of the SAP in 1974. The SAP's main achievements were the adoption of directives on equal opportunities for men and women (see also the *Defrenne* case in *Law and European Integration*) and of directives on health and safety at work.

4 Industrial relations

In the 1970s, the EU also adopted various directives and recommendations aimed at improving the conditions and legal position of employees. In the early 1980s, EU Social Policy was developed in the field of industrial relations within multi-national companies (the 1980 Vredeling Directive, for instance, proposed workers' rights to information and consultation in multi-national corporations). However, the scope of EU social legislation remained restricted to these areas during this period.

5 The Single European Act (SEA)

While the SEA (1986) was primarily concerned with market liberalization, it also increased the importance of EU Social Policy. Some member states, such as Italy and Greece, believed that the increased competition promoted by the SEA would harm their least competitive regions. Consequently, the SEA resulted in an extension of EU Social Policy at a regional level, aimed at helping poorer regions and vulnerable social groups remain competitive. This 'social dimension' of the SEA was achieved partly through the harmonization of health and safety standards at work. The SEA also established a 'Social Dialogue' between the social partners (labour and capital) to discuss the preparation of EU legislation and requires the Commission to consult labour and business on Social Policy proposals. This Social Dialogue focuses on consultation between the largest business interest group, UNICE, and the European-level trade union confederation, ETUC (see *Interest Groups*).

6   The Social Charter

In 1989, the Commission prepared the Community Charter of Fundamental Rights of Workers (known as the Social Charter), which was signed by all EU member states except the UK, and links social consensus with competitiveness. However, the Social Charter was only a political declaration, and therefore not legally binding. None the less, the Commission has used this declaration to draw up an Action Programme, containing forty-seven binding and non-binding proposals. Some of these proposals (such as those on employee participation and atypical work) have yet to be adopted.

7   The Social Protocol

Social Policy became an important issue during the negotiations for the Treaty on European Union (TEU, 1992), because many member states argue that economic liberalization necessitates corresponding social measures, in order to protect the economically weakest parts of the Community. Pro-integration member states, such as Germany, wished to incorporate the aims of the Social Charter into the TEU; other states, notably the UK, were reluctant to give up any control of social policy. After a fierce debate, the UK opted out of further Social Policy development, whilst the eleven remaining members signed the Social Protocol, which initially remained outside the Treaty. The Social Protocol enhanced the power of the social partners in the creation of EU Social Policy legislation; however, UNICE and the ETUC can exercise only limited power in a number of policy areas (for instance, there is still no right to strike and no collective wage bargaining at the EU level). The Protocol also provided for unanimity voting on legislation in the sensitive area of social security, and extended qualified majority voting (QMV) in the Council to many other areas of Social Policy, such as workers' consultation. With the change of government in the UK in 1997, the Labour Government signed the Social Protocol, and it was then incorporated into the Amsterdam Treaty as a new Social Chapter (Title XI). Although the Social Chapter has had a limited impact so far, it represents an incremental step in the development of EU competences in the Social Policy field (see *Flexible Integration*).

8   Employment policies

The reduction of unemployment has been a Community aim since the Treaties of Rome. However, a specific chapter on employment was not introduced until the Amsterdam Treaty (1997); this provides a legal basis for the implementation of a co-ordinated strategy for employment. Consequently, a number of employment guidelines have been adopted each year, including employment targets for member states. However, even though the employment policies of the member states must be consistent with Community guidelines, employment remains predominantly a national competence.

B   Environmental Policy

I   Creating an EU standard

EU Environmental Policy has often led to higher standards of environmental protection throughout Europe. While this might not always be at the same level as that of the 'greenest' member states, EU policy has consistently raised the level of protection in most of the Community. The EU's areas of competence now cover air, water and noise pollution, waste treatment, dangerous substances and technologies, and wildlife conservation.

2   Treaty basis

Unlike Social Policy, Environmental Policy was not part of the Treaties of Rome. The first Community Environmental Action Programme (EAP) was launched in 1973 as a result of pressure from the German and Dutch governments, who, having enacted anti-pollution legislation in their own countries, wanted to maintain a level economic 'playing field' by requiring other EU states to enact similar legislation. This initiative was reinforced by the recognition that pollution is a trans-national problem; in other words, air and water pollution created in one member state is likely to affect neighbouring states.

3   The Single European Act

The SEA was critical to placing Environmental Policy on the EU agenda. Through Article 95 (ex-Article 100a), environmental issues linked with trade harmonization are decided using QMV in the Council of Ministers and the co-operation procedure in the European Parliament (EP). Article 175 (ex-Article 130s) was created to legislate on environmental issues not connected with the Single Market; however, these policies must be decided using unanimity in the Council. Following the revisions in the TEU, some areas of social policy and the majority of environmental issues are now decided using the co-decision procedure in the EP (see *Institutional Actors*).

4 The European Parliament

The EP often champions areas of public concern, and has been a forceful advocate of Environmental Policy. Since environmental proposals linked with the Single Market are decided using the co-decision procedure, the EP can take a much more active role in the formation of Environmental Policy than it can in Social Policy. For this reason, the EP often works in co-ordination with the Environment DG to create policies that fall under Article 95 rather than Article 175.

5 Environmental Action Programmes (EAPs)

The fourth and fifth EAPs have significantly aided the development of Environmental Policy. The fourth EAP (1987–92) reinforced many of the environmental strategies proposed in the SEA, including the 'polluter pays' principle (requiring polluters to pay for environmental degradation) and the principle of subsidiarity (allowing EU competence over environmental issues when they cannot be handled effectively at the regional or national level – see *Constitutionalism*). The fifth EAP (1992–2000) created the principle of environmental policy integration, requiring all EU policies – especially those linked with industry, tourism, agriculture, transportation and energy – to take environmental protection into account. The sixth EAP (2001–10) is focusing on the implementation of environmental directives by member states and on 'mainstreaming': the integration of environmental concerns into other EU policies, such as Transport and Regional Policy. It also addresses four key areas of international concern: climate change, bio-diversity, sustainable use of natural resources and the connection between environment and health.

6 Environmental initiatives

In the 1990s, the EU established two initiatives that facilitated the development of EU environmental policy. The European Environmental Agency (EEA) established in 1990, and set up in Copenhagen in 1994, is responsible for gathering information on the status of the environment, distributing that information, and monitoring changes in the environment. Unlike the US Environmental Protection Agency, the EEA cannot enforce environmental legislation. It can, however, provide the Commission, interest groups and EU citizens with the information needed to prosecute polluters in the European Court of Justice (ECJ). At the same time, the Environmental Information Directive of 1990 was developed in order to reinforce the power of the EEA, and allows for the collection of environmental information from national ministries.

The problems/issues

A Social Policy

I Industrial relations

As Tsoukalis points out, EU Social Policy has historically been a dialogue between the unwilling (European businesses represented by UNICE) and the unable (labour unions represented by ETUC). He and many political scientists argue that the labour unions have neither the legitimacy nor the financial resources needed to develop a coherent social policy. Moreover, there is too much diversity in the European models of capitalism to reach a consensus on industrial relations issues. In an increasingly competitive global market, European business often argues that liberalization of labour markets is critical to keeping jobs within the EU. However, member states such as Germany and Spain are unwilling to deregulate their labour markets, because they believe this will reduce protection for their workers. Other member states with deregulated labour markets, such as the UK, therefore argue that labour regulation should remain at the national level.

However, as EU workers become more mobile, different levels of worker protection between member states form a type of non-tariff barrier to employment. The issue of labour mobility is even more important in terms of Economic and Monetary Union (EMU), as labour mobility is a method of moderating economic asymmetric shocks to the economy. Therefore, it may be necessary for the Union to further harmonize legislation in the field of industrial relations in order to eliminate these barriers to trade and facilitate EMU (see *Economic and Monetary Union*).

2 Tensions over EU Social Policy

Member states with relatively low levels of social protection (such as Greece and Portugal) often argue that EU-level social policy is too costly to implement and reduces their competitive advantage within the Union (namely, a low-wage labour force). As a result, EU Social Policy sets minimum standards for the Community, and member states are allowed to have higher standards if they wish. However, this does not necessarily solve the problem for member states with higher levels of protection, such as the Scandinavian countries. They fear that different levels of protection will make them less competitive, and that the unemployed will emigrate from poorer countries to wealthier countries, in order to benefit from their higher levels of social assistance. However, since EU labour mobility has remained relatively low, this fear may be unjustified.

3   The uneven development of EU Social Policy

While Social Policy is having a growing impact on the EU member states, the enactment of EU social regulations remains fairly limited. This is mainly because the voting procedure on the most sensitive issues remains unanimity in the Council of Ministers and consultation in the European Parliament. These legislative restrictions indicate the reluctance of member states to relinquish control over this policy area. In addition, some areas of Social Policy (such as social security rights for migrant workers, health and safety standards, and product safety standards) are far more developed than others (such as labour market policies, working conditions and industrial relations). This may be because the former are associated with legislation intended to correct for market failures. Conversely, the underdeveloped areas of Social Policy are strongly associated with controversial political choices about how a society should be regulated. Since no European consensus exists on this issue, all current EU Social Policy has a strong economic rationale (the main exception is the area of equal opportunity).

The Commission formally recognized the lack of momentum in the development of EU Social Policy through the 2000 Communication on the EU Social Policy Agenda. The Agenda outlines the Commission proposals and initiatives that are to be launched in the areas of employment and workplace health and safety, providing a timetable by which several goals in these areas are to be achieved. The Commission's publication of an annual scoreboard of its achievements, similar to the Internal Market Scoreboard, may increase EU awareness of development in this policy area.

B   Environmental Policy

I   The role of the European Court of Justice

The ECJ has ruled on Environmental Policy since the signing of the SEA. A key actor in the development of environmental regulation, the ECJ has often decided on the balance between economic development and environmental protection in the Community. Two cases highlight the ECJ's role in Environmental Policy.

- Case 21/76, *Handelskwekerij GJ Bier* vs *Mines de Potasses d'Alsace* (1976). According to Sands, the ruling by the ECJ in this case opened the way for 'forum shopping' among victims of trans-boundary pollution. This means that if pollution affects more than one member state, private individuals or interest groups can take polluters to court in the country they feel is most receptive to environmental issues. This has had a tremendous impact on the enforcement of EU environmental legislation.
- The *Danish Bottle* case (Case 302/86, *Commission* vs *Denmark*) (1989). In this case, the ECJ ruled that environmental protection was sometimes important

enough to justify trade restrictions, even if these inhibited the free movement of goods. As a result, the ECJ substantially increased the importance of environmental protection within the Community (see *Law and European Integration*).

2 Conflicts within the Commission

The Commission plays an active role in the creation of Environmental Policy, since it has the responsibility for initiating policy actions. However, the Directorate-General (DG) for Environment is often in conflict with other DGs, such as those responsible for competition or energy and transport. This is because while most DGs concentrate on facilitating deregulation, environmental re-regulation can restrict competition and other deregulatory policies. For this reason, the Commission has not always been successful in presenting a united front to the Council on environmental issues. This lack of co-ordination can undermine progress in environmental legislation. The *Danish Bottle* case is an example of this problem: despite the protests of the DG for Environment, the DG for TREN (Transport and Energy Policy) was still able to bring this case against Denmark.

3 Effects of EU Environmental Policy on trade

Within the World Trade Organization (WTO), environmental policy is often cited as the 'new trade issue', with increasingly important trade ramifications. Having raised the level of environmental standards within the Community, the EU's interest in the environmental protection standards of its trading partners is part of an effort to create a level economic playing field for EU products. As a result, the EU has established itself as an international environmental actor in the world, especially as the Commission represents the member states at international environmental conferences such as the 1992 Climate Conference in Rio de Janeiro and the one leading to the Kyoto Accords on greenhouse gas emissions, which the EU ratified in May 2002 (see *External Policies*).

C   Social and Environmental Policy

The main problem discussed in the academic literature relates to why Social Policy is so much less developed than Environmental Policy at the EU level.

I   Olson's collective action theory

Olson argues that the reason why business interest groups are more successful than public interest groups in influencing legislation is due to the way in which costs and benefits from legislation are distributed. For instance, environmental regulation usually has a concentrated (or high) cost for the producers of products that pollute and a diffuse (or small) benefit for everyone in the Community when levels of pollution drop. Because the costs are concentrated on a small group of producers, they have a strong incentive to co-ordinate their lobbying efforts to prevent un-favourable legislation. By contrast, improved environmental conditions provide only a small per person benefit for the public; therefore, EU citizens have less incentive to fight for higher levels of protection. This situation means that public interest groups generally lack funding in comparison with private interest groups, and are consequently less able to lobby effectively at the EU level. Olson's theory offers a strong explanation of why areas of social regulation (such as those on atypical work) that would adversely affect business have not been passed at the EU level. However, the theory has difficulty explaining why environmental regulation has grown so substantially at the EU level: environmental standards are consistently rising, despite the cost to business (see *Interest Groups*).

2   The 'product versus process' argument

Scharpf argues that the unequal development of environmental and social policies in the EU is due to the focus of legislation. Environmental regulation generally addresses regulations on products, and therefore affects the goods being sold in the market. Social Policy, by contrast, mainly attempts to control the processes through which goods are created: namely, labour conditions. Since the existence of different rules for products distorts competition in the EU, business is eager to harmonize rules on products, even when this leads to an upgrading of standards. However, agreement on process-related standards is difficult: since they do not directly affect the product, all member states have strong incentives not to harmonize these rules. Rich member states fear that harmonization would lower their levels of social protection, whilst poor member states fear that high social standards will make them uncompetitive. Scharpf's argument helps to explain why more environmental (= product) legislation has been passed than social (= process) legislation.

3   The historical context

Another reason why environmental legislation is far more developed than social legislation at the EU level is because member states perceive Environmental Policy to be a Union competence and Social Policy to be a national competence. Social Policy was already a well-established and important national competence before the Union was created, which has made member states reluctant to hand over compe-tence to the EU. Conversely, environmental regulation is a relatively new policy area; national governments played no traditional role in this field of legislation, and are therefore more willing to allow the EU to legislate in this area.

4 Differing impacts

Since pollution in one country tends to affect neighbouring countries, it seems logical to co-ordinate Environmental Policy at the EU level. However, because of the currently low levels of labour mobility in the EU, differences in social policies between countries do not exert such a direct influence on their neighbours. Consequently, member states do not perceive an urgent need to co-ordinate Social Policy at the EU level.

5 The California effect vs the Delaware effect

Academics such as Scharpf and Sbragia also debate whether re-regulation at the EU level will lead to a raising or a lowering of levels of environmental and social protection. In the 1980s, the US state of Delaware eliminated most of its restrictions on banking practices to increase Delaware's competitive advantage in this sector. In order to remain competitive, other US states were forced to lower standards or lose business to Delaware. This resulted in a 'race to the bottom' in US banking restrictions, meaning that rules governing banking behaviour were dramatically reduced throughout the USA. This raised fears that a lack of regulation would seriously harm US banking and the US consumer. The California effect is the reverse of the Delaware effect. During the 1990s, California proposed increasingly stringent environmental protection laws, in order to deal with air pollution problems. Since California is such a large market for the entire country, US car manufacturers responded by complying with the California level of emissions control for all new cars, rather than the more lenient standards of other states. The result was an upgrading of environmental regulation across the USA. Thus the current debate in the EU is whether EU policy, balanced between deregulation and re-regulation, will lead to a Delaware or a California effect.

6 The leader/laggard principle

Because environmental and social regulation creates a non-tariff barrier to trade, industry in member states with higher levels of social and environmental protection at the national level fear that these regulations undermine their competitiveness in the EU market. In order to create a level playing field for their products, these member states demand that their level of protection becomes the EU standard. In this way, states with higher standards force laggard states (those with lower standards) to enact more stringent levels of protection. In the EU, the leader states are traditionally Denmark and the Netherlands, led by Germany, while the laggard states are considered to be Greece, Portugal, Spain, Italy and Belgium. These 'laggard' states traditionally pass only the environmental legislation required by Brussels. Intergovernmentalists argue that poorer member states agree to these demands because they are 'bought off' by richer states with intergovernmental bargains that help them to attain such standards: an example is the Cohesion Fund, which allocates half its funding to environmental projects.

Who wins/who loses

In general, **EU citizens** benefit from re-regulatory policy as it provides them with higher standards of worker protection and an improved EU environment, through the reduction of pollution and protection of vulnerable areas. However, just because these policies benefit the public does not mean that they necessarily disadvantage **EU businesses**. High EU environmental standards on products can make the EU more competitive in 'green' goods in export markets such as the USA and Japan. Generally, however, re-regulation is viewed as an increased cost of production for EU businesses. For this reason, business lobbies actively follow and attempt to influence developments in these policy areas.

The **EU institutions**, in particular the Commission and the EP, have benefited from increased decision-making powers in the area of the environment. However, the sensitivity surrounding Social Policy has often proved to be a source of conflict between the Commission, the EP and the member states.

The delegation of social and environmental policies to the EU has affected the **member states** in varying ways. Since Environmental Policy was not a well-developed national prerogative before it became an EU competence, member states appreciated the benefits of delegating this policy area. EU-level Environmental Policy has two added advantages. Given that pollution doesn't stop at borders, an EU-level policy is more effective than national action. An EU-level policy also allows national governments to blame the EU for making tough but necessary environmental decisions. Social Policy, however, is one of the fundamental competences of the nation-state, and also differs drastically between member states. For these reasons, any harmonization in this area can be perceived as a threat to national sovereignty; this is why a consensus is normally found only when measures clearly enhance the functioning of the Common Market.

Food for thought

Since Social Policy deals with sensitive issues of importance to national sovereignty, and in light of the recent emphasis on subsidiarity, politicians have often argued that it would be more practical to keep Social Policy at the national level. However, the changes caused by the Single Market Programme (such as slowly increasing labour mobility) strengthen the need for a complementary EU-level Social Policy to be developed, in order to prevent non-tariff barriers between member states. Therefore, is economic integration a strong enough reason to transfer more competence for Social Policy to the EU level?

EU standards on environmental protection are only the minimum level that must be enacted in all member states. Through Article 176 (ex-Article 130t), member states are allowed to have more stringent regulations in environmental policy than the level required by the EU. However, when these higher standards become a non-tariff barrier to the free movement of goods, as in the *Danish Bottle* case, are higher levels of protection justified? Or should these greener member states be forced to reduce their level of protection to that of the rest of the EU? This question takes on more significance in light of EU enlargement into Central and Eastern Europe, where environmental standards fall far below EU levels.

Student-to-student tip

Although there is a lot of information available about these policies, it is difficult to find a good introductory article which adequately explains either area. For this reason, we recommend using the Commission and especially the European Parliament websites as initial resources. We also recommend contacting the European branches of environmental and social interest groups for information about recent policy developments and legislation under consideration. These groups can be found on the web or by using the *European Public Affairs Directory*, which is available in most university libraries and is updated annually (see *Interest Groups* for citation).

Summary

- While most EU legislation is deregulatory, EU Social and Environmental Policies are re-regulatory. Most EU legislation in these fields is enacted to enhance the functioning of the Single Market.
- Environmental and Social Policies have developed in different ways and at different speeds. This is primarily because national governments view Social Policy as their own prerogative, whilst environmental policy is perceived as a trans-national concern.
- Primary developments in Social Policy have been social security rights for migrant workers, health and safety standards, product safety standards and equal opportunities. Attempts at strengthening the relationships between labour unions and European businesses at the EU level have not been particularly successful. Social policy remains controversial, because there is no European consensus on how a society should be organized; areas that do not have a strong economic justification are therefore underdeveloped at the EU level.
- Primary developments in Environmental Policy have been air and water pollution, waste treatment, control of dangerous substances and technologies, and wildlife conservation. Environmental Policy has also been included in several areas of Regional Policy, including the Cohesion Fund and the new ISPA fund for pre-accession countries.

Selected bibliography

Overviews and comparisons of both policies

Hix, S. (1999) *The Political System of the European Union*, London: Macmillan, chapter 8: 223–32.

In this very concise introduction to both policy areas, Hix sketches the main theories and issues related to environment and social policy as they pertain to re-regulation.

Scharpf, F. (1996) 'Negative and Positive Integration in the Political Economy of European Welfare States', in G. Marks et al., *Governance in the European Union*, London: Sage, chapter 2: 15–39.

Scharpf outlines the product versus process argument, and offers a strong, if somewhat difficult-to-follow, explanation of the evolution of these policies.

Social Policy

Majone, G. (1993) 'The EC between Social Policy and Social Regulation', *Journal of Common Market Studies*, vol. 31, no. 2: 153–70.

Majone explains the difference between social policy and social regulation, and argues that EU social regulation is primarily justified by the need to correct market failures.

Leibfried, S. and P. Pierson (1995) 'Multi-tiered Institutions and the Making of Social Policy', in Leibfried and Pierson (eds), *European Social Policy*, Washington, DC: The Brookings Institution, chapter 1: 1–40.

This chapter provides a good balance to Majone, arguing that he overstates the extent to which EU social regulation is justified by market failures.

Leibfried, S. and P. Pierson (2000) 'Social Policy: Left to Courts and Markets?', in H. Wallace and W. Wallace (eds), *Policy-Making in the European Union*, 4th edn, Oxford: Oxford University Press, chapter 10: 267–92.

This chapter offers a concise overview of the development in EU Social Policy.

Falkner, G. (2001) 'The Council or the Social Partners? EC Social Policy between Diplomacy and Collective Bargaining', *Journal of European Public Policy*, vol. 7, no. 5: 705–24.

Falkner discusses the role played by employer and labour associations in the area of social policy, and outlines the relevant factors that lead to a social partner agreement.

Environmental Policy

Judge, D. (ed.) (1993) *A Green Dimension for the European Community*, London: Frank Cass.

Judge's volume is a great resource on environmental policy, if very historical. See in particular the chapter by Hildebrandt on the history of the policy (pp. 13–44) and the chapter by Weale and Williams which addresses various aspects, including the rationales behind the policy (pp. 45–64). For information about environmental interest groups, such as the EEB, the chapter by Mazey and Richardson (pp. 109–28) is very helpful.

Lenschow, A. (1997) 'Variations in EC Environmental Policy Integration: Agency Push with Complex Institutional Structures', *Journal of European Public Policy*, vol. 4, no. 2: 109–27.

Lenschow examines environmental policy integration in relation to other EU policies, and describes the interaction between the different Community actors, including interest groups, the EP and the Commission.

Sands, P. (1990) 'European Community Environmental Law: Legislation, the European Court of Justice and Common-Interest Groups', *Modern Law Review*, vol. 53: 685–98.

Although an older reference, Sands does a great job outlining the ECJ's role in environmental policy. In particular, he explains the significance of the *Danish Bottle* case.

Friedrich, A. et al. (2000) 'A new approach to EU Environmental Policy?', *Journal of European Public Policy*, vol. 7, no. 4: 593–612.

This article demonstrates how the Commission's ability to accommodate the interests of industry in the area of environmental policy is limited by the role of the European Parliament and the Environmental Council in the legislative process.

Supportive websites

http://www.europarl.eu.int/factsheets/default_en.htm The fact sheets are excellent: brief but highly detailed, they allow you to gain a complete oversight of any policy area in less than five minutes.

http://www.cec.org.uk/info/pubs/bbriefs/index.htm This site provides briefings on all policy fields; the information on social and environmental policies is particularly helpful.

http://www.europa.eu.int/comm/environment/index_en.htm The Environment DG website is especially well developed, with information on policy and programmes.

http://www.eea.eu.int/ The European Environment Agency website offers a comprehensive list of environmental links and information about policy development.

http://www.europa.eu.int/comm/environment/impel/index.htm Implementation and Enforcement of Environmental Law (IMPEL) is a good resource for the legal aspects of the policy.

http://www.europa.eu.int/comm/dgs/employment_social/index_en.htm The DG for Employment and Social Affairs provides links as well as documents.

17

Competition Policy

Simon Ashwell

Competition Policy has several goals, such as ensuring fair competition and encouraging the optimal allocation of resources within the EU. This policy is thus critical to the functioning of the internal market. As a result of the Single Market Programme (SMP) and the pro-competitive impact of the euro, Competition Policy has increasing importance as an area of EU competence. However, while the Commission has broad competences and regulatory powers in this policy area, the continued development of an effective EU Competition Policy is restrained by several factors, including the politicization and possible decentralization of the policy.

The facts

A   Rationale behind EU Competition Policy

Competition Policy is necessary to ensure effective competition, and thereby the most efficient allocation of resources and the highest levels of economic welfare. In Article 3 of the Treaty, the EU recognizes the need for a policy that ensures that competition within the Community is not distorted, and that creates a level 'playing field' for European businesses. Without common competition rules, the benefits of market liberalization could be minimized through industrial practices such as price fixing and market sharing by firms, as well as by government intervention in national industries.

The need for an EU Competition Policy was reinforced by the SMP. The removal of the remaining barriers to trade (especially non-tariff barriers), outlined in the 1985 Commission White Paper, required the development of new competition regulations in areas such as state aids and utilities. The economic growth and increased market liberalization of the late 1980s also led to an upsurge in pan-European mergers. These mergers required oversight by the Commission, which then attempted to regulate monopolies and to prevent unfair business practices in EU markets.

B   Theories and theoretical basis of Competition Policy

In order to analyse the theoretical basis of Competition Policy, it is necessary to understand the following concepts and their economic implications.

I   Monopoly

A monopoly exists when there is only one seller in a given market. This becomes a problem only when it is difficult for potential providers to enter this market (i.e. high barriers to entry on the supply side) and no alternative products are available to the consumer (i.e. no demand-side substitutability). In such a situation, the monopoly may act independently, determining both the price and the quantity of a good. While true monopolies (having 100 per cent of market share) rarely exist, competition policy is needed to regulate firms that can act like monopolies. The concern over cartels and mergers, for example, relates to the ability of these actors to achieve a monopolistic position, thereby dominating the market to the detriment of competition and consumers.

2   Monopoly welfare loss

This concept refers to the economic loss to the society as a whole which results from monopolistic practices. As a monopoly is the only producer of a good, it can determine both the quantity and the price of that good which is available on the market. Without any competition from other producers, consumers must accept the price set by the monopoly if they want or need that product. The loss to society is the difference between the monopolistic price and the price paid under perfect competition. The misallocation of resources resulting from monopolistic behaviour can have long-term negative ramifications on the economy.

3   Cartel behaviour

This refers to agreements between firms that undermine competition, by co-ordinating activities in order to increase profits. There are two types of cartel behaviour:

- *Price setting*: any agreement between two or more producers to protect their own market share and profits by not competing with each other. They do so by agreeing on the prices they will charge for their products.

- *Production restrictions*: a type of explicit agreement between firms in the same industry to supply a certain quantity of a product to the market. OPEC (the Organization of Petroleum Exporting Countries), for example, is able to raise the global price of oil by its members jointly agreeing to limit the production of petroleum. By co-ordinating the amount of their sales and production, the OPEC countries are able to achieve monopolistic prices for their product. This sort of restrictive activity benefits producers at the expense of the rest of society: the oil crisis caused by OPEC action was one of the main factors behind the world-wide recession in the 1970s.

4   Dominant position

According to the European Court of Justice (ECJ), a firm has achieved a dominant market position when it has the ability to behave independently of its competitors and customers. One of the benefits of the SMP is the increase in economies of scale: as more goods are produced, the scale of production becomes larger, and the cost of producing each individual unit of a good decreases. This should benefit consumers, since products should become less expensive. However, if one firm is able to increase its economies of scale to such an extent that it marginalizes all other firms, this dominant firm will attain certain monopolistic characteristics. This results in a welfare loss for society; not only does the consumer fail to benefit from economies of scale, but the pricing scheme of the dominant firm may force smaller producers out of the market, and thereby limit selection for the consumer.

5   Mergers and acquisitions

This refers to the combination of two or more firms into one. Mergers and acquisitions can have either a positive or a negative effect on social welfare:

- They can facilitate increased scales of production, which can lower costs for consumers.
- Or they can attain a dominant market position, which allows them to undercut and eliminate their competition.

C   The main instruments

The Commission has been delegated powers by the member states to develop an EU-level Competition Policy, in order to prevent anti-competitive practices in three main areas:

- monopolistic behaviour, such as restrictive agreements and concerted practices;

- mergers and acquisitions, especially when these lead to dominant market share;
- state aids, of both direct and indirect forms.

There are three Treaty articles which allow the Commission to develop competition regulations:

- Article 81 (ex-Article 85) prohibits 'restrictive practices': this refers to all agreements and decisions by firms that may negatively affect trade between the member states, by preventing, restricting or distorting competition.
- Article 82 (ex-Article 86) prohibits 'abuse of dominant position': this refers to any practices by a firm holding a dominant market position which could negatively affect trade between member states. Dominant position must be decided on a case-by-case basis.
- Article 87 (ex-Article 90) refers to the use of state aid, and prohibits the governments of member states from giving any type of economic aid to firms which might distort competition, especially if this affects trade between the member states. This article has special significance in light of the 1985 Commission White Paper, which identified state aids as a non-tariff barrier to trade within the EU.

In addition, there is important secondary legislation (see *Institutional Processes*) that is used to enforce EU Competition Policy. The Merger Control Regulation (MCR, No. 4064/89), for example, regulates the merger of any two firms that could result in the strengthening of a dominant market position in such a way as to impede competition within the EU. This regulation allows the Commission to evaluate the impact of mergers on the internal market before they are finalized, using several criteria. The main test for compatibility with the internal market is the possible effect of a merger on competition within that specific market; however, this can be difficult to determine. This is important, as the Commission has sole jurisdiction to decide on whether a merger is compatible or not.

D   Procedure

The Commission receives cases for review in three ways:

- through notification by a firm (for mergers) or government (for state aid) as required by EU law;
- through complaints brought by other companies, interest groups or individuals;
- through the Commission's own initiative.

In 2000, there were 297 anti-trust cases, 345 merger cases, and 564 state aid cases. The majority of cases resulted from own-initiative notifications. DG Competition evaluates the situation in each case to access whether:

- a case falls outside the scope of Commission responsibility;
- a case complies with EU competition law;
- a case requires the Commission to issue a formal complaint against a firm.

In order to evaluate cases, the Commission has the right to carry out inspections of firms without prior notice and can demand required documentation. However, the majority of cases are settled by administrative letters, known as 'comfort letters', which inform the parties concerned that the Commission intends to close a case, subject to conditions delineated in the letter. Most of the outstanding issues in merger and acquisition cases are resolved without the need for the Commission to call a hearing. If a hearing is necessary, the firms and/or member states involved are allowed to present their position. If the firm or member state is found guilty of anti-competitive practices, the maximum penalty which the Commission can levy is a fine of 10 per cent of the annual turnover of that firm. In 2000, the Commission levied fines totalling €199.5 million, over half of which was levied on a cartel of veterinary pharmaceutical producers.

E   Exceptions to EU competition regulations

I   For restrictive agreements

Article 81(3) allows for certain kinds of co-operation between firms to be exempted from competition rules, if they have a positive effect on society or the economy. Block exemptions have been granted to co-operation that promotes technical progress or improves the production of goods, such as R&D agreements and licensing agreements for the transfer of technology. However, only the Commission has the power to grant individual exemptions, and these are likely to include certain limits on such co-operation (such as time limits).

2   For mergers and acquisitions

The MCR applies only to mergers of a certain size, which have a pronounced impact on the internal market. Generally, the Commission examines EU mergers of companies that have:

- a joint world-wide turnover of more than €500 million and an EU turnover of more than €250 million, unless each of the companies has more than two-thirds of its turnover in just one member state;
- however, mergers below this threshold can also be examined if they have a lower world-wide turnover but involve three or more member states.

In 2000, the Commission submitted a report to the Council requesting that the thresholds for merger evaluation be re-examined to include factors such as their inter-state effect.

3   For state aids

Article 87(2–3) allows a number of exceptions to the broad prohibition on state aids, such as aid that has a social dimension. The Commission may also grant exemptions to aid that promotes:

- the development of certain activities or regions;
- important EU projects of common EU interest;
- culture and heritage (such as the French film industry).

However, Article 88 stipulates that the Commission must be notified of all state aid projects before implementation; it has the sole authority to decide whether a state aid qualifies for one of these exemptions. In order to facilitate the work of the Commission, EU Regulation No. 994/98 defined a block exemption to the notification requirement (Article 88) on aid to small and medium-size enterprises, R&D, environmental protection, employment and training.

The problems/issues

A   Scale-based efficiency as a criterion for Competition Policy

National governments and the Commission almost invariably lack the resources and the ability to apply Competition Policy efficiently and fairly. For example, politicians argue that European firms must achieve certain economies of scale in order to compete globally. However, competition regulations may be applied in ways that fail to support the goals of the SMP, by punishing those firms which pursue economies of scale, and thereby preventing the emergence of globally competitive European firms. Therefore, the Commission increasingly takes an 'efficiency defence' into account when evaluating firms – for example, the Commission may approve a merger even if the newly created firm then achieves a market-dominant position, as long as the efficiency gained through the merger produces enough economic benefit for the economy as a whole to compensate for any welfare losses produced through reduced competition.

B   Politicization

The complexities of EU policy making are exacerbated by the fact that Competition Policy has a political purpose in the EU, which goes beyond its economic objective as in the USA. Leon Brittan, former Competition Commissioner, argued that EU Competition Policy is focused on the promotion of market and European integration, in ways that could undermine its economic objectives of promoting fair competition. Therefore, he contended, the objectives of Competition Policy are often sacrificed when they conflict with other political objectives, such as European integration or the individual goals of member states. This is particularly evident in areas such as state aids, regional aid, cohesion, Environmental Policy, employment, and R&D, which favour certain national interests over others.

Despite several controversial cases (such as Case 358/94, *Air France* vs *Commission* (1997)), overall pro-market attitudes as well as tight national budget constraints (related to participation in EMU) have made EU control over state aids politically more acceptable. However, utilities in the EU remain heavily regulated. Member states justify their intervention in utilities for redistributive reasons (i.e. that all of society should benefit from public goods) and because services/utilities are often natural monopolies (i.e. industries where start-up costs are so prohibitively high that competition is minimized). These include industries such as railways and postal services in many member states.

National subsidies to utilities (as well as other natural monopolies) create a barrier to the entry of other firms into the market for these goods. Therefore, the main issue for the Commission is how to distinguish between state investment (which is legal) and state aid (which is not), rather than to force all utilities to be privately rather than publicly owned. Article 86(2) allows the Commission to justify exclusive rights in utilities as 'natural monopoly and legitimate public service obligations', thereby circumventing the political controversy which would result from the deregulation of such services.

C Decentralization and modernization

Competition Commissioner Mario Monti has indicated a strong commitment to modernizing the tools used to enforce Competition Policy. In addition to the White Paper on anti-trust provisions, Monti launched a review of merger policy in June 2000, and has made a commitment to revise block exemption regulations for research and development. Of primary concern are the distribution of functions between the national and the European level in Competition Policy, which has become an issue for two main reasons:

- The wider acceptance of the principle of subsidiarity means that the EU should not be involved in Competition Policy at a level that could be more effectively performed by the member states themselves (see *Constitutionalism*).
- DG Competition does not have the resources to handle all competition cases effectively.

While the Commission has been the only institution with the power to take action against EU cartels and abuses of dominant position since 1962, the institution is in favour of decentralizing certain areas of Competition Policy, as indicated in the 1999 Commission White Paper on modernizing rules related to Articles 85 and 86 (White Paper No. 99/027). However, decentralization is complicated by the difficulty of deciding on the relevant jurisdiction of a particular policy or piece of legislation. Within the context of the SMP, jurisdiction belongs to the EU in most areas of Competition Policy, because a growing number of mergers are multinational, and national competition policies (or lack of them) do not take the repercussions of national mergers on the SIM or other member states into account.

In November 2002, many of these issues were resolved by a new system, under which the Commission shares anti-trust law enforcement with the national authorities of member states. In the new regime, which takes effect in 2004, EU and national regulations establish a 'European Competition Network', in order to allocate cases and ensure the uniform application of EU competition law. As of 1 May 2004, firms are also no longer required to communicate all mergers to the Commission. The new system allows the Commission to intervene in any case that it feels is not being properly handled by national authorities. The decentralization of anti-trust enforcement (by comparison with the creation of a European Cartel Office) benefits the Commission by minimizing EU bureaucracy, while allowing the Competition DG to concentrate on the largest and most important anti-trust cases. In addition, this decentralization effort radically changes the way in which companies, lawyers and regulators deal with anti-trust rules.

D Differing models of capitalism

A related problem facing EU-level Competition Policy is the different national policies and traditions in this policy area. Whichever model the EU chooses for its Competition Policy, it risks discriminating against the traditions and structures of at least one member state. Of particular relevance is the difference in the approach to competition regulation in the 'Anglo-Saxon' versus the 'Continental' models of capitalism. The Anglo-Saxon model, practised in the UK, is based on US anti-trust law, in which firms are subject to strict scrutiny and fierce compliance regulations. In contrast, the Continental approach (practised in Germany and the Netherlands) has a tendency to take the wider social implications of a firm's actions, including close links between suppliers and customers, into account. Other countries, such as Italy and Belgium, have only recently developed competition agencies at all. Such diversity in competition regulations would persist if competition were delegated to the national level. Decentralization could therefore constitute a type of non-tariff barrier to trade, and result in an uneven playing field for firms. As a result, firms could be confronted by different opportunities for competing and restructuring depending on where they were located within the EU.

Who wins/who loses

Competition is one of the policy areas in which the **EU Commission** has the broadest range of powers. These powers have been both conferred on the Commission by the Treaty and delegated to the Commission by the Council. They have increased with the SMP, and have encouraged several EU Competition Commissioners, such as Van Miert, to confront member states and multi-national corporations on competition issues. Theoretically, the Commission control of Competition Policy increases efficiency by removing these decisions from the power of the member states, and thereby preventing the member states from using Competition Policy as a means of promoting their national 'champion' industries at the expense of industries in other member states. However, since the Commission acts as an agent of the member states, it is vulnerable to political pressure from powerful member states. As a result, the Commission is not always able to act as an independent arbiter in the creation and enforcement of Competition Policy. This means that while the Commission will continue to attempt to expand its competences in this field, its power over enforcement of EU competition regulations is still subject to the will of the member states.

While the **member states** have lost competences through the delegation of Competition Policy to the EU level, this has also served as a means of external stimulus for reform in areas such as state utilities and aids. Benefits between member states vary: countries such as Belgium and Italy, which have yet to develop strong anti-trust policies at the national level, benefit more from EU-level Competition Policy than states such as the UK and Germany, which have strong anti-trust offices and a history of competence in this area.

With regard to **multi-national corporations (MNCs) and European businesses**, an EU-level policy solves the internal market problems created by allowing each member state to pursue its own Competition Policy, which would constitute a type of non-tariff barrier to trade. The centralization of Competition Policy at the EU level also helps European industry by providing a common set of competition rules. This facilitates cross-border mergers and acquisitions, to the benefit of industries in all member states.

The benefit of EU Competition Policy to **EU citizens** depends heavily on the ability of the Commission to successfully balance scale-based efficiency with losses to social welfare. If EU Competition Policy works correctly, the increased competition within the EU should reduce prices and increase the selection of products. However, many academics question the ability of the Commission to control competition effectively, given the politicized position of the policy and the difficulties in determining whether an abuse of dominant position has occurred.

Food for thought

Member states often argue for the decentralization of policies, so that these policies can be tailored to the individual needs of member states and their citizens. However, the decentralization of Competition Policy could create internal barriers to trade, thus weakening the internal market. It could also encourage multi-national companies to 'shop around' for the best competition policies. This could cause a 'race to the bottom' in the regulation of competition, which would end up hurting consumers. Therefore, is the EU citizen better off through the decentralization or the standardization of Competition Policy?

EU Competition Policy is weakened by the politicization of the policy and the position of the Commission relative to the member states. Unease about these issues among member governments has lent support to proposals for a European Cartel Office. The demands are based on an enthusiasm for 'depoliticization': in other words, the purest possible application of Competition Policy principles removed from short-term political decisions and ideological economic policy considerations. Would such an office be able to harmonize the different models of Competition Policy which exist within the EU?

When anti-competitive practices take place outside the Community, the Commission is ill-equipped to deal with them (consider the problems with Microsoft). Various factors, such as divergent objectives and interpretations of Competition Policy, often limit the effectiveness of EU/US extra-territorial agreements. These problems were highlighted in the disagreement over the proposed GE/Honeywell merger, which the USA approved and the EU rejected. In addition, bilateral agreements fail to consider the interests of third countries that are affected by these policies. Might increased globalization mean that it will be necessary to delegate Competition Policy to an even higher level, such as the World Trade Organization (WTO; see *External Policies*)?

Student-to-student tip

It is surprisingly easy to find information about individual EU competition cases. The *Official Journal* of the European Communities publishes notices for all decisions made on state aid and concentration (abuse of dominant position) cases several times a month. The notices outline the details of each case, naming the parties involved and the issue of contention. Check the 'C' series legislation for the most recent developments, at http://europa.eu.int/eu-lex/ and click on 'Official Journal'. In addition, publications such as *The Economist* often contain excellent Articles about controversial mergers and EU competition cases, and Commission press releases (available at the EU website) often provide short summaries of the issues surrounding EU competition cases, when they occur.

Summary

- EU Competition Policy was established in the Treaties of Rome in order to ensure that competition within the Community is not distorted by unfair practices.

- The Council has delegated to the Commission broad regulatory powers in the field of competition. Under Articles 81–7 of the Treaties and the Merger Control Regulation (MCR), the Commission reviews three types of competition activities:
  - monopolistic behaviour;
  - mergers and acquisitions;
  - state aids.
- There are several exceptions to the broad control of competition carried out by the Commission, including block exemptions for some types of co-operation between firms and some types of state aids.
- The effectiveness of EU Competition Policy is threatened by three factors: the feasibility of scale-based efficiency as a criterion for approving mergers, problems identifying the abuse of dominant position, and the politicization of Competition Policy within the EU, especially regarding state aids.
- In addition, recent calls from member states for both the decentralization of Competition Policy and the depoliticization of the policy through the establishment of an independent cartel office could weaken or strengthen the Commission's power in this policy area.

Selected bibliography

Overviews

Pelkmans, J. (1997) *European Integration: Methods and Economic Analysis*, Harlow: Netherlands Open University and Longman, chapter 12: 183–205.
  Pelkmans provides a comprehensive introduction to the economics of the policy.
El-Agraa, A. (ed.) (2000) *The European Union: Economics and Politics*, 6th edn, London: Prentice-Hall and Financial Times, chapters 9 and 10: 187–230.
  This volume contains two chapters on Competition and Industrial Policy, which complement the work of Pelkmans.

Comprehensive analysis

Cini, M. and L. McGowan (1998) *Competition Policy in the European Union*, Basingstoke: Macmillan.
  Cini and McGowan offer the best comprehensive book for in-depth study on the subject.
Brittan, L. (1992) *European Competition Policy: Keeping the Playing Field Level*, Brussels: CEPS.
  As a former Commissioner for Competition Policy, Brittan offers a first-hand account of how the policy works.

Articles on aspects of the policy

Buigues, P., A. Jaquemin and A. Sapir (eds) (1995) *European Policies in Competition, Trade and Industry: Conflict and Complementarities*, Aldershot: Edward Elgar, introduction and chapter 1: xi–48.
  These two chapters outline the theoretical and practical conflicts between Competition and Industrial Policies.

Hay, D. (1993) 'The Assessment: Competition Policy', *Oxford Review of Economic Policy*, vol. 9, no. 2: 1–26.
  Hay provides a clear assessment of the policy following the changes resulting from the SMP.

Supportive websites

http://www.europa.eu.int/comm/competition/index_en.html The site of DG Competition, containing speeches by current Commissioner Monti and former commissioner Van Miert, and helpful press releases containing recent statistics and describing trends in Competition Policy.

http://www.europa.eu.int/comm/competition/annual_reports/ This is the link to the *Annual Reports on Competition Policy* provided by the EU Commission.

http://www.dti.gov.uk/ccp/ The British Department of Trade and Industry offers several pages with helpful links about EU Competition Policy. The analysis of EU competition regime reform, for example, cites both Commission documents and reports by the UK House of Lords; the site also contains interesting comparative reports on the effectiveness of Competition Policies in various countries.

http://www.ert.be/pe/ene02.htm In response to the Lisbon European Council (March 2000), the European Round Table of Industrialists (ERT), a group of European industrialists, published a paper listing its proposals for reforms to EU Competition Policy. The site also allows access to ERT working papers in a variety of other EU policy areas, such as enlargement and taxation.

18

Common Foreign and Security Policy

Mark Vivis

The guiding principle behind the creation of the European Community has always been to guarantee peace and stability in Europe through economic interdependence. However, successful economic integration has not led to strong co-operation in the field of foreign and security policy, since member states view security issues as a matter of national sovereignty. As a result, the EU's military influence has not kept pace with its increased economic power. In order to strike a balance between political influence and economic power, the Common Foreign and Security Policy (CFSP) was added as the second Pillar in the Treaty on European Union (TEU) in 1992. Security concerns following the end of the Cold War have also initiated further developments in the policy, including the plan for a European Security and Defence Identity (ESDI). However, as trans-national co-operation within this area threatens the sovereignty and competences of member states, the development of the CFSP within the EU has been slow.

The facts

A The Brussels Treaty Organization and the WEU

The CFSP is part of an evolving process of foreign policy co-operation amongst member states. The first attempts at military co-operation began in 1948, through the creation of the Brussels Treaty Organization. This co-operation, originally comprising the UK, France, Belgium, the Netherlands and Luxembourg, was renamed the Western European Union (WEU) in 1954, following the accession of Germany and Italy. While the original function of this organization was made redundant through the creation of the North Atlantic Treaty Organization (NATO) in 1949, the WEU has remained an organization independent of, but closely connected with, the EU. WEU membership now includes all EU member states and most candidate countries. The organization currently acts as a forum for discussions on the further development of the EU's military collaboration. The 1992 Petersburg Council played a pivotal role in the development of the WEU as the defence arm of the EU. In addition to the defence tasks already defined for the WEU in previous treaties, the Council determined that military forces of the WEU could be utilized to perform the 'Petersburg Tasks' – namely, humanitarian, peace-keeping and crisis management tasks. In 1993, the WEU was designated as the European pillar of NATO. It remains heavily militarily dependent on NATO and the USA for logistical and surveillance support.

B   The European Defence Community (EDC) and the Fouchet Plans

Simultaneous to the creation of the WEU, additional proposals for inter-European security and defence were being developed. The Cold War and concern over West German rearmament led to the Pleven Plan, a French government proposal calling for a fully integrated European army tied to a supranational institution. The Pleven Plan (named after the French Prime Minister) outlined the institutional structure of the European Defence Community (EDC); Germany, Belgium, Luxembourg, Italy and the Netherlands ratified the proposal in 1952. However, both the British govern-ment and the French National Assembly rejected the EDC, due to its supranational nature. As a result, the EDC and further plans for development in this area were abandoned until 1961, when the Fouchet Committee presented two proposals calling for a confederation of independent European states with a common foreign and defence policy. These French proposals may have been part of de Gaulle's attempt to create a purely intergovernmental European Community, independent of the USA. The institutional framework of the Fouchet Plans was ambitious, but also allowed all policy agreements to be decided by unanimity, at least initially. However, Belgium, Luxembourg, Italy, the Netherlands and West Germany rejected the plan, since it envisaged European defence as independent of NATO. At the time, such independence was perceived as a threat to the European Economic Community (EEC). As a result, no further co-operation was pursued until 1970.

C   The development of the European Political Co-operation

In 1970, the Luxembourg Summit produced the D'Avignon Report, which offered a proposal for foreign policy co-operation among the EEC member states. In a renewed spirit of co-operation, the six original member states established the

European Political Co-operation (EPC) as a purely political intergovernmental organization with no institutional basis in the Treaty. The EPC provided a forum for foreign policy co-ordination, attempting to give political direction to the EC's external relations, even though it was not initially included within the EEC legal framework. In addition, defence and security policy remained outside the parameters of the EPC, and therefore did not pose a threat to national sovereignty. The creation of the EPC led to regular meetings between the Foreign Ministers of the EEC member states and closer co-ordination between these governments on foreign policy matters. The EPC also provided a forum for the adoption of common positions, such as the Venice Declaration (1980), in which the nine member states spoke with one voice, regarding a policy on the Middle East.

However, the Islamic revolution in Iran and the Soviet invasion of Afghanistan in the late 1970s highlighted the weakness of the Community within the international political arena. In response, the member states adopted the London Report in 1981, which attempted to improve the co-operation and institutional framework of the EPC. As a consequence of the report, the governments established a troika system for the EPC, in which the Council presidency is assisted by its predecessor and its successor, in order to achieve greater policy consistency. The implementation of the report also gave the Commission a 'consultation role' on issues of external foreign policy.

However, these changes did not result in a significantly more effective organization, especially as more ambitious proposals on foreign and security policies, such as the Genscher–Colombo Plan (November 1981), were rejected as a threat to national sovereignty. Even when the EPC became part of the EC Treaty framework in 1986 through Title III of the Single European Act (SEA), it remained separate from the EC institutions and policies. However, integration into the Treaty did result in an EPC Secretariat in Brussels, and allowed the European Parliament (EP) power to scrutinize national officials and foreign ministers. The Commission's role was also expanded to ensure consistency between EC and EPC policies.

D   The creation of the Common Foreign and Security Policy (CFSP)

The current Common Foreign and Security Policy first came into being in 1993 through Title V of the Treaty on European Union, and was further refined through the Amsterdam Treaty (1997). Article 11 of the TEU states: 'The Union and its Member States shall define and implement a common foreign and security policy covering all areas of foreign and security policy.' The TEU replaced the EPC with the CFSP, which became intergovernmental Pillar II. A co-ordinated defence was also mentioned for the first time in the TEU.

The CFSP differs from the EPC in many ways. Joint actions and common positions were established as CFSP policy instruments, and the CFSP Secretariat was incorporated into the Council Secretariat, thereby emphasizing the intergovernmental character of the new policy. As a result, the CFSP meetings became part of the General Affairs Council (GAC) meetings. CFSP proposals are now discussed within the institutional framework, and more specific matters relating to defence are considered during the IGCs.

Despite the structural changes to European co-operation in this policy area, the first years of the CFSP demonstrated limited success, with notable failures in the handling of the situation in former Yugoslavia throughout the 1990s. As a result, the Amsterdam Treaty attempted to strengthen and clarify the CFSP in several ways:

- The use of qualified majority voting (QMV) instead of unanimity was expanded in order to implement CFSP decisions.
- A new policy instrument, called 'common strategy', was introduced, aimed at creating a greater long-term perspective on CFSP policy and the prioritization of policies.
- In order to prevent delays due to lack of consensus, the constructive abstention procedure was clarified, allowing countries to opt out of policy decisions (Article 23; ex-Title V, J.13).
- The Secretary-General of the Council Secretariat was replaced by the High Representative of the CFSP (also known as 'Mr/Mrs CFSP'), creating consistency in, and focus on, the CFSP.
- The Policy Planning and Early Warning Unit was created, in order to assist the High Representative.
- The European Council gained the competence to elaborate and implement common defence policies.

Significantly, the Amsterdam Treaty also strengthened the link between the Western European Union (WEU) and the CFSP. The WEU's Petersburg Tasks – crisis prevention, management and peacekeeping – were incorporated in the Treaty, thus enhancing the EU's defence competences.

E Elements of the CFSP

I Instruments of the CFSP

Because of the importance and sensitivity of defence and security issues, major CFSP policy decisions are made by the European Council, primarily during biannual meetings. CFSP legislation is determined by several instruments:

- *Common strategies.* These are decisions made by the Council upon recommendations of the Commission on issues of joint concern to EU member states. The objectives, duration and resources of each strategy are defined in a unanimous Council decision; but the strategies are implemented by joint actions and common positions, which may be taken by QMV. The EU has adopted common strategies on Russia, the Ukraine and the Mediterranean region.

- *Common positions.* The General Affairs Council (GAC) – composed of the foreign affairs ministers from each member state and the EU Commissioner on External Relations – can adopt common positions regarding the EU's stance on certain issues (such as terrorism) or geographic regions (such as the Balkans), so that the Community can speak with one voice at international conferences, for example. The member states are then responsible for ensuring that their national positions adhere to the common position.
- *Joint actions and decisions.* The GAC may adopt a joint action in situations requiring operational action by member states. Each action is specific in scope, objective, resources and duration. The GAC may also adopt decisions in this area that are binding on the member states.

2 Headline Goal

The December 1999 Helsinki European Council established the 'Headline Goal' of creating a multi-national rapid reaction force (RRF) of 50,000–60,000 men deployable to global trouble spots within sixty days of a Council request, sustainable for up to one year. The aim of this development was to create a corps-level force capable of an autonomous European mission without the assistance of NATO. The RRF was created primarily to perform the Petersburg Tasks, and was initially scheduled to be operational by 2003.

3 The ESDI and the ESDP

In an effort to develop European means for dealing with conflicts in south-eastern Europe more effectively, the 1996 NATO Council expanded on earlier suggestions for the creation of a defined European security and defence identity by creating the Combined Joint Task Forces (CJTF) as a means of using NATO military capacities in operations under the political and military control of the WEU. However, for the CJTF to function to the point where the leadership of such a force was both easily defined and well structured, the NATO foreign ministers decided to build up military co-ordination between member states, known as the European Security Defence Identity (ESDI). Following the Saint Milo Declaration on defence co-operation between the UK and France, the June 1999 Cologne European Council called for a more independent European defence programme, and the ESDI became the ESDP (European Security and Defence Policy). In addition, a Political and Security Committee (PSC), an EU Military Committee (EUMC) and an EU Military Staff (EUMS) were created, to be operational by March 2000. Priority areas of this policy included the development of independent intelligence gathering, improvement of command and control structures, and development of 'heavy lift' capacity.

4   The Political and Security Committee

The ESDP presented to the Nice European Council in 2000 an outline of progress in the development of Headline capabilities, civilian policing capabilities, the structure and role of permanent political and military organs, the inclusion of WEU functions, and arrangements for EU–NATO relations, as well as those with third countries. However, the only element of the ESDP that was included in the Nice Treaty was the PSC, as part of the amended Article 25 (ex-Article J15). The PSC, composed of senior national representatives, provides political and strategic direction for crisis management operations, with military advice and recommendations from the EUMC. At the Gothenburg European Council in June 2001, new targets were set for civilian aspects of crisis management; these targets were set to be achieved by 2003 through voluntary contributions by member states. In addition, the framework of the policy was modified so that the PSC and the EUMC could provide a liaison between the European Council, the Council Secretariat and NATO, thus strengthening a permanent and effective relationship with NATO. However, detailed agreements have not yet been reached on EU use of NATO assets and capabilities.

The problems/issues

A   Decision making in the CFSP

Initially, the second pillar of the TEU was strictly intergovernmental, and member state governments were reluctant to relinquish additional sovereignty to the EU. This meant that all decisions required unanimity, which slowed development of this policy area significantly. In order to balance the need for policy development with concerns over sovereignty, decision making was modified in Title V of the Amsterdam Treaty as follows:

- Voting on issues that affect the structure of the policy (such as the creation of new institutions) is based on unanimity.
- Voting on the appropriate means of implementing the CFSP decisions is based on 'reinforced' QMV; this includes the adoption of a common strategy or the implementation of a joint action or common position already approved by the Council. Reinforced QMV requires the sixty-two votes in favour from at least ten member states. However, the use of QMV for implementation of this legislation must first be agreed by unanimity.
- In addition, member states may decide to adopt the constructive abstention procedure, in order to opt out of decisions with which they disagree. Constructive abstention does not block the adoption of a decision, but if a member state qualifies its abstention by a formal declaration, it is not obliged to apply the legislation. However, in a spirit of solidarity, the abstaining member state is

obliged not to pursue any action that might conflict with this CFSP decision. This procedure is particularly useful for historically neutral member states, such as Denmark and Ireland.

- The Treaty of Nice (2001) introduced the concept of closer co-operation between member states in the area of security and defence policy. Closer co-operation allows member states with common interests to develop joint actions or common positions between themselves, without the involvement of all EU members (see *Flexible Integration*).

However, it is important to note that the establishment of the High Representative for the CFSP in the Council Secretariat strengthens the intergovernmental, rather than the supranational, character of the policy. For example, the member states may call on the High Representative, but not vice versa; thus, the High Representative remains the tool of the member states, not of the Commission.

The fact that the Commission and the EP have only limited roles in the development of CFSP also helps to explain the pace of decision making in this policy area. While fully associated with the CFSP, the Commission does not have the exclusive right to propose legislation, as it does in other policy areas. The EP is consulted and briefed on developments in CFSP, but it does not have the power to veto or block legislation. At the same time, the powers of both these institutions have expanded during each recent revision to the policy, and the EP and the Commission may play a greater role in CFSP as the policy becomes more established.

B   High vs low politics

The CFSP is known as a 'high politics' issue. In other words, it is a field of policy that affects the traditional core competences of the nation-state, and therefore has implications for a state's sovereignty and identity. As the EU is not a state and has no single national territory to protect, it is difficult to develop a 'homogenous' foreign policy among the different member states. This also explains why integration has tended to occur in the economic field; since economics is a 'low politics' issue, areas of commonality and shared interest between the member states are more easily identifiable. At the same time, the EU has a number of different and sometimes conflicting political, economic, social and cultural interests.

For example, certain member states have traditional or special relationships with certain parts of the world, which they seek to maintain and thus promote within CFSP. This inevitably leads to conflicting foreign policy objectives. As a result, foreign policy has continued to be conducted in national capitals rather than in Brussels, and the differing perspectives of these capitals complicate the decision-making process. Therefore, it is the lack of common interests, rather than the institutional framework, that many politicians and academics identify as the major obstacle to achieving a coherent and workable CFSP.

In addition, the CFSP lacks leadership. Some member states, primarily the larger ones, have long histories of being influential on the world stage. France and the UK, for example, have long, powerful colonial histories, and are wary of losing influence in this field of policy. Paradoxically, they are also in the best position to offer leadership to the CFSP. Although it is very concerned about national sovereignty, the UK has recently demonstrated a possible interest in taking a more active leadership role in this policy area.

C EU military force

The defence and security component of the CFSP is of primary importance. This is obviously the most sensitive 'high politics' issue, but it is also the most crucial aspect of the CFSP, as it gives 'teeth' to CFSP policy decisions. Although the EU has a number of diplomatic and economic tools it can use to control maverick nations (such as freezing diplomatic relations, suspending aid, imposing trade embargoes or economic sanctions), it still lacks the ultimate bargaining tool: namely, the threat of force. Whilst the present ESDP and the 'Headline Goal' do not seek to create a European army, the existence of a deployable military force (such as the RRF) is crucial to reinforcing the EU's political decisions. In addition, the EU must now confront the issues associated with increased co-operation with NATO and the WEU, as well as the problems that such a military force would pose for neutral member states such as Denmark, Austria, Finland and Ireland.

D The relationship with NATO

At the December 2001 Laeken European Council, the EU member states agreed to finalize security arrangements with NATO in accordance with decisions made at the 1999 Washington Summit, particularly within the field of asset and capability sharing. Historically, some EU member states have feared that the development of an EU-level foreign and security policy would undermine the relationship between NATO and the EU member states. Recent developments have indicated that the current goal of the CFSP is to allow the EU to develop a security and defence organization in the WEU that is independent of, yet still partnered with, NATO. However, several barriers to the realization of these goals still exist. For example, Sweden, Finland and Ireland (due to their historic neutrality) are not members of NATO but are members of the WEU. In addition, the UK and France hold two of the five permanent seats of the UN Security Council. For the EU to develop a comprehensive foreign policy, those two seats would need to be resigned in favour of an EU seat on the Council – an arrangement to which both the UK and France object. Duplication is also a problem within the EU, since a significant number of services (including surveillance, intelligence and logistics) are replicated in each EU country. At the same time, none of the EU member states possesses much of the heavy equipment necessary for military initiatives that extend far beyond the borders of Europe. Therefore, a relationship with NATO is still crucial to the success of any EU-level policy.

Who wins/who loses

The **smaller member states** of the European Union have much to gain from the process of creating the CFSP. It is clear, for example, that a country such as Luxembourg enjoys greater influence on the world stage when it holds the European Council Presidency than it would otherwise. In addition, Germany, for historical reasons, prefers to use CFSP and other intergovernmental methods to pursue its foreign policy goals rather than present a unilateral military force of its own. Furthermore, the CFSP allows the neutral countries to adjust their policies to reflect the new post-Cold War environment without creating military systems of their own.

Member states such as the UK and France may consider themselves losers from recent developments in the CFSP. These two member states already enjoy considerable influence on the world stage, as a result of their histories and by virtue of their permanent membership of the United Nations Security Council. However, because of the influence they enjoy, these states also have the opportunity to show leadership within the CFSP. This has been particularly evident with regard to the ESDP process, where agreement between the two big defence players in Europe has allowed rapid development within this field of policy.

In terms of the balance of power between the **Commission and the member states**, it appears that the member states currently benefit from the structure of the policy, especially since the CFSP is consolidated in the intergovernmental Pillar of the Treaty. However, the Commission has gained a number of powers since the launch of the EPC, such as the right of consultation and (since the TEU) the right to generate policy ideas. The Commission may also gain more power if the EU decides to develop a common diplomatic core. In such a system, the Commission's delegations in third countries could perform the role currently assigned to the present embassies of the member states. The EP has also recently gained the right to question officials and foreign ministers, and enjoys the right of consultation. However, both the EP and the Commission have yet to attain a position of strong influence within the CFSP.

Food for thought

Is the EU more effective as an economic rather than a military power? Through trade sanctions and financial aid, the EU has been able to use its economic power to influence political goals. During the war in Afghanistan (2002), the EU was able to quickly offer a significant aid package, but was unable to mobilize an EU military force to reinforce US troops. While it appears that the EU is more comfortable in exercising its economic power, it is likely that there will be increased demand from the rest of the world for the EU to operate as a single political entity in the international arena. This will most likely include sharing the military burden with the USA.

Is the EU really moving towards a common defence force? The field of defence and security is likely to be one of the most active areas of EU politics in the near future. In 2000, each member state decided what kind of military force it was able to offer to the RRF. This has triggered a number of additional developments, which must be finalized before the force comes into existence. The success or failure of this project will help determine the future of the CFSP; the RRF must demonstrate success if the EU wants to be seen as an equal to the USA in sharing the burden of ensuring global political stability. A successful RRF will certainly increase the EU's profile and influence within the field of conflict resolution. However, it will also expand the scope of Europe's own security arrangements, which have remained largely the preserve of NATO. Therefore, if the RRF is successful, what sort of relationship will develop between NATO and the EU?

Student-to-student tip

The CFSP is a rapidly developing area of EU policy, and many of the most significant developments have taken place in the last several years. Both the Nice Treaty and the international threat of terrorism have accelerated greater acceptance of the need for an EU military presence on the world stage. As a result, a great deal of the literature you may find about the CFSP may be out of date. Be sure to rely not only on textbooks, but also on recent academic and newspaper articles, for the most recent proposals and developments in this area. Search academic institutions for online news as they are an excellent starting point.

Summary

- The CFSP operates along intergovernmental lines within the second Pillar of the EU treaty, and involves the discussion and development of policy at the European level amongst EU member states within the fields of foreign, defence and security policy.
- The CFSP affects national sovereignty, and is therefore a 'high politics' issue. As a result, it has developed more slowly than other areas of EU policy. It has also lacked leadership by individual member states, since national capitals are reluctant to give up their role in foreign policy decisions.
- The development of CFSP is driven by several factors:
  - the increased importance of the EU resulting from its global economic strength;
  - new security concerns, such as instability in south-eastern Europe and the Middle East;
  - the emergence of common interests in relations with third countries.
- The area of defence and security within the CFSP will develop rapidly in the coming years. The ESPD process is driven partly by a desire for increased burden

sharing with the USA and partly by the need to allow the EU to fulfil an international role in the field of defence and security that is equal to its economic power.

Selected bibliography

Overviews

Forster, D. and W. Wallace (2000) 'Common Foreign and Security Policy', in H. Wallace and W. Wallace (eds), *Policy-Making in the European Union*, Oxford: Oxford University Press, chapter 17: 461–91.

This is a very good introduction to the subject, placing the CFSP within its historical context and accounting for many recent developments. It simplifies and helps explain the dynamics of the institutional structure with particular reference to ESPD.

Comprehensive books

Cameron, F. (1999) *The Foreign and Security Policy of the European Union: Past, Present and Future*, Sheffield: Sheffield Academic Press.

This is a short book (approximately 160 pages) setting out all the major aspects of the CFSP in a concise, digestible manner. It offers an up-to-date analysis of the progress in the policy so far.

Hill, C. (1996) *The Actors in Europe's Foreign Policy*, London: Routledge.

This compilation of essays analyses individual member states' foreign policy traditions and their relationship with the CFSP. It also contains a particularly useful chapter on the Commission's role in the CFSP.

Academic articles and papers

Oakes, M. (2001) *European Security and Defence Policy: Nice and Beyond*, House of Commons Library: International Affairs and Defence Section, Research Paper 01/50, 2 May 2001. Available: http://www.parliament.uk.

This research paper provides an excellent update of the CFSP debate, including an explanation of the developments at Nice as well as insights into EU–NATO relations.

Rutten, M. (2001) From St-Malo to Nice. European Defence: Core Documents, Chaillot Papers 47, May 2001, Paris: Institute for Security Studies of the Western European Union. Available: http://www.iss-eu.org/chaillot/chai47e.pdf.

This compilation by Rutten, a research fellow at the Institute of Security Studies, is an excellent source of primary source documents.

The European Foreign Affairs Review, published by Kluwer Law International.

This periodical is very helpful in keeping an eye on the most up-to-date developments in the CFSP, ESDP and European foreign policy.

Supportive websites

http://www.iue.it/EFPB/Welcome.html   This full-text database brings together documents issued by the EU in the area of foreign policy since 1985.

http://www.nato.int   Site of the North Atlantic Treaty Organization (NATO), providing updates on developments in the relationship between NATO and the EU.

http://www.weu.int   The site of the WEU, concerned with European defence, includes the reports from the WEU Institute for Security Studies: *http://www.weu.int/institute/*

http://www.cer.org.uk   The Centre for European Reform site is particularly accurate in explaining EU Security and Defence Policy.

http://www.iiss.org   This is the site of the International Institute for Strategic Studies. Unfortunately, some of its resources are subscription-based; however, they provide a good analysis of current events.

http://www.riia.org   The website for the Royal Institute of International Affairs provides excellent briefing papers in the publications section.

http://www.isn.ethz.ch/   The International Relations and Security Network (ISN) provides the Security Watch (with daily news) and Library Links. It is also worthwhile to check the associated Institute for Security and International Studies (ISIS).

19

Justice and Home Affairs

Florence Poulain

The policy area called Justice and Home Affairs (JHA) encompasses issues ranging from citizens' rights to police protection to asylum policies. While JHA issues have traditionally been the responsibility of the nation-state, they are slowly being incorporated into the Community's responsibilities. The Amsterdam Treaty (1997) attempted to accelerate this shift to the EU level by transferring several JHA issues from the intergovernmental third Pillar of the Treaty to the more supranational first Pillar. Moreover, the governments of the EU member states have agreed to develop 'an area of freedom, justice and security' (defined in Article 61) by 2004 – a goal supported by the decisions made at the special Tampere European Council (October 1999). The shift of JHA responsibilities from the national to the EU level leads to concerns about national sovereignty. EU-level JHA policy is sometimes seen as a serious intrusion on the role that nation-states play with regard to their citizens, as JHA represents some of the core responsibilities of traditional nation-states. This trend toward an EU-level JHA policy also raises some serious questions about the true nature of the EU as a political entity.

The facts

A Development of EU-level JHA policy

JHA issues have not always been part of the Community agenda. However, the goal of establishing the free movement of persons – one of the fundamental rights of EU citizenship and a basic element of JHA – is an important element of the Treaties of Rome (1957). Initially, however, this right did not apply to every person living in the member states, but only to citizens of member states involved in cross-border economic activities: namely, EC workers and their families. In 1982, the European Court of Justice (ECJ) extended this right to all EC nationals involved in economic activities, including those who were currently employed, those looking for work, and the recently unemployed.

The Single European Act (SEA) of 1986 extended the rights of EU citizens by advocating the complete removal of physical barriers to the free movement of goods, services, capital and persons by 1992, as a central part of the Single Market Programme (SMP). However, the removal of barriers to trade and to mobility within the Community created two problems:

- It increased the risk of crime across internal frontiers.
- It facilitated both legal and illegal large-scale immigration.

However, as early as 1975, some member states agreed to tackle these issues together. Given the high sensitivity of JHA-related issues, they decided to do so outside the Community framework. This allowed for the participation of only the member states interested in co-operation in this area.

B   Early initiatives on JHA

In the late 1970s and early 1980s, two initiatives developed to tackle problems associated with JHA. However, due to the controversial nature of JHA issues, both initiatives were formed outside the Treaty framework, and not all EC member states chose to participate.

- *The Trevi Group.* EC member states that wanted to proceed with increased co-operation on issues of policing and criminal justice formed the *Trevi* Group (*Terrorisme, Radicalisme, Extrémisme et Violence Internationale*) in 1975, which was composed of an informal committee of senior justice and interior officials. The *Trevi* Group addressed a wide range of issues, from terrorism to football hooliganism, organized crime and drug trafficking. Trevi also laid the foundation for future collaborations of this kind.
- *Ad Hoc Working Group on Immigration* (AWGI). Interested in addressing immigration and asylum problems, some EC governments established the AWGI in 1986. This intergovernmental body of senior officials from Interior Ministries drafted two conventions related to immigration issues: the 1990 Dublin Convention on Asylum and the 1991 External Frontiers Convention. Both conventions were signed by national governments, but they were never ratified by national parliaments, primarily because of disagreements between individual member states (most notably between Spain and the UK in territorial disputes over Gibraltar).

C   The Schengen Accords

Between 1985 and 1995, a series of far more wide-reaching agreements were negotiated outside the Community framework, in the little town of Schengen (in Luxembourg), on the issue of border controls. The first agreement, called the Schengen Agreement, was negotiated in 1985 between France, Germany, Belgium, the Netherlands and Luxembourg, with the goal of abolishing internal frontiers and establishing a common external border around their territory. In 1990, after five years of negotiations, the signatory states finally agreed to implement the Schengen Accords, as they were now called. Key features of the implementation agreement included the need to:

- devise a common list of third countries (i.e. non-EU countries) whose nationals need a visa to enter 'Schengenland' (the territory of the states that signed the agreement);
- combat illegal immigration at the external border of Schengenland;
- prevent individuals from submitting asylum requests in more than one of the signatory countries;
- co-ordinate police co-operation;
- co-ordinate judicial co-operation;
- establish the Schengen Information System (SIS, now known as the European Information System) to link relevant police databases in participating states.

The Schengen Accords acknowledged that the Treaty goal of setting up 'an area without internal frontiers, in which the free movement of goods, persons, services and capital is ensured (SEA)' meant that immigration, external borders, policing and criminal justice went beyond national borders. Therefore, these problems affected all member states, and were more effectively handled by the EU as a whole.

Membership and interest in Schengen increased, with Italy, Greece, Portugal and Spain signing the Accords in the early 1990s. However, some states (notably the UK and Denmark) remained reluctant to join Schengen, because they did not trust the border protection of the other signatories and/or wanted to preserve their sovereignty. Ireland, despite its desire to sign the Accords, was prevented from doing so by its passport union with the UK. Italy, by contrast, was refused entry until the 1990s, largely because the other signatories did not trust its ability to keep its borders secure. These problems help to explain why the Accords remained separate from the EC Treaty until 1997.

D   JHA as the third Pillar of the TEU

Even though Schengen accomplished more outside the EU Treaty in terms of co-operation than the Trevi Group and the AWGI, it was unable to make much concrete progress in creating an area of free movement of people, as long as the Accords were not incorporated into the Treaty framework. Moreover, the member states not involved in the Schengen Accords had been absent from an important aspect of common policy formulation. Consequently, at the Maastricht IGC (1991–2), the governments of the EU member states agreed to include most of the Schengen objectives – such as visa, asylum and immigration policies – in the Treaty on European Union (TEU, 1992). The TEU marked a step forward, by granting EU citizens the right to:

- circulate and live freely in the territory of any EU member state;
- take part in EP and municipal elections in their place of residence;
- benefit from diplomatic and consular protection from the authorities of all member states;
- access extra-judicial recourse through a mediator;
- petition the EP.

However, as Schengen still contained many highly sensitive issues, which member states wanted to control, JHA issues were incorporated into a new third Pillar of the Treaty, which remained completely intergovernmental. This meant that the Commission's right to initiate proposals was either non-exclusive or denied, the EP's role was almost non-existent, and the ECJ's jurisdiction on cases resulting from JHA policy was severely restricted. Given its intergovernmental character, the third Pillar presented several collective action problems:

- It was difficult for the Council to reach agreements on issues relating to the third Pillar, as it had to take decisions unanimously, and there was no independent body, such as the Commission, to initiate proposals.
- Unlike in the first Pillar, most of the decisions taken in the third Pillar were non-binding.

Consequently, even though JHA was part of the Treaty framework, the EU initially made little concrete progress in expanding JHA policy. This partly explains why the EU member states decided to transfer some JHA areas – those relating to visas, asylum, immigration and judicial co-operation in civil matters – from the intergovernmental third Pillar to the Community first Pillar in the 1997 Amsterdam Treaty. The other JHA policy areas – police co-operation and judicial co-operation on criminal matters – remained in the truncated third Pillar, mainly because member states had not managed to reach agreements on those issues, due to their sensitive nature.

E Flexible integration

For those who did not wish to take part in common policies on JHA, the Amsterdam Treaty included a flexibility clause allowing differentiated integration (see

Flexible Integration). This meant that the UK and Denmark were able to opt out of policies such as Schengen. As a result, there was no reason to keep Schengen outside the Community framework, and it was incorporated into the TEU. However, similarly to the opt-outs in other policy areas, the positions of non-participating member states have changed. In April 2002, for example, Denmark asked the Commission to define a framework for the partial implementation of certain aspects of Schengen into its national legislation.

F   The 1999 Tampere European Council

Under the Finnish Presidency, the EU agreed to a greater commitment to the development of JHA at the EU level. Tampere attempted to strengthen JHA policy in several areas:

- *The JHA Scoreboard.* Following Tampere, the Commission began publishing a biannual scoreboard, which outlines the progress being made in the field of JHA for the benefit of the Council and the EP.
- *Mutual recognition of judicial decisions.* Tampere created two new judicial instruments: the Brussels I regulation (related to jurisdiction and enforcement of civil and commercial judgments) and the Brussels II Regulation (related to jurisdiction, recognition and enforcement of matrimonial judgments). However, the EU has experienced difficulty in implementing the Tampere proposals related to common levels of sanctions across the EU, including a common definition of terrorist acts or an agreement on penalties for counterfeiting.
- *Common EU asylum and migration policy.* Tampere established several specific goals for the Community in this area, including a common EU asylum system, the management of migration flow, and the fair treatment of third-country nationals. The EU has begun to implement these goals: in February 2002, the Council amended Regulation No. 1683/95, improving the security features of the uniform format for EU visas; and the EP has issued a report on the rights of third-country nationals, as well as a resolution on improving external borders. However, despite the relocation of these policies into Pillar I, the 2001 JHA Scoreboard concluded that legislation in this area is still slowed by unanimity.
- *New JHA structures.* Tampere produced several new bodies responsible for developing JHA policy at the EU level, and included an increased role for EUROPOL. These bodies are mainly in the area of police and judicial co-operation: EUROJUST (a unit of national prosecutors, magistrates and police officers that facilitates the co-ordination of national legal authorities and co-operates with the European Judicial Network), the Task Force of Chiefs of Police, and the European Police College.

The problems/issues

A Theoretical explanations

The historical evolution of JHA policies from the Treaties of Rome to the Nice Treaty has been slow and uneven. This has raised several questions among academics, such as why integration has proceeded so slowly in the area of JHA, why JHA provisions were incorporated at Maastricht, and what explains the transfer of some JHA issues from the third Pillar to the first Pillar at Amsterdam. These can be partially explained through the integration theories (see also *Theories of European Integration*).

I Intergovernmentalism

At face value, intergovernmentalism offers the best explanation of JHA developments at the EU level, primarily because the EU member states were the only relevant actors in the area of JHA until the mid-1990s. Therefore, intergovernmentalists could argue that member states *chose* to delegate what many consider constitutes the core of their sovereignty to the Community, because they realized that they could no longer defend their territory and protect their citizens on their own.

This realization was mainly triggered by international events which took place in the 1990s and which threatened to spill over into Western Europe. They included the wave of immigrants coming from Eastern and Central Europe in the post-Berlin Wall period, and the potential for conflicts in the Mediterranean region in the aftermath of the Gulf War. Such problems were further exacerbated by the fact that the EU countries most threatened by this changing situation were ill prepared to handle such problems. Germany, the country most exposed to the immigrants coming from Central and Eastern Europe (Germany took in 79 per cent of all refugees to Europe in 1992), did not even have an asylum policy until the mid-1990s. In addition, Spain, Italy, Portugal and Greece could not be trusted to maintain proper border controls, since they could not independently finance the cost of containing illegal immigration and terrorism from the Mediterranean region.

For these reasons, the member states decided that a common approach to these issues would be most effective for the EU as a whole. However, not all issues were tackled in the same framework, as they did not attract the same level of support amongst EU member states and did not threaten them all in the same way.

2 Neo-functionalism

With its emphasis on spillover, national political elites and supranational institutions, neo-functionalist theory can be useful in accounting for other aspects of the evolution of JHA. Neo-functionalists argue that initial co-operation in the field of JHA triggered further development in this policy area, despite the initial reticence of member states. Moreover, national political elites saw that co-operation among EU member states provided an adequate solution to the JHA problems created by the completion of the Single Market. Therefore, they gradually transferred more power to the Community, and more specifically to the Commission.

Once given responsibility, the Commission was then able to maximize its power on the grounds of policy efficiency. This, one can argue, is what happened in relation to the free movement of persons, immigration and visa policies. Originally these policies were placed under both the first and the third Pillars of the TEU. During the negotiation of the Amsterdam Treaty, the Commission pointed out the serious problems in the way in which the interface between the third and first Pillars worked. The result was the movement of these issues to the first Pillar. This move was facilitated by the fact that the Commission was supported by both the ECJ and the EP, as well as pressure groups and non-governmental organizations which lobbied actively for a further 'communitarization' of JHA policies. This proved particularly effective with centre-left governments, which formed a majority in the Council during the negotiation of the Amsterdam Treaty.

B   Areas of conflict between member states

The EU has made progress in the field of immigration. A regulation setting up a common format for EU visas was brought into force in 1995, and the Eurodac database (a system for the identification of asylum-seekers) was established in 2000. Despite growing consensus among member states on many JHA issues, several areas of contention remain. The Schengen Accords, for example, require the mutual recognition and eventual harmonization of visa and asylum policy between all member states. This includes the creation of a joint list of third-country nationals who need visas to travel within the EU. The process of agreeing on this list is causing significant political conflict among the current Schengen members.

In addition, due to differences in entry requirements and benefits granted to asylum-seekers, some states receive far more asylum applications than others. In 1996, for example, the EU member states received more than 225,000 applications for asylum. Germany received over 50 per cent of all applications, whilst the next largest receiver, the UK, received only 13 per cent of total applications. In order to discourage forum shopping by asylum-seekers, application and processing procedures, as well as national asylum policies (including benefits), must be streamlined. However, a fair method for the division of labour between Schengen states in processing these applications still needs to be devised, and the application criteria must be flexible and responsive to sudden changes in the global political situation.

C Police co-operation

In the field of police co-operation, programmes such as the European Information Service (EIS) (an inter-EU database used to report criminal activities, track illegal aliens, and augment witness protection plans) have caused concerns about privacy in many member states. However, the benefits appear to far outweigh the costs: EIS increases the amount of information available to all members, facilitates more comprehensive files on international criminals, and reduces administrative duplication among member states. The result should be a more comprehensive, efficient system of European policing through co-operation, especially in the areas of arms and drug trafficking. Similar conclusions were reached at Tampere, where the European Council agreed to enhance the role of EUROPOL and establish a European Police Chief Task Force, to work in co-ordination with EUROPOL.

In light of the terrorist attacks in the USA, the EU has accelerated the development of inter-EU police co-operation at several levels. The actions taken by the Extraordinary Council meeting on 21 September 2001 included the creation of a common European arrest warrant and the acceleration of the ratification process for the 2000 Convention on Mutual Assistance in Criminal Matters. The Council adopted a Common Position on the application of specific measures to combat terrorism (2001/931/CFSP), which strengthened the commitment to fight trans-national crime made at Tampere, and called for regular meetings of the heads of Security and Intelligence Services from all member states. A Belgo-Swedish proposal to develop a second-generation EIS, which would extend EUROPOL's intelligence network to include all types of crime, was also presented. Thus, international affairs have forced the EU to definitively strengthen its commitment to common policies in the area of policing.

D The success of Tampere

Following Tampere, the EU appears to have addressed many of the goals of the original Schengen agreements. In particular, the EU has established a common EU visa and common asylum procedures, the EIS is being expanded, and co-ordinated police and judicial procedures have been developed. However, while Tampere provided the legislative structure for recent developments in co-operation on EU policing, the impetus for these developments appears to have come more from international events than from the conference. Accordingly, it may take an immigration or asylum crisis to provide enough impetus for the EU to develop this legislative field further.

Who wins/who loses

From an intergovernmentalist perspective, **member states** have gained from co-operation in two ways. First, the creation of the Single Market has made the areas of justice, freedom and security a problem that affects all member states equally. For instance, since the Community has eliminated internal frontiers, Luxembourg is as concerned as Spain by a potential flux of immigrants coming from the Mediterranean region. As a consequence, Luxembourg has more to win than to lose by co-operating with Spain on these issues. Through the EU, it can have a voice in the way Spain handles its immigration policies. Spain also has more to win by co-operating, as it need not bear the cost of maintaining an external border on its own. Therefore, by co-operating in the area of JHA, all member states can benefit from the increased prosperity that comes from completing the internal market.

Secondly, co-operation in JHA has enabled member states to gain autonomy from their national sphere. Germany, for instance, could avoid popular discontent in the 1990s by blaming stricter immigration and asylum policies on Brussels. On the other hand, the incorporation of JHA policies into the Community framework deprives member states of some of their traditional functions *vis-à-vis* their citizens.

Citizens have, over the years, gained some rights at the EU level, especially in the area of JHA policies. These range from basic economic rights (such as the right to live and to work in another Community country) to political and civil rights (such as the right to stand and vote in local elections and EP elections). Although these rights have increased considerably over the years, they are still not as comprehensive as rights granted at the national level. For instance, the TEU did not establish full and equal economic, political, civil and social rights for all EU individuals, regardless of where they reside in the EU. This inequality poses a problem, as the expansion of JHA policies has increased the area in which fundamental rights need to be protected. Consequently, the evolution of JHA has been accompanied by an increased awareness of the inadequacy of human rights protection at the EU level (see *Fundamental Rights*).

Food for thought

Establishing an area of freedom, justice and security by 2004 (as agreed in the Amsterdam Treaty) may be difficult to achieve for several reasons:

- The Commission and the EP still have only a limited role in the field of JHA. Under the first Pillar, the Commission shares the right of initiative with the Council, and the Council still takes decisions by unanimity. Under the third Pillar, the Council is the only relevant actor.
- The goal of establishing a zone of freedom, justice and security by 2004 may be hindered by the southern member states. Research shows that the latter do not always implement EU measures, due to bureaucratic and/or financial problems.
- The prospect of enlarging the EU and the complications that this entails might postpone this goal even further. In particular, many member states have expressed concern about the ability of the accession countries to enforce external borders and to fight organized crime (see *EU Enlargement*).

Student-to-student tip

It is important to remember that as JHA policy development is controversial, it is one of several EU policies where national opt-outs have been used. Therefore, not every country is developing JHA at the same speed. A case in point is the free movement of people in the EU: as the UK and Ireland did not take part in Schengen, there is no official English version of the Accords or of other official documents related to it. In addition, countries sometimes change political positions on opt-outs, as is the case with Denmark with regard to aspects of Schengen. Therefore, it is crucial to know the current positions of the member states when doing research in this policy area.

Summary

- JHA issues have progressively become a central issue within the Community. Member states have gradually agreed to give up some of their traditional functions by co-operating at the European level and/or by delegating some of their powers to the EU institutions.
- Many JHA policies began outside the framework of the EC Treaties in non-Community intergovernmental bodies. These include the Trevi Group, the AWGI and the Schengen Accords.
- The TEU was crucial to the development of the field of JHA, as it created the third Pillar of the Treaty to address these issues. The integration of JHA issues was further assisted by the transfer of many issues regarding immigration and asylum to the first Pillar in the Treaty of Amsterdam. The Tampere European Council in 1999 focused attention on many JHA issues that still required development.
- The development of JHA policy at the EU level has benefited national governments in two ways. First, JHA issues affected by the Single Market (such as immigration, internal security and free movement) are better dealt with at the EU than the national level. Secondly, by transferring some JHA policies to the Community level, national governments can now pursue unpopular policies whilst shifting the blame to 'Brussels'.
- EU citizens have also gained some rights at the EU level as a result of the expansion of JHA policies. However, these rights, especially fundamental rights, are not as well protected at the EU level as they are at the national level.

Selected bibliography

Overviews

Hix, S. (1999) *The Political System of the European Union*, London: Macmillan, chapter 11: 307–30.
    This chapter, entitled 'Citizen Freedom and Security Policies', offers a very comprehensive explan-
    ation of the political theories underlying this policy area.

Den Boer, M. and W. Wallace (2000) 'Justice and Home Affairs', in H. Wallace and W. Wallace (eds), *Policy-making in the European Union*, 4th edn, Oxford: Oxford University Press, chapter 18: 493–519.
This chapter offers a strong, general introduction to the most recent developments in JHA.

Articles on specific JHA issues

Hix, S. and J. Niessen (1996) 'Reconsidering European Migration Policies: The 1996 Intergovernmental Conference and the Reform of the Maastricht Treaty', Brussels: Migration Policy Group/Churches' Commission for Migrants in Europe.
This study of the 1996 IGC contains useful facts and background on the political situation immediately prior to the 1996 IGC.

Baldwin-Edwards, M. (1997) 'The Emerging European Immigration Regime: Some Reflections on Implications for Southern Member States', *Journal of Common Market Studies*, vol. 35, no. 4: 497–520.
This author addresses implementation problems faced by southern member states, focusing on the problems faced by the EU Mediterranean states in relation to JHA, and sheds light on many other aspects of the issues surrounding JHA policy development.

European Parliament (1996) *White Paper on the 1996 Intergovernmental Conference*, vol. 3/2, no. 27: Briefing on the Intergovernmental Conference and the Schengen Convention, JF/bo/217/96: 446–57.
A White Paper produced by the EP on Schengen, it addresses the issues that are of importance to the EU citizen, and is fairly concise and analytical compared to some Commission documents.

Hall, B. and A. Bhatt (1999) *Policing Europe: EU Justice and Home Affairs Co-operation*, London: Centre for European Reform.
Hall and Bhatt explore the external effects of migration and organized crime on the internal development of JHA. The Centre for European Reform, a think tank based in London, also offers various interesting publications at http://www.cer.org.uk.

Bunyan, T. (1997) *From Trevi to Maastricht (1976–1993): 60 Reports and Documents on Policing, Immigration, and Asylum*, London: Statewatch.
This compilation is a good source of primary source documents on JHA. Statewatch, a non-profit organization monitoring civil liberties in the EU, offers a comprehensive website with many articles of interest at *http://www.statewatch.org*.

Stetter, S. (2000) 'Regulating Migration: Authority Delegation in Justice and Home Affairs', *Journal of European Public Policy*, vol. 7, no. 1: 80–102.
Stetter explains migration policy using the principal-agent framework.

Giraudon, V. (2000) 'European Integration and Migration Policy', *Journal of Common Market Studies*, vol. 38, no. 2: 251–72.
Giraudon demonstrates how governments are able to 'venue-shop', i.e. bypass national veto-players by raising the policy area to the European level in the area of migration policy.

Huysmans, J. (2000) 'The European Union and the Secularization of Migration', *Journal of Common Market Studies*, vol. 38, no. 5: 751–77.
This article uses neo-functionalism to explain the cultural and socio-economic dimension of migration policy.

Supportive websites

http://europa.eu.int/comm/justice_home/index_en.htm This is the website address of DG Justice and Home Affairs, and also contains the full text of the Charter on Fundamental

Rights. The 2000 JHA scoreboard can be found at *http://europa.eu.int/comm/dgs/justice_ home/pdf/com2000-167-en.pdf.*

http://www.one-europe.ac.uk This pro-Europe website offers a number of interesting working papers.

http://www.cer.org.uk/ The Centre for European Reform makes individual articles on JHA from its subscription publication available online. The website offers constructive criticism of the many aspects of the EU.

http://www.ceps.be/Research/JHA.htm The Centre for European Policy Studies has begun work in this policy area, and has several reports and working papers online which offer additional information about Schengen and other JHA issues.

20

External Policies

Isabell Welpe

The EU is the largest market in the world, comprising almost 370 million consumers and producing one-third of the global GDP. The establishment of a common EU trade policy, known as the Common Commercial Policy (CCP), was crucial to the creation of a common market, and as such was one of the main goals of the Treaties of Rome (1957). Currently, it is also the only EU policy in which the EU acts as a single entity toward the rest of the world. Since the end of the Cold War, the CCP has gained increased significance as the major venue for influencing world politics. However, the EU has also chosen to strengthen its relationships with the rest of the world through philanthropy, including developmental policies and humanitarian aid programmes, which provide 55 per cent of all official international development aid. Through an analysis of EU external policies, this chapter will investigate the reasons behind, and the limits on, the EU's position as an economic and political superpower.

The facts

A   Two branches of EU external policies

The EU pursues two types of external policies with the rest of the world:

- *Trade policies.* Trade between the EU and the rest of the world is regulated by the Common Commercial Policy. This policy is made up of several components, including the Common External Tariff (CET) and trade agreements with non-EU countries. The EU Commission negotiates directly on behalf of all member states in the implementation of the CCP.

- *Development policies.* The EU provides funding for both development pro-grammes and humanitarian aid to countries throughout the world. This funding can take several forms, from financial, technical and economic co-operation with developing countries to refugee aid for displaced persons. It also includes the pre-accession aid granted to countries applying for membership in the EU.

B Trade policy – the CET and the CCP

One of the main goals of the European Community was the establishment of a Common Commercial Policy. The CCP was outlined in the Treaties of Rome, under Articles 131–5 (ex-Articles 110–16), and was inaugurated in 1968 with the establish-ment of the European customs union through a common external tariff (CET). As a result, the European-level CCP replaced the individual national trade policies of the member states. Initially, the CET was the central element of the CCP; however, as the General Agreement on Tariffs and Trade (GATT) negotiations led to a world-wide reduction of tariffs, other trade issues became more important. These include non-tariff barriers, taxation, industrial policy, labour standards, consumer protec-tion and environmental policy.

Two additional developments have had a significant influence on the nature of EU commercial policy. First, the Single European Act (SEA) replaced national trade agreements with EU-wide agreements. Secondly, the creation of the World Trade Organization (WTO) in 1993, which included the EU as a founding member (rather than just individual member states), strengthens the unity of the Union as an economic entity through its provisions. The CCP is comprised of the following instruments:

- The *Common External Tariff.* As the primary element of the CCP, the CET is crucial to the EU's status as a customs union. By removing tariffs on goods produced within the EU and utilizing single tariffs for goods produced outside the EU, the CET unifies the EU as a single economic entity in relation with the rest of the world.
- *Common trade agreements* with the rest of the world and a common application of trade policy instruments. These include bi- and multilateral trade agreements, such as those developed through the WTO and with the candidate countries of Central and Eastern Europe (see *EU Enlargement*).
- *Common rules* on goods imported into the EU – such as limits on the import of genetically modified organisms.

C Trade agreements

The main function of the EU Commission within this policy is to negotiate trade agreements on behalf of the EU member states. There are two types of EU trade agreements: multilateral agreements (such as WTO agreements) and bilateral agreements (such as the preferential trade agreements with the candidate countries – see *EU Enlargement*). The Commission takes a significant role in multilateral trade agreements, as the representative of the EU in GATT/WTO negotiations. In addition, the EU participates in several bilateral trade agreements, which are preferential trade agreements with several states, such as the ACP states or Russia. These agreements are often criticized for favouring the EU over partner countries. The EU has also recognized a special economic relationship with the European Economic Area (EEA), through which the EEA states receive preferential trade conditions. Similarly, the EU has included Turkey and Malta in a customs union with the EU. The Community has also developed preferential trade agreements with the former colonies of member states through the Lomé Conventions (see below).

D   Trade instruments

Under the CCP, tariffs, import quotas and anti-dumping policy on imports from non-members are the exclusive competence of the EU. This means that, according to Treaty Article 133 (ex-Article 113), the Commission negotiates tariffs with third countries (countries outside the EU) on behalf of all member states. While the policy is described as having a liberal objective, the CCP does utilize several 'protectionist' policy instruments:

- *Anti-dumping measures.* 'Dumping' refers to a situation in which an exporter sells a product to another country at an economic loss. The EU uses these measures to minimize the distortion to the markets caused when countries subsidize otherwise inefficient producers through the export of their goods. Such measures are frequently used instruments of trade defence, and are legal under GATT procedures. However, as dumping is difficult to prove, these protective measures sometimes appear to unfairly penalize the exporting countries and create tensions between the EU and its trading partners.
- *Voluntary export restrictions (VERs).* These are bilateral agreements restricting the quantity of exports from one country to another. VERs are considered to be a more politically feasible solution than anti-dumping measures, because the parties involved negotiate the amount of exports that will be permitted into the restricting country. However, the dominant position of the EU in the world market makes beneficial VERs difficult to negotiate for smaller non-EU countries.

In addition to these 'protectionist' policy instruments, the EU also uses minor measures to restrict trade, including trade sanctions, countervailing duties and safeguard clauses.

E The World Trade Organization (WTO)

The WTO replaced the GATT in 1995. With 144 members and thirty observers (as of June 2002), the WTO is the only intergovernmental body responsible for enforcing the global trading rules set out in the World Trade Agreement (WTA). Importantly, members of the WTO can register complaints through the WTO's dispute settlement process, should they believe that another member is violating the WTA. Judgments are made by specially appointed panels of experts and are subject to appeal. Over 150 cases were registered between 1995 and 1999, many of which were used to settle EU–US trade disputes, such as the Banana Wars (see below).

One of the primary functions of the WTO is to serve as a forum for trade negotiations between members. GATT/WTO negotiations have taken place in several successive rounds. The lengthiest and most contentious round was the Uruguay Round from 1986 to 1993, in which the WTO's position on agricultural trade (supported by the USA and the Cairns Group) posed a threat to the EU's Common Agricultural Policy (CAP). By speaking with one voice, the EU was able to make far fewer concessions on production and export subsidies than could have been achieved by each member state acting independently (see *The Common Agricultural Policy*).

Due to the protest of tens of thousands of anti-globalization demonstrators, as well as the equity concerns of many developing nations, the Millennium Round of WTO negotiations failed to be launched as planned in Seattle in 1999. The WTO Ministerial Conference in Doha, Qatar, launched a new trade round in November 2001, which plans to address issues including agriculture, intellectual property and the environment.

F EU Development Policy

The EU is the largest provider of world aid (over 50 per cent of the world total), which is administered and distributed by the Commission. While the EU has pursued development policies since the Treaties of Rome (1957), a specific legal status for development policy was not formalized until 1993, by Articles 177–81 of the Treaty on European Union (TEU). Development Policy aims at promoting economic and political progress in developing nations, and attempts to establish a balance between aid and other EU policies (such as the Common Agricultural Policy) that may have an impact on these countries. The policy takes two approaches to development assistance:

- The *commercial approach* is based on the Generalized System of Preferences (GSP). This system grants customs reductions or exemptions to developing countries on manufactured or semi-manufactured goods, as well as processed agricultural products and textiles. The GSP does not require reciprocity on the part of the developing country. The objective of the system is to promote economic growth, industrialization and national income from exports through economically favourable trading agreements. The GSP has also developed the possibility of applying incentives based on social and environmental goals.

- The *thematic approach* supports universal activities, such as the fight against AIDS, sustainable development and environmental conservation. The EU co-operates with many non-governmental organizations (NGOs), primarily through the co-funding of such projects.

G European Community Humanitarian Office (ECHO)

The EU provides emergency humanitarian aid for people suffering from either natural or man-made disasters through ECHO, which was set up in 1992 under Title XX of the EU Treaty. EU humanitarian aid takes the form of three main instruments:

- *Exceptional aid* – to address the immediate results of a disaster, such as the need for medicine, food and shelter. The EU can provide such aid within 48 hours of a disaster.
- *Food aid* – to prevent starvation in areas suffering from famine. The EU allocates large amounts of food as well as funds for this type of aid.
- *Refugee aid* – to assist people displaced as a result of war or famine. The EU helps such individuals to either emigrate or return home once conditions improve.

ECHO encompasses more than 2,000 projects in eighty countries, and thereby helps raise the global profile of the EU. ECHO also works with over 200 partners, including the UN and many NGOs. In 2001, the Commission created the EuropeAid Co-operation Office to co-ordinate the implementation of all Commission external aid instruments. With an initial budget of €7.6 billion, EuropeAid's activities include management of the European Development Fund (for ACP countries), as well as oversight of legislation benefiting more than 150 countries.

The EU is also one of the principal donors to specialized UN agencies. In 2001 ECHO provided €544 million for humanitarian actions, many in conjunction with UN activities. However, as the EU as an entity has only observer status in the UN, it is significantly constrained in its interactions with the UN at the policy-making and operational level. This has resulted in a lack of effective co-ordination between EU and UN humanitarian activities.

H ACP countries and pre-accession aid

Two of the most substantial beneficiaries of EU Development Policy are ACP countries, through the Lomé Conventions, and Central and Eastern European countries (CEECs), through the pre-accession aid instruments.

1   The Lomé Convention/Cotonou Agreement

The Lomé Convention is a north–south co-operation between the EU and seventy-one ACP countries, most of which are former European colonies. The Convention, which has been renewed four times, provides non-reciprocal trade benefits to the ACP countries, allowing them to import many goods into the EU duty-free. The EU is the largest market for ACP country exports; however, as these arrangements offer preference to ACP countries over other non-EU countries, they are increasingly incompatible with WTO agreements. In addition, the Commission expressed increasing concern over the effective use of EU funds through the Lomé Conventions (especially in regard to increased corruption) in the 2000 Green Paper. With the expiration of Lomé IV in 2000, the Commission successfully negotiated the Cotonou Agreement in June 2000, incorporating humanitarian programmes as well as good governance criteria into the co-operation. The Cotonou Agreement is valid for twenty years, and will provide €13.5 billion in aid to the ACP nations through the European Development Fund (EDF) and the European Investment Bank (EIB) within the first five years of the agreement. In order to comply with WTO provisions, the new agreement also proposes a gradual integration of ACP economies into the global economy.

2   Pre-accession aid to CEECs

The EU is the biggest source of financial assistance for the CEECs. Aid includes tailored programmes such as PHARE (Assistance for the Economic Reconstruction of Poland and Hungary), as well as loans from the EIB. These funds, which made up 3 per cent of the EU budget in 2002, aim at preparing the CEECs for EU accession, and were increased in 2002 in light of the Commission's formal recommendation for full membership of ten accession countries by 2004 (see *EU Enlargement*).

The problems/issues

A   The independence of the Commission

One crucial element in the success of the CCP as a policy has been the independent role played by the Commission in creating trade policy. This independence, however, is limited in several ways: member states can influence international negotiations, and are present at WTO negotiations; they also have partial competence in key areas of global trade, such as services and intellectual property. As such areas compose an increasingly important aspect of international trade, their inclusion as part of the EU's competences is crucial to the success of future trade negotiations. Concerns about the Commission's limited resources also affect its ability to oversee some CCP programmes, such as the anti-corruption initiatives that make up part of the Cotonou Agreement.

B   The limitations of economic power

The EU has substantially less influence in international financial matters than in trade. Unlike in the WTO, the EU has no seat in the International Monetary Fund (IMF), and the Commission cannot speak on behalf of the EU member states. The consequences of the EU's weakness in this area became clear during the 1997 Asian financial crisis, in which the USA was the only important actor able to intervene. Economic and Monetary Union (EMU), however, is likely to increase EU power in the area of finance and investment, and to change the imbalance of financial power between the EU and the USA.

Academics such as Hill argue that EU economic power is inconsistent with its political power because of a 'capabilities–expectation gap'. This means that the world perceives the EU as a single giant economic actor, which in turn generates expectations about its role in world affairs. However, the EU cannot fulfil these expectations without a coherent policy in other areas (such as the Common Foreign and Security Policy (CFSP)). A further weakness is caused by internal tensions within the Community. As the Uruguay Round of GATT (1986–93) demonstrated, internal tensions – between the member states, within the Commission, and between the Commission and the Council – can handicap the EU's bargaining power in negotiations. The likelihood of such tensions increases whenever commercial decisions become politicized, as in the case of agricultural policy. As a result, the EU becomes less effective in conducting its commercial policy.

C   Economic strength for political ends

The EU has often attempted to use the CCP as an economic means to political ends. Examples of this include the use of sanctions against South Africa during Apartheid, the humanitarian and good governance stipulations associated with the Cotonou Agreement, and trade concessions with Russia and China in order to facilitate political dialogue. This strategy is also the foundation of the negotiation processes with the countries of Central and Eastern Europe who wish to join the EU. The Commission has often pushed for political and economic reforms in these countries, in exchange for trade concessions and accession to the Community. These instruments are sometimes called the EU's 'soft security policy', since they are much more consensual and less controversial than the military solutions developed in the CFSP.

D   Relations with the USA

The EU's economic impact on the world becomes clearer when compared with the USA. The USA became concerned with what it termed 'Fortress Europe' after the signing of the SEA in 1986. As a result, the USA has tried to force a reduction of EU tariffs on some products several times, and in the last few years, the USA and the EU have engaged in various trade wars. These wars may indicate that the USA views the EU as a rival economic power; otherwise, it would be able to force the EU to follow its political will by means of its extra-territoriality. At the same time, the EU remains a major ally of the USA, especially since it is the largest market for US exports and the largest source of foreign direct investment (FDI) into the USA. The USA is also the EU's largest single trading partner. Given the combined impact of the EU and the USA on world trade, it is crucial that both parties find ways to co-operate. Although the EU and the USA have committed themselves to a transatlantic economic partnership, several areas – including a number of US laws and policies on the Internet and e-commerce – have the potential to create future trade disputes. The fast entry of genetically modified crops into US agriculture, and the EU's concern over these products, is another potential source of conflict.

E The Banana Wars and US steel tariffs

The EU and the USA have clashed over trade issues several times. The term 'Banana Wars', for example, refers to a long-standing dispute between the USA and the EU over banana quotas. In 1993, the EU extended the banana quotas of individual member states to cover the entire Community. The new quota system favoured the former European colonial states to such an extent that Central and South American banana producers were effectively denied access to the EU market. The system also angered the US banana brokers, a strong US agricultural constituency, which lost profits due to this arrangement. Consequently, the USA protested against the EU measures, resulting in a WTO judgment in 1997 which stated that the EU quotas were illegal under WTO rules. Instead of dealing with the real issue behind the dispute – namely, that EU quotas unfairly favoured former colonies – the Commission modified the regime to address some of the minor technical objections raised by the WTO judgment. Since the changes were so insignificant, US and Central American banana producers have again complained to the WTO, threatening retaliatory measures if the EU doesn't comply with the WTO judgment.

However, the USA has demonstrated that it is willing to enact protectionist policies of its own. In March 2002, the USA announced that it was raising tariffs on most steel imports by up to 30 per cent, in order to protect the failing US industry from inexpensive foreign steel. In response, the EU has registered a complaint with the WTO, stating that US steel producers are not suffering from a rise in imports, but rather from internal inefficiencies. The EU steel industry, by comparison, underwent significant restructuring during the 1980s and 1990s, which has resulted in an 18 per cent growth in exports since 1988. The success of the WTO petition is of critical importance to the EU steel industry, because the US tariff could not only eliminate the EU's ability to export its specialized steel products to the USA, but also cause the EU steel market to be flooded with all the excessive imports of foreign steel which the USA has blocked through these tariffs. The EU has already taken safeguard measures to prevent such a flood of imports, through changes in quota and tariff levels. However, such protectionist actions by the world's largest economies will inevitably have negative ramifications for steel producers outside the EU and the USA that have been suffering from depressed global steel prices since the late 1990s.

Who wins/who loses

For the **EU**, the external policies have two positive effects: they allow the Community to raise its international profile by co-ordinating development and humanitarian activities, and they reduce the possibility of unilateral decisions being taken by individual member states, which could have a negative impact on the perception of the Union as an economic entity. Since the integrity of the internal market can be guaranteed only through a uniform external trade policy, the EU as a whole has benefited from the enhanced international bargaining power resulting from the CCP. This has been particularly beneficial for small member states, which consequently find themselves much less vulnerable to pressure from larger, outside countries.

However, the benefits of the external policies for the **rest of the world** are unclear. Certainly, the development programmes and humanitarian aid sponsored by the EU are welcomed by recipient nations. At the same time, these nations are often disadvantaged under aspects of other EU policies, such as the CAP. The creation of the WTO, which should balance the needs of all members, has resulted in significant benefits for the USA, which has won several important trade disputes against the EU (such as the Banana Wars) under WTO regulations. Yet for smaller countries outside the EU, the bipolar dominance of the USA and the EU in world trade has minimized their ability to negotiate economically advantageous trade agreements. This bipolar dominance also leaves third countries helpless to counteract the consequences of trade disputes between the EU and the USA, such as the protectionist steel tariffs.

Food for thought

The distinction between foreign and security policy and commercial policy is fading. Europe's security interests today seem to focus equally on securing economic prosperity and achieving military security in neighbouring countries. At the same time, the rise of international terrorism has increased interest in the development of the CFSP and military co-operation. Can it still be argued that EU security goals are best achieved through commercial rather than foreign policy?

Student-to-student tip

The most interesting aspects of the CCP can be explored through the reaction of countries to protectionist tariff increases or dumping practices. The Commission often issues press releases (available on the EU website) in response to US protectionist activities or WTO rulings, and these documents offer a great deal of background on individual trade issues. Of particular interest are trade wars between the USA and the EU; when these wars occur, national media in both the EU and the USA often provide a broad perspective and good background information on the issues. Development policy and humanitarian aid also receive a great deal of coverage in the daily EU Commission press releases, which are published on the EU website, *http://europa.eu.int website*.

Summary

- EU external policies can be divided into two categories: those dealing with trade (such as the CCP) and those dealing with aid (such as development policy and humanitarian work carried out by ECHO).
- The CCP is one of the main policies that the EU pursues with the rest of the world, and the only one where it can be said to have superpower status. It is a critical component of the Single Internal Market, and enhances the presence of the EU in global politics.
- The main function of the EU within the CCP is to negotiate trade agreements on behalf of member states. The Commission negotiates two types of agreements: multilateral agreements (i.e. GATT/WTO rounds) and bilateral agreements (i.e. preferential trade agreements with individual countries). However, the goals of these two types of agreements often contradict each other.
- An important element of the external policies is the EU's preferential relationship with some third countries, such as the CEECs or members of the Lomé Conventions. These relationships have caused disagreements with other EU trading partners, as witnessed in the Banana Wars of the 1990s.
- The EU's economic strength is not counterbalanced by equal political power; this has led the Commission to use these economic external policies as tools for political ends. Development policy and humanitarian aid are excellent examples of the EU using its economic power not only to positively influence unstable political situations around the globe, but also to enhance its political stature through its reputation as one of the world's largest aid providers.
- The relationship between the USA and the EU in this policy area is of crucial importance to the global economy, and recent developments, including the creation of the WTO, have demonstrated the expansion of EU power in trade negotiations.

Selected bibliography

Brühlhart, M. and D. Mccalese (2000) 'EU External Trade Policy', in A. El-Agraa (ed.), *The European Union: Economics and Policies*, 6th edn, New York: Prentice-Hall, chapter 21.
This is an excellent chapter on EU trade policy, including the CCP and all related issues.
Penketh, K. (1992) 'External Trade Policy', in F. McDonald and S. Dearden (eds), *European Economic Integration*, New York: Longman, chapter 14.

Concise and well structured, Penketh is one of the best sources to learn about the history of the CCP and the EU's external trade policies.

Woolcock, S. (2000) 'European Trade Policy', in H. Wallace and W. Wallace (eds), *Policy-making in the European Union*, 4th edn, Oxford: Oxford University Press, chapter 14: 373–99.
This chapter outlines the EU's economic role, and provides a good overview of the EU's trade policy. This volume also contains a chapter on the Banana Wars.

Neal, L. and D. Barbezat (1998) *The Economics of the European Union and the Economies of Europe*, Oxford and New York: Oxford University Press, chapter 8: 171–88.
A detailed account by two American economic historians, this chapter examines the development of the CCP and its effects throughout the world.

Supportive websites

http://europa.eu.int/pol/comm/index_en.htm   The EU website for the external policies provides an excellent overview of the CCP, its legal bases and its implementation details, while also offering a great deal of information about EU Development Policy.

http://www.parliament.uk   House of Commons, Research Paper 99/28, provides an excellent account of the EU–USA trade dispute over bananas.

http://www.oecd.org/publications/e-book/1100181e.pdf   This OECD site has helpful definitions, and offers clarification of current issues, such as 'The European Union's Trade Policies and their Economic Effects'.

http://www.wto.org   The World Trade Organization (WTO) provides expert advice on barriers to trade.

http://www.iie.com   The Institute for International Economics offers policy briefings on trade policy.

Part VI

CURRENT INTEGRATION AND FUTURE IMPLICATIONS

21

EU Enlargement

David Akast

The European Union (EU) is scheduled to expand considerably over the next several years, increasing the size of the Union from fifteen to possibly twenty-seven member states. In comparison to previous waves of enlargement, the proposed expansion is without precedent, in terms of both size and scope. Enlarging to the east and south serves to fulfil the Community's historic mission to promote peace, democratic values and market economies. Enlargement is also viewed as an opportunity to increase the Single Market and to promote investment and growth. These benefits do not come without challenges: the magnitude of the next enlargement will have a dramatic effect on the structure of EU institutions and policies, as well as on the economies and political structures of the applicant countries. The EU's ability to successfully cope with such change is yet to be determined.

The facts

A   Previous enlargements

Since the original six member states signed the Treaties of Rome (1957), there have been four waves of enlargement:

    1973: Denmark, Ireland and the UK
    1981: Greece
    1986: Portugal and Spain
    1995: Austria, Finland and Sweden

These enlargements followed a similar pattern. After the initial application was received, the Commission issued an opinion regarding the application, and the Council decided whether or not to open negotiations – only then could enlargement take place. Within this pattern, groups with close economic ties would typically join the Community together, as was the case with Spain and Portugal.

B   The fifth enlargement

The present negotiations have not followed this pattern. This is partly because the Union was unprepared for the pace and scale of change in Central and Eastern Europe following the collapse of the Soviet system in 1989. In addition, the countries applying for EU membership (known as 'candidate countries') were much less ready to join the EU than had been the case with countries in previous enlargements, both politically and economically. Consequently, the current EU member states were concerned about the ability of the candidate countries to fulfil their EU membership obligations and adopt all necessary EU legislation. For this reason, the EU has created a set of economic and political targets, known as the 'pre-accession strategy', that the candidate countries must achieve prior to accession.

The candidate countries are Bulgaria, Cyprus, the Czech Republic, Estonia, Hungary, Latvia, Lithuania, Malta, Poland, Romania, Slovakia and Slovenia. Turkey is officially an applicant country (this means that the EU has agreed that Turkey may have a formal relationship with the EU which may eventually lead to full membership), but a date has not yet been set for the commencement of official accession negotiations. Croatia and the Former Yugoslav Republic of Macedonia (FYROM) have also signed agreements with the EU that offer the prospect of EU membership. Albania, Bosnia, Hercegovina and the Former Yugoslav Republic (FYR) are also eligible for similar programmes. It is therefore possible that these countries will apply for EU membership within the next decade.

C   A concise history of the current enlargement

1989. The fall of the Berlin Wall marked the beginning of the end of the Soviet system and the artificial division of Europe, and led the countries of Central and Eastern Europe (CEECs) to initiate a programme of radical political and economic reform. The EU established the European Bank for Reconstruction and Development (EBRD), which provides low-interest loans to the CEECs for development of the private sector, and offers aid to the CEECs through the PHARE programme (Poland and Hungary: Action for the Reconstruction of the Economy) of initially 300 million ECU to help finance restructuring projects in the CEECs.

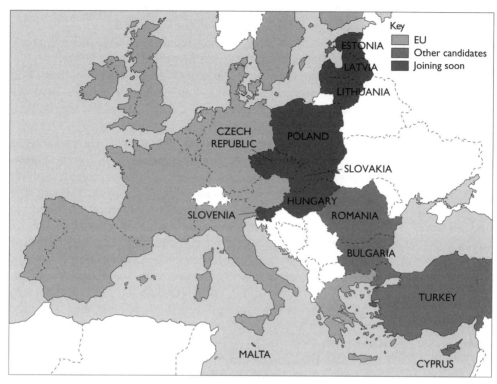

Key
- EU
- Other candidates
- Joining soon

The European Union – Current and Future Member States, 2003

1991. The EU signed the first of the Association Agreements (also known as the Europe Agreements) with Poland and Hungary. These agreements provided a framework for the economic and political relationship between the EU and the signatory countries, the ultimate aim of which was free trade with the EU. Further association agreements were signed with Bulgaria, the Czech and Slovak Republics and Romania in 1993; and with the Baltic states (Estonia, Latvia and Lithuania) and Slovenia in 1996. (Malta, Cyprus and Turkey had concluded similar agreements between 1970 and 1973.) These agreements resulted in an asymmetric trading relationship between the EU and the CEECs, by liberalizing tariffs and quotas more quickly on the EU side than was required of the CEECs. However, by delaying liberalization of the 'sensitive sectors' (agriculture, chemicals, coal, steel and textiles) in the EU – areas in which the CEECs had the majority of their trade and a comparative advantage – these trade agreements still worked to the advantage of the EU.

1993. The Copenhagen European Council agreed to allow the CEECs to join the EU, and introduced the concept of 'conditionality': accession would take place only when the applicant country was able to take on the economic and political obligations of EU membership. These conditions are known as the 'Copenhagen Criteria', and require that each candidate fulfil the following conditions:

- *Political*: the existence of stable institutions guaranteeing democracy, the rule of law, human rights and respect for and protection of minorities.
- *Economic*: the existence of a functioning market economy as well as the capacity to cope with competitive pressures and market forces within the Union.
- *Legislative*: the ability to take on the obligations of membership, including adherence to the aims of political, economic and monetary union – in other words, the ability to adopt the *acquis communitaire* (the body of EU legislation).

1997. In July the Commission published the *Agenda 2000 Report*, which examined the future of the Community's main policies, the financial outlook for the period 2000–6, the necessary institutional reforms, and the impact of enlargement. Agenda 2000 also contains the Commission's opinions on applications from Bulgaria, the Czech Republic, Estonia, Hungary, Latvia, Lithuania, Poland, Romania, Slovakia and Slovenia. The Commission proposed that membership be offered to the six candidates that were most prepared for accession. Agenda 2000 thereby established the model for all subsequent enlargement negotiations. The Luxembourg European Council recommended that accession talks be started with the Czech Republic, Estonia, Hungary, Poland, Slovenia and Cyprus (known as the 'Luxembourg Six'), and launched the pre-accession strategy aimed at helping the candidate countries adopt the *acquis communitaire*. Membership negotiations with the Luxembourg Six began in March 1998.

1999. In March the Berlin European Council established two new pre-accession instruments to channel aid to the candidate countries: one for structural reform (ISPA), with an annual budget of €1,040 million, and one for agricultural reform (SAPARD), with an annual budget of €520 million. During the Helsinki European Council in December, membership negotiations began with Bulgaria, Latvia, Lithuania, Malta (whose application was reactivated in 1998 after being withdrawn in 1996), Romania and Slovakia. These candidate countries are referred to as the 'Helsinki Six'. Turkey, which had originally submitted an application in 1963, was recognized as a 'candidate country' for the first time.

2000. At the Zagreb Summit, the EU offered Stabilization and Association Agreements (SAAs) to the Balkan states (Albania, Bosnia-Hercegovina, Croatia, FRY and Macedonia), and indicated that they might lead to EU accession. All five states started negotiations on the SAAs, with Macedonia signing in April 2001 and Croatia in October 2001. Although all have expressed interest in joining the Union, none of these countries has yet applied for membership. In December 2000, the Nice Treaty outlined the institutional reforms necessary for accession, including the number of Members of the European Parliament (MEPs) to be assigned to each candidate country and the weight of voting under QMV for the new members (see *Institutional Actors*). It also indicated that the EU desires the first wave of accession to take place before the next European Parliament (EP) elections in 2004.

2001. The Gothenburg European Council reached a compromise on the timetable issue, according to which the EU would be ready for the first wave of enlargement by 2002. It was later rescheduled to 2004, since neither the EU nor the candidate countries were prepared to enlarge in 2002.

2002. In October, the Commission recommended the conclusion of the accession negotiations by the end of the year with Cyprus, the Czech Republic, Estonia, Hungary, Latvia, Lithuania, Malta, Poland, the Slovak Republic and Slovenia, since the Commission had determined that these countries should be ready for EU membership by 2004. Bulgaria and Romania, by contrast, should be prepared for accession by 2007. The Commission established an elaborate 'monitoring' mechanism to ensure the successful implementation of EU legislation before accession, including 'security clauses' allowing the EU to suspend any chapter in the accession negotiations related to the Single Market and Justice and Home Affairs (JHA).

D   The enlargement process

In order to facilitate accession, the EU agreed to pre-accession strategies and partnerships with each candidate country. The pre-accession strategies include two key elements:

- Accession partnerships, which outline national programmes for each candidate country, in order to co-ordinate and facilitate the achievement of the accession criteria.
- Financial assistance, in the form of PHARE (for institutional development and financial investment), SAPARD (for agricultural development) and ISPA (for environmental and transport infrastructure).

The EU held bilateral negotiations with each candidate country to define the terms under which these countries would adopt and implement the *acquis communitaire*. As the EU has developed, it has accumulated more and more legislation that must be accepted by the candidate countries prior to entry. Hence, the criteria for entry are significantly more extensive today than they were during previous enlargements. Therefore, the negotiations focused on whether the EU would allow the candidate countries transitional time frames and arrangements for contentious policy issues, as it had in previous enlargements. In order to facilitate this process, the *acquis* was divided into thirty-one sections, known as chapters. The most difficult chapters on subjects including agriculture, regional policy and financial/budgetary provisions were scheduled to be addressed in 2002. By June 2002, twenty-eight of the thirty-one chapters had been completed provisionally.

The problems/issues

The fifth wave of enlargement poses many challenges to the EU. Taken together, the candidate countries are almost half the size and have almost half the population of the current EU, but produce only one-tenth of the combined GDP of the Community. The geographic and economic realities of enlargement have forced the EU to recognize the need to reform both its policies and its institutions, in order to ensure that a larger Union does not result in a weaker one.

A Policies

The Common Agricultural Policy (CAP) and EU Regional Policy (Structural and Cohesion Funds) are the main EU redistributive policies, and constitute almost 80 per cent of the EU budget. With the EU budget limited to 1.27 per cent of EU GDP, accession will require this funding to be distributed among a larger number of actors without being significantly increased through the contributions of the accession countries. While a small amount of funding has been reserved under the current financial perspective (2000–6) for any member state that joins before 2006, there is no consensus on how the EU budget will be divided after this period. For this reason, CAP and Structural/Cohesion Fund reform has become an important enlargement issue.

I   The Common Agricultural Policy (CAP)

As the percentage of the workforce engaged in farming is at least four times higher in the candidate countries than in the EU, enlargement may dramatically increase the number of farmers receiving CAP assistance and could result in a return to agricultural overproduction. As a result, enlargement would also significantly increase the proportion of the EU budget spent on agricultural subsidies, slow down agricultural reforms in the candidate countries, and distort world food prices – which would have negative ramifications for the EU's relationship with the World Trade Organization (WTO) (see *The Common Agricultural Policy*). In addition, the CAP is a regressive policy: the burden of paying for the policy falls most heavily on the poor. If the policy is expanded to include the CEECs, it will increase the agricultural prices in a region that already suffers from relatively low incomes, and where people spend a large portion of their incomes on basic necessities.

2   The Structural and Cohesion Funds

If the current structure of regional funding were extended to the candidate countries, each would qualify for Cohesion Fund and Objective 1 Structural Funds assistance (see *Regional Policy*). An extension of the current policy to the CEECs could equal a 30 per cent increase in the current budget of the Structural Funds alone. Therefore, if this policy is not reformed and the EU budget is not expanded, enlargement would result in funds being diverted from the current recipients to new member states – a prospect actively resisted by the current Cohesion countries (Spain, Greece, Ireland and Portugal), for which EU regional funds account for up to 3 per cent of their GDP.

Because of the difficulty in reforming these redistributive policies, increasing the EU budget appears to be the simplest means by which to deal with these issues. However, modifying the EU budget presents its own challenges, especially when one considers the widely diverging budgetary interests of the current member states. The net contributors (such as Germany, the Netherlands, Austria and the UK) are unlikely to sanction any increases, while the net recipients may fight to preserve their privileged positions (see *The EU Budget*). Therefore, the budgetary implications of extending these policies must be resolved before enlargement takes place. In addition, many of the applicant countries still have inadequate bureaucratic structures to absorb and manage these funds. Grants of this magnitude could be economically destabilizing to accession countries, which do not have a developed regulatory or administrative capacity; moreover, these countries would find it very difficult to match the current projects' co-funding requirements of the Structural Funds (at 50 per cent) and the Cohesion Fund (at 15 per cent).

While, in theory, the cost of extending these policies to the candidate countries may appear excessive, the actual cost may be more modest, for two important reasons: many farms in the CEECs are too small to qualify for the CAP, and current EU policy limits regional aid to any country to a level of less than 4 per cent of its GDP. In addition, the Commission has proposed a short-term solution to these problems. In order to address both the financial and social implications of extending the CAP, the Commission has proposed a shift away from direct payments toward rural development programmes, and has suggested that CAP funding to the accession countries be phased in gradually. This would allow all member states to receive an equitable benefit from the CAP by 2013. Furthermore, the Commission has proposed that regional funding be phased in between 2004 and 2006, so that the candidate countries have time to develop the administrative infrastructure to handle these funds efficiently. However, more fundamental reforms to these policies have yet to be addressed by the Commission.

B   Institutional reform

EU enlargement has emphasized the need to reform EU institutions, since additional members may further slow down the decision making and dilute the process of European integration. The Nice Treaty (2001) attempted to address these problems by adopting the following reforms:

- *The Commission.* According to the Nice Treaty, the Commission will consist of one commissioner per member state, starting in 2005. When the Union has reached twenty-seven members, the number of commissioners will be smaller than the number of member states; therefore members will be selected on a rotation system, based on the 'principle of equality'.
- *The Council of Ministers.* The Nice Treaty also established the number of weighted votes for each new member state under Qualified Majority Voting

(QMV) (see *Institutional Actors*). The reweighting of votes in the Council has important implications for the formation of blocking minorities, which can play a critical role in the direction and development of EU policy. However, the effect that this new system will have on the potential for blocking minorities is unclear.

- *The European Parliament*. The upper limit of 700 members in the EP (established in the Amsterdam Treaty) was raised to 732 in the Nice Treaty. However, all of the candidate countries will not join at the same time, and this has implications for the voting system during the transition period, including blocking minorities (see *Institutional Actors*).

These reforms may not be sufficient to prevent gridlock in the institutional decision-making processes of an enlarged EU. Nor do these changes ensure that the Community can continue to 'deepen' and expand EU-level policies. Further institutional innovations will therefore be the focus of upcoming European Councils, and constitute a major theme in the 2002 Convention on the Future of Europe (see *Constitutionalism*).

Who wins/who loses

This question is critical to the analysis of the enlargement process. Because the decision to proceed with enlargement must be determined by unanimity, all current member states must agree that enlargement will benefit them, or that they will be compensated for any negative ramifications of enlargement. Since the EU budget has been capped at 1.27 per cent of EU GDP, the possibility of using side-payments to compensate the losers from enlargement has been greatly reduced. Below is a cost–benefit analysis for both the EU and the candidate countries.

A   The current EU member states

I   Economic benefits

- *Trade gains*. Even though two-thirds of candidate country exports are sent to the EU, the Community's trade gains after enlargement are estimated to be only between 1 and 2 per cent of EU GDP. However, an additional 115 million citizens represent a huge new market for EU producers. At the same time, these trade gains will be unevenly distributed among the member states: Germany and other historic CEEC trading partners will receive significantly more than member states such as Portugal and Spain.
- *Efficiency gains*. Increasing trade will be beneficial in terms of increasing competitiveness, the availability of goods, allocative efficiency and output.

2   Economic costs

- *Budgetary constraints.* Even after reform, expanding the CAP and Regional Policy funding places a huge budgetary burden on the existing member states. This presents a problem both for the poorer current EU members (who may lose their present funding) and for member states that are net contributors to the EU budget. In addition, programmes for financial and technical assistance, such as PHARE, are likely to be long-term financial commitments, considering the low economic base of the new members.
- *The 'sensitive sectors'.* Some EU industries, particularly agriculture and textiles, will face increased competition from new member states, which enjoy a comparative advantage in these sectors. Portugal, for example, with a large textile industry and as a recipient of regional funding, will be a net loser from the enlargement process.
- *Reduction of foreign direct investment (FDI).* Such investment will be diverted from the current member states (especially those in peripheral areas) to the CEECs, due to the presence of a highly educated, lower-cost labour force that will attract MNCs.

3   Political benefits

- *International political prestige and democratic legitimacy.* Enlargement will increase the prestige of the EU as a global player, enhancing its visibility in global trade agreements. In addition, the induced gains of policy reform and institutional reform may enhance the Union's legitimacy and decision-making competence.
- *Stability and peace across Europe.* An increased zone of stability and peace in Europe will encourage economic growth. It will also internalize environmental and migratory problems, which have been of increasing concern for those EU countries that border the candidate countries.

4   Political costs

- *Increased democratic deficit and difficulty with decision making.* If institutional reform is delayed, the 'democratic deficit' in the EU will worsen with enlargement. The increased diversity of members may make decision making even more difficult and less transparent, potentially weakening integration.
- *Slowdown of the deepening process.* Some member states, such as France, worry that rapid enlargement of the EU (widening) will slow down the process of further economic and political integration (deepening) in policies such as EMU and the CFSP.

- *New borders.* By extending its borders, the EU will face greater difficulty in combating international crime (the Mafia, smuggling, etc.), as these problems are greater in many of the applicant countries. In addition, the EU will now border more politically volatile areas of the world (see *Justice and Home Affairs* and *Common Foreign and Security Policy*).

B The applicants

I Economic benefits

- *Access to EU markets.* The CEECs will gain access to the vast, wealthy markets of the existing members (370 million people).
- *Trade gains and reduced risk premium.* It has been estimated that the CEECs' trade gains after enlargement will amount to 1.5 per cent of total GDP. The 'sensitive sectors' make up a significant portion of these countries' output, and are likely to gain once the Single Market is expanded to include them. Arguably, the most significant gain is a lower-risk premium on investment in the CEECs. The risk premium is the 'excess' rate of return charged by investors on loans to these countries, because of the uncertain economic and/or political environment. Enlargement will result in increased investor confidence in the region and, consequently, more investment. It has been estimated that the risk premium could be reduced by up to 15 per cent.
- *Price stability and increased investment.* Membership in the EU will facilitate the macroeconomic convergence process for the CEECs, leading to price stability. In addition, increases in FDI are likely to increase with the reduction of the risk premium. This, in turn, will encourage transfers of technology, management skills and retraining programmes already being advanced by the PHARE programme. Such transfers are particularly relevant to those countries emerging from decades of central planning, poor economic performance and state ownership.

2 Economic costs

- *Adoption of the acquis.* The process of incorporating EU regulations into the legal structure of the CEECs is a complex and costly task; the applicant countries also lack the administrative infrastructure required to complete the adoption of the *acquis* quickly and effectively.
- *Market pressures.* If current market barriers are removed, EU membership could magnify structural weaknesses in these economies, which may not be able to withstand the strong competition in the Single Market. In addition, less competitive industries will suffer short-term losses through the removal of state aids.

- *Culture of dependence.* Joining the EU and receiving economic aid in the form of the CAP and the regional funds may lead to a culture of dependence in these countries, delaying internal reforms.

3 Political benefits

- *Keeping reforms on track.* Joining the EU serves as a commitment device to continue economic and political restructuring.
- *Elimination of the artificial division of Europe.* Enlargement can be seen as a final *rapprochement* between Germany and the nations of Eastern Europe. EU membership is also an alternative to the legacy of being a 'buffer zone' between Russia and the West. This is of particular importance to the CEECs, who will gain increased security and stability from EU membership.
- *Adoption of social and environmental norms.* This benefit is hard to categorize, since it is a welfare gain, but it is one that can come at a very large cost. For example, nuclear power plants in some CEECs may have to be closed because of EU environmental standards, resulting in the loss of jobs and significant increases in the cost of energy in these countries.

4 Political costs

- *Loss of national sovereignty.* After liberation from fifty years of totalitarian rule, new members may resent being forced to adopt EU rules and regulations that they had no part in creating.
- *Reform fatigue.* The huge costs of restructuring markets and monolithic enterprises may force the governments of the CEECs to be fiscally frugal. As a result, the Copenhagen Criteria may lead to 'reform fatigue' among the citizens of these countries and reduce support for accession. However, an October 2001 Eurobarometer poll of the candidate countries indicated that two-thirds of those polled would still vote in favour of EU membership in a referendum on the issue.

Food for thought

What is the best method for enlarging the European Union? Some CEECs are clearly more prepared than others to take on the requirements of membership. If enlargement takes place in phases (as is currently proposed), what happens to those countries that are initially excluded from the EU? Will this hinder their attempts to reform? In addition, if membership is confined to current applicants, this may have serious economic and political implications for the countries that remain outside the EU, such as the Ukraine and Russia. Some academics propose that there might be alternatives to joining the EU. Full membership is not required to obtain the majority of the economic benefits listed in the *Who wins/who loses* section. The only big economic gains that require full membership are precisely those that pose the most political problems within the EU: namely, participation in the CAP and Regional Policy. However, would the candidate countries be willing to accept second-class EU citizenship?

When should the EU stop expanding? In light of the Turkish application for EU membership, the academic debate on the practical, political and social boundaries of Europe has taken on greater significance. The debate focuses on the unifying force behind EU expansion: namely, whether Europe is defined by geography, democratic principles, shared cultural values or merely economic efficiency. The current candidate countries have already tested assumptions about the boundaries of Europe: the human rights violations in Slovakia, the Muslim majority in Turkey, the *de facto* division of Cyprus, and new EU borders with the Middle East challenge the traditional perceptions of Europe. Moreover, the EU must consider the possibility of further applications from former Soviet Republics and perhaps even Russia.

Student-to-student tip

It is important to remember that economic estimates vary significantly between authors, depending on the empirical methodology employed. Therefore, it is best to view all estimates with some scepticism. For a comprehensive analysis of the political situation, it is also important to understand the impact of enlargement on individual member states and candidate countries. Although the costs and benefits may seem straightforward, the position of individual countries can vary significantly. Therefore don't assume that Poland's priority issues are the same as Latvia's or Malta's.

Summary

- The candidate countries involved in the fifth wave of enlargement are at different stages in their economic and political development. The EU has agreed to offer membership by 2004 to ten countries: Cyprus, the Czech Republic, Estonia, Hungary, Latvia, Lithuania, Malta, Poland, Slovakia and Slovenia. Bulgaria and Romania should be ready to join in 2007. Turkey, although it has been accepted as an official applicant country, has not been offered a date for the beginning of formal membership negotiations.
- Membership of the candidate countries (excluding Turkey) would increase the current EU population and area by one-third, but would increase the EU's GDP by less than 10 per cent, posing a budgetary challenge to the Union.
- The main costs and benefits involved in the enlargement process are as follows:
  - For the current EU member states, costs are an increased budgetary burden, under current CAP and regional fund criteria (and the potential deepening of the democratic deficit of the Union) if the structures are not adapted to a larger organization; while the benefits are expected trade gains, the spread of stability and peace across the continent and an increase in international political prestige.

- For the applicant countries, costs are the adoption of the *acquis*, the market pressures from the West, and possible reform fatigue; while the benefits are access to a market of 370 million consumers, transfers from the EU budget, the reduction of risk premiums and the consequent inflows of FDI, external pressure for economic and political transition reforms and the end of the artificial division of the continent.
- While the structure for enlargement has been established, difficult individual negotiations with some applicant countries have yet to take place. These include agreements on transition periods in sensitive policy areas such as agriculture and regional aid.

Selected bibliography

Overview

Sedelmeier, A. and H. Wallace (2000) 'Policies towards Eastern Europe', in H. Wallace and W. Wallace (eds), *Policy-Making in the European Union*, 4th edn, Oxford: Oxford University Press, chapter 16: 427–60.
An excellent introduction to the subject, this chapter facilitates a rapid and clear view of the enlargement process and the problems surrounding it.

Comprehensive book

Mayhew, A. (1998) *Recreating Europe: The European Union's Policy towards Central and Eastern Europe*, Cambridge: Cambridge University Press.
While a very comprehensive volume, covering thoroughly most aspects of enlargement, Mayhew is very biased in favour of eastward enlargement.

Articles and reports on enlargement issues

Baldwin, R., J. François and R. Porter (1997) 'The Costs and Benefits of Eastern Enlargement: The Impact on the EU and Central Europe', *Economic Policy*, vol. 24: 125–76.
A 'must read' on the subject, this article is the most thorough attempt to quantify the actual economic costs and benefits from enlargement. The authors conclude, some believe optimistically, that enlargement will result in financial gains for the enlarged Union.
EBRD (2002) *Annual Transition Report*, London: EBRD.
The annual report from the European Bank of Reconstruction and Development outlines the main developments in each of the transition countries, and is very useful when searching for economic data on the CEECs.
Preston, C. (1995) 'Obstacles to EU Enlargement: The Classical Community Method and the Prospects for a Wider Europe', *Journal of Common Market Studies*, vol. 33, no. 3: 451–63.
Preston presents a straightforward comparison between previous enlargements and the current one.
Schimmelfennig, F. (2001) 'The Community Trap: Liberal Norms, Rhetorical Action, and the Eastern Enlargement of the European Union', *International Organization*, vol. 55, no. 1: 47–80.
Drawing on both intergovernmentalist and constructivist writings, Schimmelfennig introduces the concept of rhetorical action to explain how opponents of eastwards enlargement found it difficult to argue against widening, in light of the EU's own legitimacy.

Tucker, J. A. et al. (2002) 'Transitional Winners and Losers: Attitudes towards EU Membership in Post-Communist Countries', *American Journal of Political Science*, vol. 46, no. 3: 557–71.
> This article discusses the support for EU membership in post-Communist states, in light of the economic performance of the countries since the fall of Communism.

Steuneberg, B. (ed.) (2002) *Widening the European Union: The Politics of Institutional Change and Reform*, London and New York: Routledge.
> Written from an institutionalist rational choice perspective, this book brings together several prominent authors discussing most topics related to institutional change and EU enlargement.

Supportive websites

http://www.bcemag.com   This site is provided by *The Economist*, and outlines the main economic indicators from the transition countries.

http://www.ebrd.com   The site of the London-based EBRD provides very helpful data and reports.

http://europa.eu.int/comm/enlargement/index_en.html   The site of the Commission's Task Force for the Accession Negotiations (TFAN), it offers information on the issues and procedures involved in the negotiations.

http://wiiwsv.wsr.ac.at/Countdown/   *Countdown* is a site devoted to Eastern European enlargement, and includes links, bibliographic references and a directory of academic researchers.

http://www.cer.org.uk   The Centre for European Reform is a think tank devoted to improving the quality of the debate on the future of the EU. Their Enlargement section is often updated, and has many interesting articles.

http://www.euractiv.com   This site's section on Enlargement provides valuable information.

http://www.dbresearch.com   The EU Enlargement Monitor from the Deutsche Bank has a very interesting 'Scenarios' section, describing possible ways in which EU enlargement may progress.

22

Flexible Integration

Jorge Juan Fernández García

European integration can be achieved in a number of different ways. One possibility is for all member states to be involved in every policy, in the same way and at the same time. However, past experiences, such as the Empty Chair crisis in 1965, demonstrate that this type of integration can lead to blockages in policy making, since member states find it difficult to reach the consensus needed to take collective action through the EU institutions. Policy-makers have therefore experimented with other, more flexible forms of integration. While flexible arrangements have existed since the 1970s, a number of flexible provisions were institutionalized in the Treaty of Amsterdam (1997). These provisions are legal instruments that allow groups of member states to pursue further integration amongst themselves without the need for consensus among all member states. The creation of these flexible provisions marks a significant break with the historical pattern of integration. It not only affects the way in which policies are created, but also alters the relationship between the member states and the EU, as well as the relationships among the member states themselves.

The facts

A Defining flexible integration

According to Stubb, 'the aim of flexibility is to allow different groupings of member states to pursue an array of public policies with different procedural and institutional arrangements'. This means that member states are involved to differing extents in EU integration, and therefore have different rights and obligations in certain policy areas or expenditure programmes. An example is Economic and Monetary Union (EMU): as of January 2003, only twelve of the fifteen member states participate in EMU.

B   Different concepts of flexible integration

The term 'flexible integration' is used by politicians and academics to refer to many different kinds of integration arrangements. Therefore, it is important to distinguish between the different concepts of flexible integration. There are three main types (as defined by Stubb), and each concept is based on a different premise, relating to a particular method of integration.

I   Multi-speed

This is 'a mode of flexible integration, according to which the pursuit of common objectives is driven by a group of member states, which are both able and willing to go further, the underlying assumption being that the others will follow later'. A good example is EMU: although those member states that have not joined EMU are waiting to decide whether and when to join, it is expected that they will join at some point. Therefore, the unity of the Union and of its policies will eventually be re-established. According to the multi-speed model of flexible integration, the different levels of policy implementation between member states are temporary rather than permanent.

2   Variable geometry

This is 'a mode of flexible integration which admits unattainable differences within the integrative structure by allowing permanent or irreversible separation between a hard core and lesser developed integrative units'. An example of this is the Western European Union (WEU), the European defence organization, of which most member states are members. However, some states, due to commitments to neutrality, have decided not to join. Variable geometry differs from multi-speed because it does not assume that all countries will eventually sign up to all policies. In practice, variable geometry creates a core of countries that lead the integration process and a group of outsider member states that cannot or will not participate in these policies. Note that, in this model, the group of countries that form this core are always the same.

3   Europe à la carte

This is a 'mode of flexible integration whereby respective member states are able to pick-and-choose, as from a menu, in which policy areas they would like to participate, whilst at the same time holding only to a minimum number of common objectives'. Examples of these 'opt-outs' include the UK opt-out for EMU and the Social Charter, and the Danish opt-out for defence, citizenship issues and EMU in the Treaty on European Union (TEU). The difference between *Europe à la carte* and variable geometry is that the core in *Europe à la carte* will not always be composed of the same countries. Instead, each policy field will have a different core.

C   When the EU discusses flexible integration

Stubb's analysis of the flexibility debate demonstrates that flexibility occurs whenever at least one of the following five issues is debated at the European level: EMU, Justice and Home Affairs (JHA), Common Foreign and Security Policy (CFSP), enlargement, or the exclusion of reluctant member states. Therefore, flexibility becomes an issue every time the Union is about to undergo further integration (deepening) and/or an expansion of membership (widening).

D   The history of the debate

The flexibility debate evolved because the strong differences of opinion between the member states were hindering policy making within the Union. The debate developed in three stages.

I   The political debate in the 1970s

The flexible integration debate started with speeches, articles and documents prepared by policy-makers in the 1970s.

- The first contribution was made in November 1974 by the West German Chancellor Willy Brandt, who argued that the Community was suffering from stagnation in policy creation. In order to move forward, Brandt proposed that the Community should find ways of promoting 'graduated integration'. However, he emphasized that this differentiation should not be a permanent feature of the Union: eventually, the slower or less willing countries should join the core. Thus the Brandt proposal was a multi-speed solution.
- The second event was the Tindemans Report of January 1976. Belgian Prime Minister Leo Tindemans argued that it was not 'absolutely necessary that in every case all stages of integration should be reached by all member states at the same time'. Tindemans drew attention to the fact that some states were prepared to move ahead faster than others, and those who were able to progress had a duty to do so. However, he firmly stated that he was not promoting *Europe à la*

carte. Like Brandt, Tindemans believed that all member states should be subject to a final common objective, which they would all reach in due time.

- The third development was the lecture given by Ralph Dahrendorf at the European University Institute of Florence in November 1979. He advocated a *Europe à la carte*, but not in the way in which the term has entered the current terminology (as defined above). Dahrendorf viewed *à la carte* as a method of integration that would 'more often than not... in the end lead to common policies'. More recently, his terminology has been misused by politicians who do not favour the EU; in its current usage, *Europe à la carte* is seen instead as a loose 'pick-and-choose' option that may not lead to further European integration.

2   Academic efforts to define flexible integration in the 1990s

In the early 1990s, academics began to study these concepts from the points of view of different academic disciplines (law, political science, international relations, economics, etc.). They were able to make clear progress in narrowing the various terms and strategies to the three different conceptual models discussed above. These were later used in the 1996 intergovernmental conference (IGC).

3   The political debate before the 1996 IGC

Schäuble and Lamers, British Prime Minister John Major and French Prime Minister Edouard Balladur put flexibility on the agenda for the 1996 IGC. All three visions of Europe were important, but it was the Schäuble and Lamers paper that provoked the largest – mainly negative – reaction. Their paper was the basis for the responses submitted by Major and then Balladur:

- The political debate on the practical implementation of flexibility started in September 1994, when two Conservative German politicians, Wolfgang Schäuble and Karl Lamers, published the document 'Reflections on European Foreign Policy'. The authors argued that a stronger and more democratic Union was required to cope with both EMU and the strains of enlargement. This could be achieved only by an inner core of member states leading Europe forward. Member states' reactions to this were negative, because the paper named Germany, France and the Benelux countries as this inner core of member states.
- In response, John Major advocated *Europe à la carte*, a concept which complemented the British preference for intergovernmental integration. Major's version of *Europe à la carte* did not conform to Dahrendorf's original definition, but instead proposed a pick-and-choose organization. This was to be centred on the Single Market, which the UK had always considered to be the core purpose of the EU.

- In November 1994, Balladur contributed to this debate with his proposal for 'concentric circles' of integration. These concentric circles consisted of two tiers of full member states, as well as a third tier with the status of 'partners'; this third tier could even include Russia and Turkey. The aim would eventually be to integrate all three tiers into one.

E The practical tools of flexible integration

While these ideas have been used on various occasions to justify putting different flexible forms into practice, it is also important to differentiate between flexible arrangements and flexible provisions.

I Flexible arrangements

These are anomalies and exceptions to full integration that occur outside or within the framework of the EC/EU treaties amongst several of the member states. Examples of such flexible arrangements outside the treaty framework include the Schengen Accords and the European Monetary System (EMS). Not all member states participate in these areas, and none of these arrangements is covered by a provision in the EC/EU treaties. Main examples within the legal framework defined by the treaties are the third stage of EMU and the Social Protocol.

2 Flexible provisions

These are the legal instruments of flexible integration that were institutionalized in the Amsterdam Treaty, establishing general rules for such anomalies and exceptions. The provisions consist of a set of criteria that the member states must fulfil in order to launch closer co-operation (CC) initiatives.

F Provisions institutionalized in the Amsterdam Treaty on CC

The constitutional framework of CC was introduced into the Amsterdam Treaty through general and specific clauses. The general clauses aim at establishing a clear framework for using CC, and are set out in a new Title VII ('Provisions on Closer Co-operation') in the TEU. The specific clauses supplement the general clauses by spelling out in detail when CC may actually occur within each Pillar. The set of common requirements establishes that CC must do the following:

- further the objectives of the Union;
- respect the single institutional framework;
- be used only as a last resort;
- concern at least a majority of member states;
- not affect the *acquis communitaire* (i.e. current legislation);
- not affect the competences, rights, obligations and interests of the non-participating member states;
- be open to participation by all member states;
- comply with the Pillar-specific additional criteria laid down in Article 11 (ex-Article J.1) and Article 40 (ex-Article K.12) of the TEU.

Additionally, the Treaty of Nice (2001) determined that the co-operation proposed must not:

- be applied in areas of exclusive Community competence (i.e. internal market);
- affect Community policies, actions or programmes;
- concern EU citizenship or discriminate between EU citizens;
- go beyond the limits of Community competences;
- constitute a trade restriction or distortion of competition between member states.

The Commission is responsible for submitting proposals for CC to the Council, based on an application from the interested countries. However, while the Commission (rather than the member states) decides whether new countries can join a CC initiative under Pillar I, it can only issue an opinion under Pillars II and III (in CC proposals, the Commission enjoys a bigger role in JHA than in CFSP).

G   The Nice Treaty changes on the provisions on CC

The Nice Treaty made changes to the CC provisions, primarily because the provisions had never been utilized, due to the very specific and restrictive conditions placed on the use of CC. Consequently, the changes have made it easier for groups of member states to launch CC initiatives. The main changes are:

- The extension of CC to the Second Pillar (CFSP), to allow the implementation of a joint action or a common position among the member states. However, this extension is fairly limited, as it may not involve matters with military or defence implications.
- The minimum number of eight participants in CC proposals is the same as in the Amsterdam Treaty, but this number will not change when the EU is enlarged to twenty-seven countries.
- Prior to Nice, any attempts to initiate CC had to be taken by unanimity in the Council of Ministers. This veto mechanism was abolished at Nice—so the

decision on whether general provisions have been met is now decided by qualified majority voting (QMV). Hence, CC can be adopted even if some countries vote against it.

- In policy areas subject to the co-decision procedure in the First Pillar (EC), CC may be initiated only with the assent of the European Parliament (EP), which gives the EP extra powers in this field.

The problems/issues

A   The impact of CC provisions on the EU institutions

- *The Council of Ministers.* Philippart and Sie Dhian Ho explain that in policy fields subject to unanimity in the Council, CC could help prevent blockage in policy making by enabling CC participants to circumvent a member state's veto. Where QMV is the rule, CC could still be useful, as it provides a 'softer' solution: for policies falling under QMV, the outvoting of member states in politically sensitive areas can be especially traumatic, and raises questions of democratic legitimacy. CC thus offers an important alternative if no consensus exists in the Council.
- *The European Commission.* CC provisions allow for some countries to pursue deeper integration through their own initiative. This might diminish the role of the EU Commission as the traditional policy-initiator. On the other hand, if the Commission wants to be seen as the key promoter of European integration, it will need to be involved in the CC framework. If it does get involved, some countries may feel that the Commission favours the core member states, rather than protecting the common interests of all members. CC could therefore undermine the status of the Commission as a neutral arbiter of the needs of all member states.
- *The European Parliament.* The EP is only consulted on issues concerning CC provisions, which increases the Union's democratic deficit.
- *The European Court of Justice.* The ECJ has been given jurisdiction over CC issues in the Nice Treaty, and can now pass judgments on all matters under Pillar I.

B   The impact of CC on the EU system of governance

If CC increases the complexity and the opaqueness of the Union, the structure and activities of the EU may become even less transparent for citizens and for third countries. In areas such as Pillar II (CFSP), in which there is already very little parliamentary supervision, the use of CC provisions could increase the Union's lack of accountability.

On the other hand, the institutionalization of CC should minimize the temptation for member states to form agreements outside the institutional treaty framework.

This could be positive, since such agreements also lack transparency; the absence of both any parliamentary supervision and independent judicial review in these agreements also raises questions about the Union's democratic deficit. Consequently, it is unclear whether CC will increase or diminish this deficit.

C Possibilities for use of the CC provisions

The CC provisions have never been used, but the changes incorporated at Nice have made CC more accessible. Potential policy areas where CC could allow for new policy developments include:

- *First Pillar*: professional training, youth, culture, public health, tourism, energy, civil protection, trans-European networks, industry, research and technological development, environment.
- *Second Pillar*: the incorporation of the WEU or the Eurocorps in the Union, the development of a common regime for armaments, immigration policy.
- *Third Pillar*: police and judicial co-operation with respect to crime, terrorism or drugs, exchange of information, harmonization of extradition, hot pursuit rules, and of penal law.

However, there may be areas where the use of flexibility is inappropriate, or even harmful to the integration process.

Who wins/who loses

On the surface, **member states** are most likely to either gain or lose from flexible integration. Depending on how the CC provisions are applied, the potential winners and losers could vary. CC could lead to the development of a hegemonic core of wealthier member states, which would disrupt the dynamics of European integration. The larger, more powerful countries could decide to pursue deeper integration, leaving the weaker countries without a voice in the decision-making process. Problems will occur for those countries that are able but not willing to pursue deeper integration. CC may mean that such countries lose their ability to block legislation, and therefore also lose their bargaining powers in the decision-making process. The diplomatic relationships between the 'ins' and the 'outs' of any particular flexible arrangement could also harm negotiations between member states in other policy areas. The dominance of the member states in the CC process also increases the democratic deficit.

The **Commission** could be a loser, especially if its role as initiator is diminished. In addition to the increased democratic deficit, CC could create an opaque organization, thereby increasing the lack of transparency, which would make **EU citizens** losers as well. The **EP** and the **ECJ** also appear to be losers, since they have been removed from most of the CC process. Although they have regained some powers at Nice, these institutions remain marginalized.

Unless the CC provisions spill over into all the member states, the **process of European integration** could suffer, especially as member states regain control of the integration process from the supranational institutions.

Food for thought

Will CC provisions contribute to a successful deepening and widening of the Union? Enlargement is a formidable challenge for a Union which is attempting to reconcile different visions of Europe. Some members wish to proceed faster than others, and there is also disagreement over the direction that Europe should take. In addition, flexible integration could lead to further fragmentation or even disintegration of the Union. In what respects will EU enlargement accelerate the already existing trends towards a 'multi-speed union'?

Will the existence of different speeds of integration have an impact on the long-term characteristics of the Union? Diversity could cause problems for the integration process, such as the possible development of a second-class membership for the newcomers. While there may be another solution to handling such diversity besides flexible integration, the EU might simply stop developing without flexible integration.

Student-to-student tip

The best way to understand flexible integration is to study practical examples. In particular, policies such as EMU, Schengen and the Social Protocol all demonstrate ways in which the EU could further develop policies at different speeds and in different configurations. It is important to note that member states also change their minds about participation in these programmes, especially with changes in government. The UK, for example, signed on to the Social Protocol following the election of a Labour government. Therefore, it is useful to examine a member state's participation in a policy area in terms of the matrix of willing/unwilling and able/unable.

Summary

Flexibility is the result of some member states wishing to proceed with further integration in some areas when others do not. Flexible integration has been applied through flexible provisions and flexible arrangements.

- Flexible arrangements have been in use since the 1970s. They have occurred outside (e.g. Schengen, EMS) or within the treaty framework through opt-outs (e.g. third stage of EMU, Social Charter). These are anomalies to the dynamics of integration.
- Flexible provisions were institutionalized in the Amsterdam Treaty. They are now legal instruments, which can be used to establish a new pattern for European integration. The provisions have not yet been used, in part because the conditions to launch CC were considered too restrictive. The conditions were therefore changed in the Nice Treaty.

Conceptually speaking, there are three different modes of flexible integration:

- *Multi-speed* means some countries go ahead in a given policy field while others wait and join later. However, all member states will eventually join. In this concept, the separation is temporary.
- *Variable geometry* allows for a core of countries to go ahead with policy integration. Here, the separation is permanent, and the core is always composed of the same member states.
- In *Europe à la carte*, the separation is also permanent, but the core in any given policy area can be composed of different countries.

Selected bibliography

Articles

Stubb, A. (1996) 'A Categorisation of Differentiated Integration', *Journal of Common Market Studies*, vol. 34, no. 2: 283–95.
A must-read, this article clarifies the terminology, and is an excellent source of historical examples of flexible integration.
Stubb, A. (1998) 'The Amsterdam Treaty and Flexible Integration', *ECSA Review*, vol. 11, no. 2.
This eleven-page article analyses the different options adopted by the policy-makers.
Philippart, E. and M. Sie Dhian Ho (2000) *The Pros and Cons of Closer Cooperation in the EU: Argumentation and Recommendations*, Working Document W104, The Hague: Netherlands Scientific Council for Government Policy. Available at *http://www.wrr.nl/HTML-EN/BasisPU-EN.html*.
The authors highlight the pros and cons that the use of CC could have for the Union, explaining the reasoning behind them.
Milner, F. and A. Kölliker (1999) *How to Make Use of Closer Cooperation? The Amsterdam Clauses and the Dynamic of European Integration*, Brussels: EU Commission Forward Studies Unit. Available at *http://www.europa.eu.int/comm/cdp/working-paper/index_ en.htm*.
This document applies Public Goods theory to the different policy options where CC could be applied, in order to explain and anticipate why some outside member states might join some flexible provisions.

Books

Stubb, A. (2002) *From Amsterdam to Nice and Beyond: Negotiating Flexible Integration in the European Union*, London: Macmillan.
This is an excellent insider account of the process of negotiations on flexible integration within the Union during the last two treaty negotiations.
Bruess, F. and S. Griller (1998) *Flexible Integration in Europe – Einheit oder 'Europa-a-la-carte'*, Vienna: Springer.
Published in conjunction with the Austrian Society for European Research, this volume offers a variety of perspectives on the most controversial aspects of flexible integration. Unfortunately, it is currently available only in German.
Dewatripont, M. et al. (1996) *Flexible Integration: Toward a More Effective and Democratic Europe*, London: Centre for Economic Policy Research.
In a concise 190-page volume compiled before the 1996 IGC by a team of academics from six countries, Dewatripont offers a very positive but somewhat dated perspective on flexible integration.

Part VII

CONCLUSION

23

A European Union for EU Citizens

Jess Clayton and Jorge Juan Fernández García

In almost every chapter of this book, the winners and losers from various aspects
of EU integration have been analysed. This discussion often deals with the
balance of power between member states, the Commission and the European
Court of Justice; this also reflects the benefits which a particular policy provides
for particular constituencies. Interestingly, the only consistent statement made
throughout the book in this section deals with the perceived and real benefits of
these policies and structures for EU citizens. Even with respect to issues such as
fundamental rights and social policy, which speak directly to the needs of the
citizens, it has been difficult to demonstrate a clear and direct benefit for the EU
citizen in any policy area. The reality of this perception is illustrated by the
Eurobarometer polls of EU citizens that consistently indicate antipathy and
confusion about the role and importance of the Community. As a result, citizens
of the member states still identify themselves primarily with their nation-state,
and only nominally with the EU. Two questions arise from this discussion: why
haven't EU citizens developed an EU identity similar to their national identity?
and why is the development of EU identity important to the future of the EU?

A The development of an EU identity

The answer to the first question above is complicated and multi-fold. The development of an EU identity, defined as a connection between the EU citizen and the EU
as a supranational entity, is based on both the perceived benefits of EU membership
and the ability of the EU citizen to participate in the evolution of the Community.
In both areas, the current structure of the EU fails to support these connections with
the EU citizen.

I Benefits of EU membership

Large-scale benefits of EU membership are difficult to demonstrate concretely to individual citizens. For example, the creation of the Community has helped to ensure over fifty years of peace and stability in Europe. However, the benefits of peace (i.e. the lack of war) are difficult to demonstrate, especially to the current generation, which has never known the suffering caused by World Wars I and II. Yet, the very structure of the EU – namely, the integration of economies – serves as one of the best barriers to future conflict.

Similarly, the economic prosperity generated by regional economic integration is extremely difficult to demonstrate, especially since the creation of the EU has not prevented economic slowdowns and recessions. It is also hard to prove that economic prosperity in Europe is the direct result of the Community, rather than other global economic forces. Yet it can be argued that EU regional integration has dramatically increased intra-EU trade, which has in turn led to a larger selection of goods for consumers, greater competition in the marketplace and a corresponding lowering of prices in all member states. The EU has also allowed the individual nations of Europe to emerge as a united global economic player of equal significance to other superpowers, such as the United States.

In addition, while some policy areas have created more visible benefits for EU citizens, the impact of policies in these areas on the creation of an EU identity appears to be neither consistent nor considerable:

- EU-level environmental policy has greatly eliminated trans-boundary pollution by creating uniform environmental standards across Europe. While Europeans enjoy the benefits of better environmental standards, these benefits are not always attributed to the EU.
- Regional policy, in the form of the Structural and Cohesion Funds, has contributed to the creation and improvement of infrastructure, such as new roads and water treatment plants, throughout the EU. However, because of the co-operation between the EU and national or regional authorities in such projects, the credit for these projects is often given to national entities.
- Economic and Monetary Union (EMU) in the form of the circulation of the euro acts as a concrete symbol of EU membership in the wallet of every citizen. However, many citizens still perceive the euro as an inconvenience, without recognizing its benefits.
- Some policies – such as the Common Agricultural Policy (CAP) – provide noticeable benefits for a small number of citizens, at the expense of the majority of citizens.

It is easy to understand why it would be difficult for EU citizens to identify with the Community on such issues as peace and economic growth, especially as it is difficult to prove that these benefits would not have occurred without the presence of the EU. However, even the most concrete benefits of EU membership are often taken for granted by EU citizens. For example, the Treaty principle on the free movement of people has led to the creation of a common EU passport and the ability of EU citizens to live, study and work in any member state. While language barriers remain, a growing percentage of EU citizens take advantage of opportunities arising from this right, without the conscious realization that such activities are a direct benefit of EU membership.

Perhaps more significantly, the lack of development of certain policy areas at the EU level has inhibited the growth of an EU identity. An important example is EU Social Policy, which has been confined to the creation of common standards for workers, such as equality of pay between men and women and workplace safety requirements. However, since social policy includes such activities as welfare, education and health care, it is an arena where member states are most able to demonstrate the benefits of citizenship. As a result, many member states have strongly guarded against the encroachment of EU policies into these areas. The same can be said of other policy areas that citizens strongly identify with the nation-state, such as the military and police co-operation.

2   Participation of citizens in the construction of the EU

Perhaps the largest barrier to increased EU identity among the citizens of Europe has resulted from the structure of the EU itself. Since the EU is based on an international treaty rather than a constitution, many of the benefits associated with citizenship – namely, fundamental rights, democratic processes, etc. – are missing from the Treaties. More importantly, the decision-making process in the EU has evolved over time to incorporate the changing needs and power dynamics of the main policy-makers. The resulting political system is not only overly complicated, but it also lacks the transparency and simplicity needed to be readily understood by the average citizen. As a result, the EU citizen is unable to develop the fundamental connection with the EU as a polity – namely, the ability to actively participate in the creation of EU policy and the future of the Community.

While both contribute to the problem, it is the democratic deficit more than the lack of transparency in the EU which inhibits the growth of EU identity. The democratic deficit is exemplified by the fact that decision-makers in the EU are far removed from the EU citizen:

- The European Parliament (EP), which is the only EU body elected directly by EU citizens, is the weaker half of the legislative branch of governance. In addition, the candidates for membership in the EP are primarily selected by the heads of national parties. As a result, EP elections are often more about national politics than EU issues (the same can be said of national referendums on the acceptance of EU treaties).
- The Council of Ministers, whose members are even further removed from the citizen, still holds the majority of the decision-making power in the EU. Since the Council is made up of individuals from the cabinets of the current national

leadership, the democratic deficit is greater in the Council. This has ramifications throughout the EU, especially since the Council decides on the membership of the Commission, the European Court of Justice, and most other supporting institutions.

In comparison with the significantly more direct representation inherent in most national systems of governance, it is not surprising that the average EU citizen feels disconnected from developments in the EU. The combined effect of the complexity of the EU as a political system and the democratic deficit in decision making within that system have thus created substantial barriers to the development of an EU identity.

B   The need for an EU identity

If the benefits of EU membership are difficult to demonstrate, and the EU citizen feels unconnected to the political process in the EU, the question then becomes, Why is it necessary to create an EU identity? Critics argue that citizens are already alienated from national politics; therefore it should not matter if they perceive no connection with the EU. However, unlike participation in the nation-state, partici-pation in the European project is a choice, which is often put to the vote during national referendums on EU treaties. The referendums during the confirmation of the Maastricht and Nice treaties seemed to demonstrate that EU citizens were not content with their passive role in the development of the Community. The eastward enlargement of the EU presents another difficult challenge to the fragile consensus on the benefits of the European project for the EU citizen that the EU is attempting to maintain.

I   The effects of enlargement on EU identity

While enlarging the Union serves to fulfil one of the fundamental goals of the Treaties of Rome, it also threatens to undermine the fragile agreement that cur-rently exists between the EU and its citizens. The tacit agreement of the people of Europe to participate in the European project is the foundation upon which the European Union was built. Without the support of EU citizens, the Community ceases to be a viable project. Eastward enlargement in the present political system would increase the democratic deficit and significantly slow down policy making. This may be unacceptable to the EU citizen, who already lacks confidence in the benefits of enlargement. While the Treaties of Amsterdam and Nice have made institutional reform a condition of enlargement, the institutional reform agreed upon in these treaties – namely, the determination of MEP seats for accession countries and the reconfiguration of the Commission – does not address the current barriers to the development of an EU identity, such as transparency and the democratic deficit. Moreover, some of the instruments added to the Treaties in order to correct these problems, such as Closer Co-operation and subsidiarity, could have the opposite effect, by fragmenting the Community and thereby undermining the common bonds that connect all EU citizens to each other.

2   Building identity through a constitution

The effects of enlargement on EU identity and the future of the European project were acknowledged by the Laeken Declaration in December 2000, which led to the 2002 Convention on the Future of Europe. The Convention has been designed as an open debate between citizens and their political leaders on the development of an EU constitution to replace the EU treaties. Those in favour of a constitution argue that it would address the main concerns of the EU citizen, by simplifying the legal and legislative structure of the EU, thereby increasing transparency. It would also delineate more clearly the scope of subsidiarity within the EU system, in order to decrease the democratic deficit. Some proposals include the incorporation of the Charter of Fundamental Rights, the non-binding political declaration made by the Community in conjunction with the Treaty of Nice.

An EU constitution would have the advantage of being able to clearly spell out the rights and duties of all concerned parties, including citizens, in a way that recognizes the reality of enlargement. However, despite the obvious advantages of a constitution to an enlarged Union, the old barriers to such a legal realignment of the Community remain. The creation of an EU constitution still appears to be the first step down the path of federalism – and many EU citizens resist the idea of changing an economic union into a federalized superstate. Such a scenario not only threatens the status of the nation-state, but also undermines its *raison d'être*. At the same time, it is questionable whether any of the problems inherent in the current system can be changed without a legal restructuring. Without a constitution, the EU faces the increasingly difficult task of obtaining the tacit agreement of the people of Europe to continue with the European project. Without this agreement, there is no foundation upon which to build the future of Europe.

Summary

The question of who wins and who loses from European integration is fundamental to the future of the EU. Moreover, the fact that the most important participants in the construction of the EU – its citizens – do not understand or appreciate the benefits they gain from the European project threatens to undermine the premise upon which the Community was built. The summary at the end of the *Who wins, who loses* section of the chapter on Constitutionalism may state it best:

> For the **EU citizen**, constitutionalism can be viewed either positively or negatively. If the EU adopts a constitution, which both involves EU citizens in its creation and extends the protection of fundamental rights, then constitutionalism will work to their

advantage. However, a constitution that is not based on the will of the citizens would lack legitimacy, and could further alienate EU citizens.

Therefore, if the EU is interested in maintaining the tacit agreement of the citizens of Europe to participate in the European project, it may not be enough to develop an EU identity or to eliminate the democratic deficit in the decision-making process. Instead, it may be necessary to demonstrate strongly and consistently that, in the analysis of who wins and who loses from EU integration, EU citizens always win.

Selected Treaty Highlights

Alexis Xydias

Treaty of Paris	Treaties of Rome	Single European Act	Treaty on European Union (TEU, Maastricht)
Date signed: 18 April 1951, Paris.	**Date signed**: 25 March 1957, Rome.	**Date agreed**: 2–4 December 1985, at the Luxembourg Council. **Date signed**: 17 February 1986, in Luxembourg (Italy, Greece and Denmark signed 28 February 1986 in The Hague).	**Date agreed**: 10 December 1991, at the Maastricht European Council. **Date signed**: 7 February 1992, Maastricht.
Date of enforcement: 23 July 1952.	**Date of enforcement**: 1 January 1958.	**Date of enforcement**: 1 July 1987, after ratification problems in Ireland.	**Date of enforcement**: 1 November 1993, after a long, problematic ratification process: EMS crisis, negative referendum (Denmark), traumatic parliamentary ratification in the UK and constitutional challenges from German High Court (Karlsruhe judgment).
Impetus: World War II creates the need for peace and stability in Europe. 1950 Schuman Declaration.	**Impetus**: Political pressures as a result of the apparent success of ECSC; EDC proposal; Beyen Plan; Spaak Committee.	**Impetus**: 1981 Genscher–Colombo Plan; the Stuttgart Declaration, June 1983; 1984 Spinelli Draft Treaty, Fontainebleau Summit, June 1984; Adonino Report; enlargement negotiations with Portugal and Spain; the 1985 White Paper.	**Impetus**: The success of the 1992 programme; the collapse of the Soviet Union; events in Eastern Europe; German reunification.

continued

Alexis Xydias—cont'd

Treaty of Paris	Treaties of Rome	Single European Act	Treaty on European Union (TEU, Maastricht)
IGC: Negotiations among states began in June 1950 and ended in April 1951.	**IGC:** IGC of Rome.	**IGC:** Launched at the Milan Summit of June 1985, the IGC met from September to December 1985.	**IGC:** Outcome of two parallel IGCs, one on EMU and one on EPU. Both began in Rome, in December 1990, and finished in December 1991, in Maastricht, at the end of the Dutch Presidency.
Centrepiece of the Treaty: Creation of the ECSC.	**Centrepiece of the Treaties:** Creation of a common market (free movement of goods, services, persons and capital).	**Centrepiece of the Treaty:** Completion of the common market for goods, services, people and capital by 31 December 1992.	**Centrepiece of the Treaty:** The adoption of a common currency by 1 January 1999 at the latest.
Outcome: (i) Institutional: The establishment of a common market (not an FTA) for an ECSC, with a High Authority (executive), a Council of Ministers, a Common Assembly (delegates of national parliaments), a Court of Justice, and a Consultative Committee.	**Outcome:** (i) Institutional: Two communities created: EURATOM and the EEC, which established the formation of a common market by 1970. Established the Commission, Assembly, Council and ECJ for each community. Creation of the EIB and the ESF.	**Outcome:** (i) Institutional: **Council:** Expansion of QMV into areas connected to the SMP.	**Outcome:** (i) Institutional: Establishment of a European Union (EU) on three different pillars: First Pillar: the EC (combining the ECSC, the EEC, EURATOM) Second Pillar: CFSP Third Pillar: JHA The Treaty formally accepted the name 'European Union', thus signalling an increased importance for non-economic functions.

EP: Introduction of co-operation and assent procedure for legislation, enhancing the EP's role.

ECJ: Establishment of the CFI, to streamline the ECJ's workload.

European Council: First formal Treaty recognition of the European Council as institution (Art. 2 SEA).

Council: Expansion of QMV in most new areas of the Treaty, such as education and public health.

EP: Introduction of the co-decision procedure in a limited number of areas, such as free movement of workers, and Single Market measures. Extension of EP's right of 'assent' to almost all international agreements, especially those with budgetary consequences, and certain legislative matters. EP granted the right to approve the election of a new Commission.

ECJ: Given powers to impose fines on member states if the Commission brings an additional action for failing to comply with the ECJ's original infringement judgment.

Other institutions: Recognition of the European Council. Decision to establish the ECB to run monetary policy within the euro-zone from 1999 onwards. Creation of the CoR and the European Ombudsman. The Court of Auditors was given full status as an institution.

continued

Treaty of Paris	Treaties of Rome	Single European Act	Treaty on European Union (TEU, Maastricht)
(ii) Policies: A common policy for the integration of the coal and steel sectors, two sectors with central importance for both economic and defence reasons.	**(ii) Policies**: Aim: the creation of a common market by 31 December 1969. Establishment of a common agricultural policy, a limited social policy, a transport policy, and an association policy to provide for the economic and social development for territories. Include a provision for Council decisions to be taken by QMV, after a transitional period, in areas such as the CAP and transport policy.	**(ii) Policies**: Creation of a common market (= free movement of goods, capital, services and persons) by 31 December 1992. New Community competences: Economic and Social Cohesion, Research and Technology. New Title outlining new procedures for foreign policy co-operation, known as 'European Political Co-operation'.	**(ii) Policies**: Establishment of EMU (= common currency), with deadlines, detailed provisions and opt-outs for the UK and Denmark. Extension of EC competence into a variety of areas: visas for third-country nationals, Education, Culture, Public Health, Consumer Protection, Industrial Policy, Development Co-operation, Industrial Policy, vocational training, TENs, Environment, etc. Establishment of new treaty provisions on energy, tourism and civil protection. Extension of EC competence among eleven states in the form of the EC Social Protocol. Introduction of the principle of subsidiarity. Establishment of the Cohesion Fund. Development of the notion of EU citizenship.

Treaty of Amsterdam

Date agreed: 16–17 June 1997, at the Amsterdam European Council.

Date signed: 2 October 1997, Amsterdam.
Date of enforcement: 1 May 1999.

Impetus: Prospective eastern enlargement; the TEU required another IGC to deal with the unfinished duty of institutional reform from the TEU and a new decision-making process; the Yugoslav crisis demanded a reassessment of CFSP.

IGC: After the Westendorp Reflection Group Report, the Turin European Council opened the IGC in March 1996; it finished in June 1997, at the end of the Dutch Presidency.

Centrepiece of the Treaty: Preparation to create the political and institutional conditions to enable the EU to meet the challenges of enlargement.

Outcome: (i) Institutional:
Commission: Members agree to reduce commissioners by one per country by the next accession, compensating larger members with more votes in the Council. Position of the EU Commission President is strengthened through increased power in the appointment of other commissioners and in the allocation of portfolios.

Nice Treaty

Date agreed: 7–11 December 2000, at the Nice European Council.

Date signed: 26 February 2001, Nice.
Date of enforcement: The EP, for the first time in the history of the EU, did not explicitly ask the national parliaments to ratify the Treaty of Nice. The first Irish referendum in 2001 rejected the Treaty, delaying implementation. The Treaty was approved by the second Irish referendum on 19 October 2002.

Impetus: Need to facilitate working procedures and to make decision making more flexible in view of an enlarged EU (same objectives as Treaty of Amsterdam).

IGC: From 14 February until 11 December 2000.

Centrepiece of the Treaty: Unresolved issues from Amsterdam, in order to prepare for enlargement.

Outcome: (i) Institutional:
Commission: Limited the number of commissioners to one per country from 1 January 2005 onwards, until twenty-seven member states is reached. At this point there will be fewer commissioners than there are member states, and commissioners will be selected by a system of rotation that will be fair to all countries (this system has yet to be decided on).

continued

Treaty of Amsterdam	Nice Treaty
Council: Extension of QMV – most notably in the field of CFSP (decisions are taken by unanimity, but on issues relating to policy implementation, QMV became the rule), but also in employment, countering social exclusion, equality of opportunity and treatment for men and women, public health, transparency, fraud, establishment and research framework programmes.	Enhanced powers for the President: he or she will decide the internal organization of the Commission, distribute responsibilities among its members, appoint the vice-presidents, be able to request the resignation of any single commissioner with the approval by the full Commission. The President of the Commission will be appointed by the Council acting by QMV instead of the unanimity needed in the past.
EP: Number of MEPs is capped at 700. EP powers increased through the extension, modification and simplification of the co-decision procedure. Co-decision becomes the norm for new legislation, and the co-operation procedure is used only for EMU matters. In most cases, co-decision with the EP goes hand in hand with QMV in the Council. Assent procedure limited to the accession of new member states, some big international agreements, adoption of uniform procedure to elect MEPs.	**Council**: Reweighted votes in the Council in favour of the larger countries, although smaller countries will still have more votes relative to population. National votes have been set for member states currently in negotiations to enter the Union. The system of QMV can be modified only from 1 January 2005 onwards. A proposition under QMV would be carried if it represents a double majority. The Treaty provides for the possibility of a member of the Council to request verification that the qualified majority represents at least 62 per cent of the total population of the EU. If this condition is not met, the decision will not be adopted.
ECJ: Increased jurisdiction in the field of JHA.	**EP**: Reallocated seats and increased the number of MEPs from 626 to 732. This will apply starting in the European elections of 2004. Extension of co-decision to seven additional areas.
	European Council: As from 2002, one European Council meeting per Presidency will be held in Brussels. All European Council meetings will be held in Brussels.
(ii) Policies: New EC competences are developed in the field of employment and anti-discrimination policy, and a new title on Employment is developed.	**(ii) Policies:** QMV is increased to encompass twenty-nine new provisions, including important aspects regulating asylum-seekers, regulation of the ECJ in order to streamline its work, and senior appointments (including the President of the Commission).

New provision on suspension of rights is introduced as a sanction against a member state found guilty of a 'serious and persistent breach' of respect for human rights and the rule of law.

JHA: Establishment of an area of 'Freedom, Security and Justice', which transfers immigration and judicial co-operation in civil matters from the intergovernmental third Pillar, JHA, to the supranational EC first Pillar (five years after the Treaty enters into force). The UK and Ireland secured the right to opt out of EC competences in this field. Schengen Accords incorporated into Treaty: the UK and Ireland secured the right to maintain border controls.

CFSP: Adoption of the WEU's Petersburg Tasks as EU policy and the creation of 'Common strategies'. The Treaty introduces 'constructive abstention' and the 'emergency break' in CFSP decisions, in addition to closer relations with WEU. A High Representative, who is part of a troika responsible for external representation, is created, together with the Council's Presidency and the Commission.

A flexibility provision is developed, allowing member states to establish closer co-operation (subject to conditions).

Consultative powers of the CoR are extended.

A new IGC to reform the composition and functioning of the institutions should be called one year before the EU enlarges.

Forty-one Treaty articles (10 per cent of all Treaty articles) still use unanimity voting; areas include taxation, co-ordination of social security systems for cross-border workers, common commercial policy, maritime transport, economic and social cohesion policy (until 1 January 2007), policy on asylum and immigration (until 2004).

Enhanced co-operation ('flexibility') is developed to allow CC to proceed with a minimum of eight participants, instead of the majority of member states (as previously required).

Charter of Fundamental Rights is recognized, but not as a legally binding instrument.

A new IGC will be called in 2004 to deal with the delineation of power within the EU, the status of the Charter of Fundamental Rights, simplification of the treaties, and the role of national parliaments in the European system.

Historical Overview

Kristina Zorita

5 June 1947	The US Marshall Plan is launched in order to finance the reconstruction of Europe. Formally known as the ERP, it distributes approximately $US 12,500 million to sixteen European states over three years. This funding is conditional upon the elimination of trade barriers and the systematic organization of European financial recovery. The Eastern Bloc does not participate in this programme.
17 March 1948	The Western Union Treaty (also known as the Brussels Treaty) is signed between France, the UK and the Benelux countries, in order to promote collective defence.
16 April 1948	The Treaty creating the OEEC is signed by sixteen countries, in order to manage the funds from the Marshall Plan. In December 1960, the OEEC becomes the OECD, after a new OECD Treaty is signed in Paris, to include the USA and Canada as members.
25 January 1949	COMECON is established in Moscow between five countries in the Eastern Bloc as a counterweight to the economic aid being received by Western Europe through the Marshall Plan.
4 April 1949	The North Atlantic Treaty Organization (NATO) is signed in Washington, DC, by twelve countries.
5 May 1949	The Treaty of Strasbourg, signed by ten European countries, creates the Council of Europe.
9 May 1950	Schuman Declaration: in a plan inspired by the French political theorist Jean Monnet, the French Foreign Minister Robert Schuman proposes that France and the Federal Republic of Germany place their coal and steel resources under a common High Authority, and invites other European countries to participate in the project. This date is now celebrated as Europa Day.
19 September 1950	The European Union of Payments is launched to aid trade liberalization and make European currencies convertible.
18 April 1951	The Treaty of Paris: 'the Six' (Belgium, France, Germany, Italy, Luxembourg and the Netherlands) establish the ECSC.

27 May 1952	The European Defence Community Treaty is signed by the Six in Paris, on the basis of the Pleven Plan, proposed by French Prime Minister René Pleven in October 1950.
25 July 1952	The ECSC enters into force.
30 August 1954	The EDC fails when the French National Assembly rejects the EDC Treaty.
23 October 1954	The Six and the UK sign a treaty allowing the Federal Republic of Germany to join the Western Union, renaming it the Western European Union (WEU).
6 May 1955	The WEU Treaty enters into force.
14 May 1955	The Soviet Union institutes the Warsaw Pact with the participation of seven Eastern European countries in response to the inclusion of the Federal Republic of Germany in NATO.
1–3 June 1955	Messina Conference: the Six and the UK meet to discuss European economic integration, through the establishment of a common market for all their products and by extending economic integration to all sectors of the economy. The UK drops out of the talks.
29 May 1956	The Spaak Report, drawn up by the Belgian Foreign Minister Paul-Henri Spaak, is approved. The report lays the foundations for the creation of the EEC and EURATOM.
25 March 1957	The Treaties of Rome, establishing the EEC and EURATOM, are signed by the Six.
1 January 1958	The Treaties of Rome enter into force.
3–11 July 1958	The Stresa Conference lays the foundations for the CAP.
4 January 1960	Following the Stockholm Convention, EFTA is established through the initiative of the UK. It enters into force on 3 May 1960. Founder members include the UK, Denmark, Sweden, Norway, Portugal, Austria and Switzerland. Iceland joins in 1970, and Finland in 1986.
9 August 1961	The UK applies to join the EC, followed by Denmark, Ireland and Norway. French President Charles de Gaulle successfully opposes accession negotiations.
2 November 1961	Presentation of the Fouchet Plans: France proposes a confederation of independent European states with a common foreign and defence policy, as part of de Gaulle's attempt to create a purely intergovernmental EC, independent of the USA. The proposal fails to be adopted on 18 January 1962.
14 January 1963	French President de Gaulle announces that France will veto UK accession to the Community.
5 February 1963	The *Van Gend en Loos* ruling by the ECJ specifies that the Community constitutes a new legal order, and that the member states have restricted their sovereignty in order to participate.
20 July 1963	The first Yaoundé Convention, an Association Agreement between the EC and seventeen African countries and Madagascar, is signed in Yaoundé, Cameroon. The first elements of the Convention enter into force in June 1964.
12 September 1963	An Association Agreement is signed between the Community and Turkey, effective 1 September 1965.
15 July 1964	The ECJ rules on the *Costa* vs *ENEL* case, arguing for the supremacy of EC law over national law.

8 April 1965	The Merger Treaty is signed in Brussels, combining EURATOM, the ECSC and the EEC into the EEC, and merging the executives of the three communities into a common Council and Commission.
1 July 1965	The Empty Chair crisis begins, when the transition period into the Common Market (stipulated in the Treaties of Rome) expires, and decisions could begin to be taken by QMV. France recalls its permanent representative in the Community and refuses to participate in all Community institutions, in order to prevent further supranational developments.
28–9 January 1966	The Luxembourg Compromise ends the Empty Chair crisis, when France returns to the Council in return for agreement on the retention of the unanimity vote whenever 'national interests are at stake'.
11 May 1967	The UK reapplies for membership of the Community.
1 July 1967	The Merger Treaty enters into force.
1 July 1968	A customs union is launched in the Community, as the last intra-EC customs duties on manufactured goods are eliminated, and the CET is introduced.
1–2 December 1969	The Hague Summit approves the enlargement of the Community (to include the UK, Denmark, Ireland and Norway) and the establishment of Economic and Monetary Union by 1980.
22 April 1970	The Treaty of Luxembourg becomes the first budgetary treaty, providing for the gradual introduction of an 'own-resources' financial system for the EC (based on customs duties, agricultural levies and VAT) to replace member state contributions. The Treaty also extends the budgetary powers of the EP.
27 October 1970	The Six accept the Davignon Report on political co-operation, and allow the Community to speak with one voice in all major international forums.
17 December 1970	The ECJ clarifies the idea of fundamental rights within EC law in the *Internationale Handelsgesellschaft* ruling.
1 January 1971	The Yaoundé II Convention between the Community and nineteen ACP countries enters into force.
22 March 1971	The Council adopts the Werner Plan (proposed in 1970), laying the foundation for EMU by 1980.
25 May 1971	The ECJ rules on the *Defrenne* vs *Sabena* case, establishing the direct effect of Treaty articles on the national legal systems of member states and reinforcing the equality between men and women in the workplace established in the Treaties of Rome.
15 August 1971	Nixon declares the inconvertibility of dollars into gold, formally ending the BWS, which had been the international monetary system since World War II.
24 April 1972	The Community launches the currency 'Snake' (agreed in March 1972), allowing fluctuations between currencies of $\pm$ 2.25 per cent.
19–21 October 1972	The Paris Summit defines new fields of EC activity: regional, environmental, social, energy and industrial policies. The HOSG at the summit also set several future goals, including a reaffirmation of their intent to achieve EMU by 1980.
19 December 1972	An Association Treaty between the EC and Cyprus is signed, effective 1 June 1973.

I January 1973	The first enlargement of the Community takes place, with the UK, Denmark and Ireland joining, Norway having withdrawn its membership application following a national referendum on 26 September 1972.
6–27 October 1973	In response to the Yom Kippur War between Israel and Egypt, OPEC decides to massively reduce petroleum supplies, triggering a world-wide recession.
9–10 December 1974	The Paris Summit establishes the European Council, thereby institutionalizing summit meetings. This summit also agrees to the direct elections to the EP by universal suffrage and the establishment of the ERDF.
28 February 1975	The Lomé I Convention replaces and expands the Yaoundé Conventions governing relations between the EC and forty-six ACP countries. It is signed in Lomé, Togo, and remains in force from I April 1976 to I March 1980.
22 July 1975	The Second Budgetary Treaty establishes a Court of Auditors and expands the role of the EP in budgetary decisions. It enters into force on I June 1977.
7 January 1976	The Tindemans Report on the creation of a People's Europe is published by Belgian Prime Minister Leo Tindemans, at the behest of the Council of Europe.
28 March 1977	Portugal formally applies for membership in the Community, followed by Spain on 28 July.
5 April 1977	The EP, the Council and the Commission sign a joint declaration on the respect of fundamental rights.
4–5 December 1978	The Brussels Summit establishes the EMS, operative from I January 1979, following proposals by France and Germany at the Bremen European Council on 6 and 7 July. All member states (except the UK) decide to participate in the main feature of the system, the ERM, based on the ECU as the unit of currency.
20 February 1979	The ECJ establishes the principle of mutual recognition in the *Cassis de Dijon* ruling.
4 April 1979	A memorandum on the accession of the EC to the European Convention for the Protection of Human Rights and Fundamental Freedoms is adopted by the Commission, but never signed by the Council.
7–10 June 1979	The first EP elections by direct universal suffrage take place.
31 October 1979	The Lomé II Convention is signed between the Community and fifty-eight ACP countries, and remains in effect from I March 1980 to 28 February 1985.
I January 1981	The second enlargement of the Community takes place, with Greece joining the EC.
13 October 1981	EC Foreign Ministers reach agreement on the London Report, which strengthens and expands the EPC.
7 November 1981	The Genscher–Colombo Plan is presented, outlining a German–French initiative aimed at political co-operation in defence.
23 February 1982	Greenland, as a territory of Denmark, decides to leave the EC, remaining a part of EFTA.
14 September 1983	The Spinelli Report, a draft treaty establishing the European Union, is presented to the EP and ratified by it in February 1984.
17–19 June 1983	A 'Solemn Declaration on the European Union' is issued by the member states at the Stuttgart Summit, expressing their wish to move towards a European Union.

25–6 June 1984	The Fontainebleau Summit agrees to grant the UK a budget rebate on its contribution to the Community budget, and leads to the Dooge Committee (on institutional reform) and the Adonino Committee (on the development of a People's Europe). The summit also increases the Community budget by raising the ceiling on VAT.
14 November 1984	For the first time, the EP refuses to discharge the Commission on the execution of the 1982 Community budget.
8 December 1984	The Lomé III Convention is signed in Togo between the Community and sixty-six ACP countries, remaining in effect from May 1986 to February 1990.
1 January 1985	Jacques Delors is appointed President of the Commission.
29–30 March 1985	The IMPs are created, to assist Greece and Italy.
14 June 1985	The Schengen Agreement on the elimination of border controls among signatory countries is signed by the Benelux countries, Germany and France in Schengen, Luxembourg.
28–9 June 1985	The White Paper on 'completing the internal market', presented by the Commission and listing 279 concrete measures needed to realize the internal market, is approved at the Milan Summit. The HOSGs call for an IGC on institutional reform.
1 January 1986	The third enlargement of the Community takes place, with Spain and Portugal joining the EC.
17 and 28 February 1986	The Single European Act (SEA), which modifies the Treaties of Rome, is signed.
14 April 1987	Turkey formally applies to join the Community.
1 July 1987	The SEA enters into force.
11–13 February 1988	An extraordinary European Council meeting in Brussels leads to an agreement on the financing of EC policies, and to the Delors Package 1 – a multi-annual programme of expenditure (for 1988–92). The package also leads to a reform of the CAP and a restructuring of the Structural Funds.
29 March 1988	The Commission presents the Cecchini Report, outlining 'The Costs of non-Europe'.
27–8 June 1988	The Hanover European Council appoints a Committee for the Study of EMU (later known as the Delors Committee).
20 September 1988	UK Prime Minister Margaret Thatcher gives her 'Bruges speech' against Delors' federalist approach.
24 October 1988	The Council establishes the CFI to assist the work of the ECJ.
12 April 1989	The Commission presents the Delors Report on EMU.
	The EP adopts the Declaration of Fundamental Rights and Freedoms.
14–16 July 1989	The seven most industrialized countries (G-7) ask the EC to co-ordinate aid for economic restructuring in Poland and Hungary, leading to the establishment of the PHARE programme.
9 November 1989	The Berlin Wall falls, and the German Democratic Republic opens its borders.
8–9 December 1989	The Charter on Fundamental Social Rights of Workers is adopted by all member states (except the UK) at the Strasbourg European Council.
15 December 1989	The Lomé IV Convention is signed between the EC and sixty-nine ACP states.
28 April 1990	An extraordinary European Council summit in Dublin decides on a common approach to German reunification.
29 May 1990	The EBRD is established to provide financial support to the CEECs.

19 June 1990	The Schengen Accords on the elimination of internal EC border checks are signed.
1 July 1990	Launch of Stage I of EMU: liberalization of capital movements. Four member states (Spain, Portugal, Greece and Ireland) are granted an exceptional regime, given their insufficient progress towards financial integration.
3 October 1990	The reunification of Germany results in the territory of former East Germany becoming part of the Community.
14–15 December 1990	The Rome Summit launches two intergovernmental conferences (one on EMU, the other on political union), which lead to the TEU, also known as the Maastricht Treaty.
16 January–28 February 1991	The Persian Gulf War is fought to liberate Kuwait, and includes forces from several EU countries.
8 December 1991	The USSR collapses, following a coup in Moscow, on 19–22 August.
16 December 1991	The first Association ('Europe') Agreements are signed with Poland, Hungary and Czechoslovakia.
7 February 1992	The TEU is signed in Maastricht, The Netherlands.
18 March 1992	Finland formally applies for membership in the Community, followed by Sweden and Austria.
2 May 1992	A Treaty on the EEA is agreed between the EU and five EFTA members, in Porto, Portugal.
20 May 1992	Switzerland applies to join the EU (and later withdraws its application).
June/September 1992	Referendums on the ratification of the TEU: whilst Ireland supports the Treaty on 18 June, France approves it by a tiny margin on 20 September, and Denmark rejects it on 2 June. The Treaty leads to a democratic deficit crisis within the EU.
September 1992	The Italian lira and British pound leave the EMS, due to German Bundesbank monetary policy.
11–12 December 1992	The Edinburgh European Council agrees to the Danish and British opt-outs from several policy areas in the TEU and a financial perspective for 1993–9 (the Delors Package II). The summit also opens accession negotiations with Austria, Finland, Sweden and Norway, and establishes the Cohesion Fund for the four poorest member states.
1 January 1993	The Single European Market enters into force.
18 May 1993	A second national referendum allows Denmark to ratify the TEU.
21–2 June 1993	The Copenhagen Summit leads to the creation of the Copenhagen Criteria (political and economic conditions that must be satisfied by the CEECs in order to join the EU).
August 1993	Major ERM/EMS crisis leads to the introduction of wider currency bands, from $\pm$ 2.25 per cent to $\pm$ 15 per cent.
1 November 1993	The TEU enters into force.
1 January 1994	Launch of Stage II of EMU: establishment of the EMI.
9–10 March 1994	The CoR, created in the TEU, meets for the first time.
31 March 1994	Hungary applies to join the EU, becoming the first CEEC to formally submit an application.
28 November 1994	Following a national referendum, Norway again refuses to join the EU.
9–10 December 1994	The Essen European Council creates the pre-accession strategy for the accession countries.
1 January 1995	The fourth enlargement of the Community takes place, with Austria, Finland and Sweden joining the EU.
23 January 1995	The Santer Commission is formally appointed.

26 March 1995	The Schengen Accords come into force in seven EU member states (Germany, France, Belgium, Luxembourg, the Netherlands, Spain and Portugal).
12 July 1995	Jacob Söderman is appointed as first ombudsman of the EU.
26 July 1995	The member states sign the EUROPOL Convention on EU police co-operation.
27–8 November 1995	The Barcelona Declaration is signed by fifteen EU and twelve Mediterranean states, agreeing to a long-term three-pillar partnership (economic and financial affairs, political issues, and cultural and educational ties) with North African and Middle Eastern states.
1 January 1996	A customs union between the EU and Turkey is launched.
5 March 1996	The *Brasserie du Pêcheur* and *Factortame* rulings by the ECJ establish a precedent for state liability rulings in EC law.
1 June 1997	The European Central Bank (ECB) is inaugurated in Frankfurt, Germany.
16 July 1997	The Commission presents 'Agenda 2000 – for a stronger and wider Europe' to the EP, in addition to the Commission's opinions on the applications of candidate countries.
2 October 1997	The Amsterdam Treaty is signed by EU Foreign Ministers.
12–13 December 1997	The Luxembourg Summit launches accession negotiations with Poland, Hungary, the Czech Republic, Slovenia, Estonia and Cyprus.
3 May 1998	At a special European Council meeting in Brussels, it is agreed that eleven states will participate in the third stage of EMU, which includes the introduction of the euro on 1 January 1999.
1 January 1999	Launch of Stage III of EMU: the euro (€) becomes official currency in Austria, the Benelux countries, Finland, France, Germany, Ireland, Italy, Portugal and Spain.
15 March 1999	The Santer Commission resigns, following a very critical report by the Committee of Independent Experts on allegations of fraud, mismanagement and nepotism.
24 March 1999	NATO begins an air campaign against the Federal Republic of Yugoslavia in response to the Kosovo crisis.
24–5 March 1999	An overall agreement on Agenda 2000 is reached at a special European Council in Berlin, Germany.
1 May 1999	The Treaty of Amsterdam enters into force.
5 May 1999	The Prodi Commission is formally appointed.
3–4 June 1999	The Cologne Summit adopts the first EU common strategy concerning Russia, and decides to provide the EU with defence capabilities. Mr Javier Solana is designated as the first Mr CFSP.
10–11 December 1999	The Helsinki Summit opens accession negotiations with Romania, Slovakia, Latvia, Lithuania, Bulgaria and Malta, and recognizes Turkey as an applicant country.
23 June 2000	The Cotonou (Benin) Agreement replaces the Lomé Conventions.
28 September 2000	Following a national referendum, Denmark refuses to join the euro.
7 December 2000	The Charter of Fundamental Rights of the EU is signed by the EP President, the European Council and the Commission.
11 December 2000	The Treaty of Nice is agreed upon at the Nice Summit in France.
2 January 2001	Greece becomes the twelfth member of the euro-zone.
26 February 2001	The Nice Treaty is signed.
7 June 2001	Following a national referendum, Ireland refuses to ratify the Treaty of Nice.

15–16 June 2001	The Gothenburg European Council agrees on a framework for successful completion of the enlargement negotiations. The European Council also addresses issues of sustainable development, in terms of economic, social and environmental policy.
11 September 2001	The World Trade Towers and the Pentagon are attacked.
21 September 2001	An extraordinary European Council meeting is held in Brussels to determine the EU's response to the terrorist attacks in the USA.
9–13 November 2001	The WTO holds a ministerial conference in Doha, Qatar.
14–15 December 2001	The Laeken European Council determines that negotiations with candidate countries ready for accession are to be concluded by the end of 2002. EU member states agree to finalize security arrangements with NATO and to develop the operational capability of the common ESDP. The European Council also adopts a declaration and initiates the Convention on the Future of Europe.
1 January 2002	The euro (€) successfully enters into circulation in the twelve participating member states, and completely replaces national currencies on 28 February 2002.
28 February 2002	A year-long Convention on the Future of Europe begins.
31 May 2002	The EU ratifies the Kyoto Protocol on the world-wide reduction of greenhouse gas emissions.
23 July 2002	The ESCS Treaty expires after fifty years.
9 October 2002	The European Commission recommends the conclusion of accession negotiations with Cyprus, the Czech Republic, Estonia, Hungary, Latvia, Lithuania, Malta, Poland, the Slovak Republic and Slovenia by the end of 2002, as it considers these countries ready for accession in 2004.

Index

Bold type: definitions or explanations of the entry.